The Structural Design of Language

Although there have been numerous investigations of biolinguistics within the Minimalist Program over the last ten years, many of which appeal to the importance of Turing's Thesis (that the structural design of systems must obey physical and mathematical laws), these studies have by and large ignored the question of the structural design of language. They have paid significant attention to identifying the components of language – settling on a lexicon, a computational system, a sensorimotor performance system, and a conceptual-intentional performance system; however, they have not examined how these components must be inter-structured to meet thresholds of simplicity, generality, naturalness, and beauty, as well as of biological and conceptual necessity. In this book, Stroik and Putnam take on Turing's challenge. They argue that the narrow syntax – the lexicon, the Numeration, and the computational system – must reside, for reasons of conceptual necessity, within the performance systems. As simple as this novel design is, it provides, as Stroik and Putnam demonstrate, radical new insights into what the human language faculty is, how language emerged in the species, and how language is acquired by children.

THOMAS S. STROIK is Professor of English Linguistics at the University of Missouri, Kansas City. His previous publications include *Locality in Minimalist Syntax* (2009).

MICHAEL T. PUTNAM is Assistant Professor of German and Linguistics at the Pennsylvania State University. He is the author of *Scrambling and the Survive Principle* (2007), and has edited three books including *Exploring Crash-Proof Grammars* (2010).

T0370775

The Structural Design of Language

Thomas S. Stroik
Michael T. Putnam

CAMBRIDGE
UNIVERSITY PRESS

Shaftesbury Road, Cambridge CB2 8EA, United Kingdom

One Liberty Plaza, 20th Floor, New York, NY 10006, USA

477 Williamstown Road, Port Melbourne, VIC 3207, Australia

314–321, 3rd Floor, Plot 3, Splendor Forum, Jasola District Centre, New Delhi – 110025, India

103 Penang Road, #05–06/07, Visioncrest Commercial, Singapore 238467

Cambridge University Press is part of Cambridge University Press & Assessment, a department of the University of Cambridge.

We share the University's mission to contribute to society through the pursuit of education, learning and research at the highest international levels of excellence.

www.cambridge.org
Information on this title: www.cambridge.org/9781009342469

First published 2013
First paperback edition 2022

A catalogue record for this publication is available from the British Library

Library of Congress Cataloging-in-Publication data
Stroik, Thomas S.
The structural design of language / Thomas S. Stroik, Michael T. Putnam.
     pages   cm
Includes bibliographical references.
ISBN 978-1-107-03483-9
1. Grammar, Comparative and general – Syntax.   2. Generative grammar.
3. Minimalist theory (Linguistics)   4. Biolinguistics.   I. Putnam, Michael T.
II. Title.
P291.S693   2013
415–dc23

                                                                    2012034002

ISBN   978-1-107-03483-9   Hardback
ISBN   978-1-009-34246-9   Paperback

Contents

Preface

> Discovery commences with the awareness of anomaly, i.e., with the recognition that nature has somehow violated the paradigm-induced expectations that govern normal science. It then continues with a more or less extended exploration of the area of anomaly. And it closes only when the paradigm theory has been adjusted so that the anomalous has become the expected.
>
> Thomas S. Kuhn, *The Structure of Scientific Revolutions* (1962: 52–53)

We would like to begin our book with a somewhat startling observation: theories of generative grammar and theories of modern physics appear to exhibit similar anomalies involving putative violations of the Principle of Locality. In physics, both gravity and quantum particle entanglements have been analyzed, at one time or another, as processes that allow action at a distance, in violation of the Principle of Locality, which requires all physical processes to be immediate and immanent. And in generative grammar, displacement phenomena, such as *Who does Sam think that Jesse believes that Chris expects Pat to talk to __ tomorrow* (where the prepositional object *who* has been separated from its preposition), have been explained in terms of long-distance grammatical operations that connect a displaced constituent to its displacement site – operations that violate the Principle of Locality by allowing action at a distance.

We find the fact that generative grammar and modern physics are investigating similar questions about (non-)locality to be particularly interesting because it raises the possibility that we will be able to gain some valuable insight into how to analyze locality in grammar by looking at how work in physics has dealt with locality. So let us consider what we can learn about locality from physics. Locality issues in physics go at least as far back as Newton. In his Law of Gravity, Newton formulates gravity to be an instantaneous force that acts on bodies at any distance. Newton's Law of Gravity, then, is a non-local law. Despite the explanatory successes of Newton's theory of gravity, Einstein, committed to local realism, rejected Newton's analysis of gravity on conceptual grounds. As Einstein proves in his Special Theory of Relativity, no information can be transmitted faster than the speed of light; as a result, no force (including the force of gravity) can be an instantaneous force acting at a distance. Therefore, Newton's Law of Gravity must be wrong. Although the Special

Theory of Relativity undermines Newton's theory of gravity, it does not replace Newton's non-local theory with a local theory of gravity. The reason it does not do so is that the Special Theory of Relativity, even though it adds a fourth (time) dimension to physical laws, does not re-conceptualize Newton's three spatial dimensions. As a consequence, the non-local spatial relations that stand at the heart of Newton's Law of Gravity remain the same in the Special Theory of Relativity, which leaves the latter theory unable to provide an alternative explanation for gravity. To give a non-local account of gravity, Einstein had to re-conceptualize not just the laws involved in transmitting information, but the nature/structure of space and time. In his General Theory of Relativity, Einstein shows that space and time are not flat, as they are for Newton; rather, space-time is locally curved by whatever mass is present. For Einstein, gravitational effects do not arise from an attraction-force acting at a distance, but from the local curvature of space-time. What is important to point out about Einstein's re-analysis of Newton's non-local theory of gravity is that this analysis required more than reformulating the laws that explain how information is transmitted in space and time, it required a radical redesign of the structure of space and time itself.

A similar story can be told about quantum entanglements, in which two particles that intersect continue to be informationally connected no matter how far apart they become positioned. Of note, this informational alignment (in terms of physical properties such as momentum, spin, polarization, etc.) is non-local and instantaneous; hence, it appears to violate the light-speed limit on the transmission of information. Einstein (once again the champion of the Principle of Locality) took exception to quantum entanglement, calling it "spooky action at a distance." Even though Einstein and others sought to give a local explanation for quantum entanglement by introducing "hidden variables" into quantum equations, these maneuvers have failed. Some promising, local solutions to the non-locality of entanglements, however, have been advanced recently. These solutions, it is interesting to note, come from string theory/M-theory and from multiverse theories; that is, the solutions are grounded in radical re-conceptualizations of space and time. At present, it is not clear whether or not any of the proposed analyses of quantum entanglements will eventually succeed in giving a local explanation for entanglement; what is clear, though, is that if there are to be local solutions to quantum particle entanglement, they will have to be structure-based (a Turing solution) and not rule-based (a Galileo solution). That is, obviating non-local anomalies in a given physical domain cannot be done by reconfiguring the laws or principles that operate within the domain; it requires, instead, reconfiguring the domain because the anomalies are in the domain (not of the domain).

As we note above, generative grammar is like modern physics in that it seems to permit non-local processes. Although it has been recognized by generative theorists since Ross (1967) that non-local grammatical processes are problematic because they overgenerate syntactic structures, solving this problem has been approached largely as a computational problem in need of a Galileo-type solution. Hornstein (2009: vii) makes this poignantly clear when he states,

Thus, Chomsky (1977) assumed that Ross's (1967) constraints were more or less empirically adequate and wanted to "explain[ed them] in terms of general and quite reasonable 'computational' properties of formal grammar" (p. 89) ... So too we will assume here that Government and Binding Theory (GB) correctly limits the properties of [Universal Grammar/Faculty of Language] and our aim is to explain them on the basis of simpler, more general, more natural cognitive operations and principles.

Hornstein, following Chomsky, proposes to explain, among other things, the problems Ross identifies with non-local operations by reconfiguring operations and principles, seeking to redress the problems of non-locality by constraining operations and principles so they become less non-local, which is exactly what the "hidden variable" analyses of quantum entanglement sought to do (unsuccessfully). Hornstein's trust that getting the operations and principles right will resolve locality-related anomalies in grammar, unfortunately, misses the crucial point we have taken from physics that such anomalies are not law/rules/operation/principle anomalies, they are structural anomalies. To address these anomalies requires a reformulation not of operations and principles, but a reformulation of the domain over which operations and principles apply; in other words, it requires a reformulation of the biological base of human language, which we call Universal Grammar/Faculty of Language.

In this book, we take on the challenge of looking at the structural design of the Faculty of Language, arguing that the design proposed in Chomsky (1995, 2005, 2008) is a flat (Newtonian) structure that creates locality anomalies. As we point out, Chomsky's design for the Faculty of Language posits a structure that consists of three discrete, independent modules – a Lexicon, a computational system, and two interpretative External Interfaces (the Conceptual-Intentional interface and the Sensorimotor interface) – that have only operational connections with one another; consequently, any information shared by the modules must necessarily be "spooky action at a distance." We show that this design is flawed and needs to be reformulated as a curved design in which there are structural overlaps that allow information to be shared locally within and among the components of the Faculty of Language, which for us include the Lexicon, a computational workspace, and two performance systems (the Conceptual-Intentional performance system and the Sensorimotor performance system).

A crucial part of our argument for a radical re-conceptualization of the structural design of the Faculty of Language comes from evolutionary biology. We take seriously the suggestions made by Thompson (1917) and Turing

(1952) that mathematical and physical laws play a role in shaping biological form and structure by investigating the formal properties that determine the biological structure of the Faculty of Language: in fact, we make Turing's Challenge (to determine the formal properties of the Faculty of Language) the center of our analysis.

Of note, because we adopt Thompson's and Turing's views of biology, we also follow the constraint-based theories of evolution spawned by these views – theories such as those advocated by Fodor and Piattelli-Palmarini (2010), by Dawkins (2009), and by Deacon (2012). By adopting constraint-based theories of evolution, we accept that, as Fodor and Piattelli-Palmarini (2010: 21) observe,

Contrary to traditional opinion, it needs to be emphasized that natural selection among traits generated at random cannot by itself be the basic principle of evolution. Rather, there must be strong, often decisive, endogenous constraints and hosts of regulations on the phenotypic options the exogenous selection operates on.

And we accept the related observation made by Deacon (2012: 427):

Even in the case of the simplest organisms, an undirected, unconstrained process for sorting through the nearly infinite range of combinatorial variants of forms, and testing for an optimal configuration by trial and error of natural selection, would fail to adequately sample this space of possible combinatorial variations, even given the lifetime of the universe. In contrast to this vast space of possible combinatorial variants, the process of biological development in any given lineage of organisms is highly constrained, so that only a tiny fraction of the possible variations of mechanisms can ever be generated and tested by natural selection.

As Deacon and Fodor and Piattelli-Palmarini argue, evolution is not driven primarily by external forces (or exogenous natural selection); hence, evolution is not primarily an adaptationist process; it is driven instead by internal structures, self-organization, and self-assembly, all of which, in accordance with Thompson's and Turing's suggestions, conform to mathematical and physical laws.

We stress the importance of our constraint-based assumptions about evolution to highlight differences between the design of the Faculty of Language we propose and the one Chomsky proposes for standard Minimalism. Even though Chomsky often invokes his debt to Thompson and Turing in his formulation of the operations used in Minimalist syntax, his design of the Faculty of Language is strictly an adaptationist design (on top of being a Newtonian design, as we have discussed previously). For Chomsky, the Faculty of Language is designed to satisfy the Strong Minimalist Thesis (SMT), which holds that language is an optimal solution to interface conditions. What this means is that the computational system in the Faculty of Language produces output that optimally meets the interactive (and interpretative) needs of the external Conceptual-Intentional and Sensorimotor interfaces. In other words, under SMT assumptions, the computational system (a biological system) is designed to meet system-external (exogenous) conditions; it is designed to adapt to interface requirements imposed from outside of the computational system. An additional "adaptation-ist" problem with Chomsky's design of the Faculty of Language is that this design currently uses a "free" Merge operation to build syntactic structure – an operation that permits the computational system to build structures licentiously and relies on the interface systems to filter out unusable structures. However, as Deacon notes above, biological processes that freely produce combinatorial variants are untenable.

The case we are making here is that biolinguistic theories of syntax, partic-ularly those currently proposed in the Minimalism framework, are built on a shaky foundation. Although such theories have devoted substantial attention to identifying the core "cognitive operations and principles" of grammar (as Hornstein 2009: vii asserts), they forego any analysis of the structural domain for these operations and principles, accepting without question the structural design advanced by Chomsky. Sadly, this design, as we have been arguing, suffers from being Newtonian and adaptationistic; consequently, much of the work done on operations and principles under Chomsky's design also suffers.

In this book, we are going to reverse Hornstein's analytical approach. Rather than pursue syntactic operations and principles in and of themselves, we pursue the structural design of syntax (of the Faculty of Language) and we investigate operations and principles only after we have ascertained the structural domain in which these constructs apply. Our analysis of the Faculty of Language will show that this faculty is not Newtonian and adaptationistic, but curved and constraint-based.

We build our analysis of human language around two core arguments. First, we argue that the design of the Faculty of Language that has evolved for human language has been, as Fodor and Piattelli-Palmarini observe of all phenotypic developments, "drastically limited by internal constraints" (2010: 25). In par-ticular, we argue that the Faculty of Language is located within (and not separate from, as Chomsky proposes) the hominid performance systems that pre-existed language, and therefore, the evolution of the Faculty of Language has been constrained by these performance systems. Second, we argue that all the operations used in computing human language follow the same sorts of locality conditions that apply to all biological operations, as described by Dawkins (2009: 247):

The development of the embryo, and ultimately the adult, is achieved by local rules implemented by cells, interacting with other cells on a local basis. What goes on inside cells, similarly, is governed by local rules that apply to molecules, especially protein molecules, within the cells and in the cell membranes, interacting with other such molecules. Again, the rules are all local, local, local.

Of note, unlike Chomsky's design of the Faculty of Language, ours permits only bottom-up, strictly local operations that build structures on top of structures non-teleologically, without regard for their own output. In this way, our system of rules follows Dawkins (2009: 220), who notes of biological rules that

> The body of a human, an eagle, a mole, a dolphin, a cheetah, a leopard frog, a swallow: these are so beautifully put together, it seems impossible to believe that the genes that program their development don't function as a blueprint, a design, a master plan. But no: as with the computer starlings, it is all done by individual cells obeying local rules. The beautifully "designed" body *emerges* as a consequence of rules being locally obeyed by individual cells, with no reference to anything that could be called an overall global plan.

According to Dawkins, biological rules/operations are non-teleological (not being farsighted), but they are not blind. They are, however, intensely nearsighted. They are sensitive to, and constrained by, input conditions that allow material to be added to a biological structure only if the new material has an informational match with the existing structure. As Dawkins describes this biological accretion, cells in general bristle with "labels" (chemical badges) that enable them to connect with their "partners" (Dawkins 2009: 234). That is, cells, which possess a complicated array of "adhesion molecules" that are information-rich, participate in structure-building only if their information appropriately matches other cells. It is important to underscore the fact that for Dawkins, biological structures are built adhesively, not combinatorily. That is, biological rules are unary processes/operations that add material to a structure to grow that structure, and not binary processes/operations that combine two independent biological structures to form a third structure. The reason that this is important for our analysis of human languages is that our design of the Faculty of Language permits only Dawkins-type syntactic operations that are unary and adhesive (as we discuss at length in this book), while standard Minimalism has binary, combinatory operations. Hence, our structural design of the Faculty of Language aligns with constraint-theories of biology in ways that Chomsky's design (the design widely accepted in all versions of Minimalism) cannot, which provides a strong motivation for re-conceptualizing the structural design of the Faculty of Language along the lines we do.

Our primary objective in this Preface has been to establish the need to investigate the structural design of the Faculty of Language both in terms of the physics of locality and in terms of constraint-based theories of biology. We acknowledge from the get-go that our admittedly radical investigation will raise a host of controversial and uncomfortable questions about the design of human language that will encounter serious resistance, and we recognize upfront that there are many issues about structural design that will not be covered in this book, and these issues will be flagged as being problematic for us. However, we take some (perhaps undeserved) comfort from Kuhn (1962: 157), who points out that "if a new candidate for a paradigm had to be judged from the start by . . . people who examined only relative problem-solving ability the sciences would experience very few major revolutions." Aware that much work on the structure design of the Faculty of Language remains to be done, we move ahead with our analysis, confident that our call for shifting the paradigm of generative grammar deserves careful attention because our analysis promises productive connections with theories of biology that Chomsky's analysis cannot deliver. If, as Kuhn (1962: 157) asserts, "the issue is which paradigm should in the future guide research on problems many of which neither competitor can yet claim to resolve completely," we are certain our structural design of human language is built on principles most able to survive.

Acknowledgments

Every book manuscript has a unique story behind it, and this one is no different. The idea for this book actually came out of a pizza shop in downtown Kansas City, Missouri back in the spring of 2005. We discussed the idea of writing a "manifesto" of sorts regarding the contribution that the Survive Principle could make to the biolinguistic turn in generative linguistics. Since that day we have been working collaboratively on our "manifesto."

We have been fortunate to discuss some of our core (and peripheral) ideas developed in the book with many scholars, colleagues, and friends at a number of venues. Their critical feedback and probing questions undoubtedly aided us in revisiting many facets of our claims and ultimately pushed us to improve them. We would like to thank the following individuals for helping us clarify and shape our ideas: Klaus Abels, Marc Authier, Vicki Carstens, Mike Diercks, Sam Epstein, Antonio Fábregas, Helen Goodluck, Kleanthes Grohmann, John Hale, Wolfram Hinzen, Diego Krivochen, Winnie Lechner, Tim Osborne, Maria del Carmen Parfita Couto, Lisa Reed, Daniel Seely, Joe Salmons, Elly van Gelderen, Marjo van Koppen, Jerry Wyckoff, and Gilbert Youmans. There are others who have delivered helpful and insightful comments on our project at various stages of its development, and the omission of anyone's name is due to poor memory on our part.

Our ideas have also benefited from being presented at conferences and invited presentations. We would like to recognize and mention these venues and institutions for allowing us to present our work and, as a result, enhance it as a result of the feedback we received while there: DEAL (Descriptive and Explanatory Adequacy in Linguistics), Exploring Crash-Proof Grammars (Carson-Newman College), Johann-Wolfgang Goethe Universität, LASSO 37, MALC-2007, MALC-2009, Syntaxfest (Cyprus 2006), University of Michigan (Syntax Support Group), University College London, Universität Stuttgart, and University of York. In addition to these conference venues, the majority of the arguments concerning the structure of the Lexicon previously appeared in an article authored by Thomas Stroik entitled "The Lexicon in Survive-minimalism" (2009b). Our discussion of syntactic structure in relation to the system we develop and discuss in this book is based largely on our co-authored (Putnam and

Stroik 2010) book chapter "Syntactic relations in Survive-minimalism." We would like to thank John Benjamins Publishing Company for allowing us to republish these core ideas in this manuscript.

Thomas Stroik would like to thank, first and foremost, the University of Missouri-Kansas City for granting him a research leave in 2009–2010 to work on this book manuscript – with special thanks to Karen Vorst, Jeff Rydberg-Cox, and Ginny Blanton for making this leave happen. He would also like to thank the Department of Linguistics at University College London for providing him with a Visiting Professorship while he worked on the book in the fall semester of 2010. And to Michelle Boisseau, his wife, he says, "You are the heart and soul of everything I do. This book is for you."

Michael Putnam is thankful for his family, friends, and colleagues in their unyielding support of him and this project. This project (as is the case with most endeavors of this duration and length) took on a life of its own, and without supporters in your corner, it is virtually impossible to finish a book. Michael would like to thank his colleagues and students at Penn State University (especially Carrie Jackson and Richard Page), Richard Gray, John Littlejohn, Zachary Reichert, and Brad Weiss for being a constant source of reason and encouragement. A special thanks goes out to Ron Then and Nick Henry for their assistance in creating an index for this book. In addition to these individuals, Michael would like to issue a very special thanks to his parents for their continued unconditional support of his work throughout his career. Finally, Michael would like to thank his wife, Jill, and daughter, Abby, for their unyielding patience and love throughout this project – "I couldn't have done it without you guys!"

Abbreviations

AP	adjectival phrase
ATB	across-the-board
BAE	Bare Argument Ellipsis
CI	concatenated items
C-I	Conceptual-Intentional
CoN	Copy-to-Numeration
CoSD	Copy-to-syntactic derivation
CP	Complementizer Phrase
CS	computational system
CUD	Copy's Uniformity of Directionality
DM	Distributed Morphology
DP	Determiner Phrase
EF	edge feature
EM	External Merge
FL	Faculty of Language
FLB	Faculty of Language broad
FLN	Faculty of Language narrow
FM	Feature Matrix
GB	Government and Binding
HP	Head Phrase
HPSG	Head-driven Phrase Structure Grammar
IM	Internal Merge
LEX	Lexicon
LF	logical form
LFG	Lexical Functional Grammar
LI	lexical item
MLC	Minimal Link Condition
NP	Nominal Phrase
NUM	Numeration
PF	phonetic form
PHON	phonological-feature set

PP	Prepositional Phrase
PSF	performance system feature
PSI	performance system item
QP	Quantifier Phrase
QR	quantifier raising
SCT	Strong Computational Thesis
SD	syntactic derivation
SEM	semantic-feature set
SM	Sensorimotor
SMT	Strong Minimalist Thesis
SYN	syntactic-feature set
TDI	Type Driven Interpretation
VP	Verb Phrase
WB	WorkBench

1   The biolinguistic turn

1.1   Introduction

Human language gives us the ability to express anything we can think, and to communicate these thoughts via a set of mutually comprehensible signals. Although all animals communicate, this boundless expressibility sets our species apart. (Fitch 2010: 5)

Human language is full of wonders, none more fascinating or arresting than its "boundless expressibility." The fact that any given human language can render a larger number of sentences than there are particles in the universe gives some indication of the magnitude of language. And the fact that humans can produce and use linguistic expressions that point, in some sense, to things that neither exist in the universe nor can be conceptualized by humans – such as "squared circles" or "colorless green ideas" – demonstrates the transcendence and the uncontainability of language. The fact of the matter is that human language is so expressive that it cannot be circumscribed by human experience or by human culture; it is, in some sense, larger than life. Given the sheer reach of human language, one cannot help but wonder how very young children can acquire the complex system of language (when they cannot master much simpler systems such as checkers or chess) and how our long-ago ancestors could have developed a biological system as complex as language in their evolutionary journey from early hominid to modern human.

   In this book, we investigate the "boundless expressibility" of human language, attempting to explain how it evolved and how children acquire it. Needless to say, we are not the first scholars to pursue these investigations: numerous philosophers, scientists, and linguists have preceded us: Plato, Aristotle, Descartes, Humboldt, Darwin, and Chomsky, among others; and numerous philosophers, scientists, and linguists continue to study the evolution and development of human language (see, in particular, Hornstein 2009; Bickerton 2009; Fitch 2010; Lieberman 2010; Searle 2010; Chomsky 2010; Ramachandran 2011). However, we bring a unique perspective to this investigation: we focus not on the expressibility of language or on the linguistic structures that underwrite this expressibility, but on the design properties of language communication systems (how language systems align with conceptual and Sensorimotor performance systems) and we argue not only that human language possesses the same basic structural design properties of all other animal communication systems' but also that the "boundless expressibility" unique to human language surprisingly evolves out of these design properties.

Our analysis of human language builds on Chomsky's (1995, 2005, 2010) Minimalist assumption that the design of language is grounded in conceptual necessity. We depart from Chomsky, though, in the application of this assumption. For Chomsky, conceptual necessity applies primarily to the computational system (CS) of human language: that is, it applies to the operations humans use to build linguistic expressions larger than single lexical items and to the domains over which the operations apply. Chomsky invokes conceptual necessity to determine whether human language needs operations other than the Merge operation; and he invokes conceptual necessity to determine whether human language requires levels of syntactic representation beyond some level of logical form; and he invokes conceptual necessity to justify computational domains such as "phases." Although we agree with Chomsky that the computation system (the syntax) of human language should be conceptually justified, and not merely operationally justified – in fact our previous work takes a vigorous look at the sorts of mechanisms permissible in a conceptually necessary CS (see Stroik 1999a, 2009; Putnam 2007; and Putnam and Stroik 2009, 2010) – here we do not limit the assumption that human language is grounded in conceptual necessity to the CS; rather, we generalize this assumption, applying it to the overall design of language systems. In particular, we start with Chomsky's observation that a language system consists of Conceptual-Intentional and Sensorimotor performance systems and a variety of mechanisms that build and send structurally elaborate strings of words to these performance systems for interpretation, and we investigate what conceptual necessity can tell us about how the components of a language system must interrelate with the performance systems for the language system to work. If the biological systems of human language consist of two performance systems (one that oversees linguistic form and one that oversees linguistic meaning), together with a Lexicon and with a CS that puts words together into larger linguistic units, we need to determine how these components interrelate. Are these systems separate subsystems, external to one another (as Chomsky assumes)? Or are they intersective systems with overlapping properties? In this book, we view the structural design properties of human language through the lens of conceptual necessity, discovering that the language system is embedded within the performance systems and that this particular structural relationship stands at the heart of the evolvability of human language, as well as its "boundless expressibility."

1.2   Theory-shaping

Modern biolinguistics, according to Boeckx (2006: 16–17), began with Chomsky's (1959) review of Skinner's *Verbal Behavior* and with his (1965) book, *Aspects of the Theory of Syntax*. It was in these works that the biolinguistic thesis started to take shape – the thesis that "the aim of a theory of grammar is to outline the biologically given cognitive structure that enables human children so reliably and effortlessly to project grammars from the [linguistic] data they receive" (Boeckx 2006: 19). Committed to the biolinguistic thesis, generative grammars from the Aspects model through the Government and Binding framework (see Chomsky 1981) and through the initial developments of the Minimalist Program (MP) (see Chomsky 1995, 2000) have continued to focus on ontogenetic language acquisition. All of these models of grammar have attempted to explain, first and foremost, how first-language grammars develop in children.

In the last decade, however, there has been a turn in the biolinguistic thesis. Even though early work by Chomsky did passingly raise questions about the evolution of language, recent work by Deacon (1997, 2012), Jenkins (2000), Hauser, Chomsky, and Fitch (2002), Chomsky (2005, 2009, 2010), Bickerton (2005, 2009, 2010), Boeckx (2006, 2009), Hinzen (2009a, 2009b), Reuland (2009), Hornstein (2009), and Fitch (2010), among others, has shifted the biolinguistic thesis to include serious consideration of phylogenetic language acquisition. Now the aim of a theory of language is to explain not only how children can biologically acquire a grammar, but also how our species could evolutionarily acquire human language.

As currently developed, the biolinguistic program seeks to answer five interrelated questions (discussed in Jenkins 2000 and in Boeckx 2008b, 2009):

1. What is the knowledge or Faculty of Language (FL)? (Humboldt's Problem)
2. How is this knowledge or Faculty of Language acquired? (Plato's Problem)
3. How is this knowledge put to use? (Descartes' Problem)
4. How is this knowledge implemented in the brain? (Broca's Problem)
5. How did this knowledge emerge in the species? (Darwin's Problem)

We cannot stress enough how much bringing Darwin's Problem (language evolution) into the biolinguistic program has changed the way we conceive of questions 1–4; it changes how we look at the structural design of FL and of the use and acquisition of FL. What Darwin's Problem adds to the biolinguistic program is the challenge that Saussure (1915, 1966) sought to avoid, the challenge of untangling the complex relationship between time and the development of language. Of the many tangles in the evolution of language, the two most pressing involve, as Bickerton (2005, 2009) and Gärdenfors and Osvath (2010) argue, first the emergence of symbolic communication and then the emergence of structured symbolic communication. The use of symbols, rather than signs, to communicate is, according to Bickerton (2009: 50), "the Rubicon that had to be crossed for our ancestors to start becoming human"; using symbols allowed our ancestors to extend their domain of communication beyond their immediate experiences, which in turn permitted them to engage in the long-range planning and the collaboration needed for survival. This Rubicon was crossed nearly 2 million years ago (see Bickerton 2009; Corballis 2010; and Bingham 2010), when a branch of hominids developed symbols, perhaps gestural symbols, to communicate. Although our ancestors appear to have mastered the use of symbols long ago, they do not seem to have developed the ability to combine these symbols in the structured ways we modern humans do until relatively recently. So while the development of a symbol-based protolanguage may indeed have been the essential first step towards the evolution of modern humans, it was not until our ancestors evolved the ability to combine their symbols in unbounded ways, thereby providing an unbounded stock of concepts about which and with which to communicate, that modern humans fully emerged.

One of the truly amazing facts about the development of modern language from protolanguage is how quickly this development took place. As Boeckx (2009: 46) observes, "everyone who has thought about the evolution of language seems to agree that it . . . happened within a very short space of time." The consequence of this compressed evolutionary time line, for Hornstein (2009), is that it places significant constraints on language development:

A common assumption is that language arose in humans in roughly the last 50,000–100,000 years. This is very rapid in evolutionary terms. I suggest the following picture: FL is the product of (at most) one (or two) evolutionary innovations which, when combined with cognitive resources available before the changes that led to language, delivers FL (2009: 4).

Hornstein's speculations severely limit what evolutionarily plausible theories of grammar should look like. Given his speculations, theories of grammar that assume complex sets of language-specific rules (such as Chomsky's 1965 Standard Theory or Gazdar et al.'s 1985 Generalized Phrase Structure Grammar and its aftermath) or complex sets of filters (such as Chomsky and Lasnik's 1977 work) or the optimality theoretic syntax of Pesetsky (1998) or complex sets of language-specific modules (such as Chomsky 1981 and Chomsky and Lasnik 1993) will be evolutionarily implausible because the development of these complex structures would be too time-intensive. Instead, a theory of grammar should be a theory of FL that, as Hauser, Chomsky, and Fitch (2002) maintain, consists of pre-linguistic cognitive processes (called Faculty of Language broad, FLB) able to subserve language processes and an extremely small set of language-specific processes (called Faculty of Language narrow, FLN).

But how exactly do we go about developing a theory of FL? For Chomsky (2005: 11), this question is "The general question ... How far can we progress in showing that all language-specific technology is reducible to principled explanation, thus isolating the core properties that are essential to the language faculty, a basic problem of linguistics?" Chomsky argues that there are three factors that reduce language-specific technology in FL: (i) genetic endowment, (ii) experience, and (iii) principles not specific to the FL. Of these three factors, it is, according to Chomsky, third-factor principles such as "language-independent principles of data processing, structural architecture, and computational efficiency ... [that provide] some answers to the fundamental questions of biology of language, its nature, use, and perhaps even its evolution" (2005:9).

Investigating the third-factor principles underlying FL, however, requires, from Chomsky's perspective, that we approach language as a natural, biological object. The consequence of treating language as part of the natural world is that the design structures of language must obey physical laws (which we call Turing's Thesis following Jenkins 2000 and Ott 2009) and that the computational processes involved in language must, as Galileo's Thesis requires, follow mathematical laws (see Boeckx 2006 for a discussion of Galileo's Thesis). This means that the structural mechanisms and the computational operations posited for FL must meet thresholds of simplicity, generality, naturalness, and beauty, as well as of biological and conceptual necessity. Or, as Hornstein (2009: 3) states, "FL will be natural if it is based on principles and operations that promote computational tractability, that are built from parts that are cognitively general and atomic, and that are basic enough to be (plausibly) embodied in neural circuitry." The goal of this book is to investigate how Hornstein's challenge can be met.

Since our response to Hornstein's challenge is largely shaped with Turing's Thesis in mind (and the constraints this thesis places on the structural design of human language), we would like to take a close look at Turing's Thesis and how it applies to our analysis of language. In his study of morphogenesis, Turing (1952: 37) makes the observation that "The purpose of this paper is to discuss a possible mechanism by which the genes of a zygote may determine the anatomical structure of the resulting organism ... [the] theory does not make any new hypothesis; it merely suggests that certain well-known physical laws are sufficient to account for many of the facts." As Turing admits, his thesis (which grounds biology in physical, and arguably structural, laws) is not a new thesis. Versions of this thesis have been advanced by others, such as Thompson, who notes that

Cell and tissue, shell and bone, leaf and flower, are so many portions of matter, and it is in obedience to the laws of physics that their particles have been moved, moulded, and conformed ... Their problems of form are in the first instance mathematical problems, their problems of growth are essentially physical problems, and the morphologist is, *ipso facto*, a student of physical science (1917/1992:10).

The importance of Turing's Thesis to our work is that it brings physical constraints and structural design into biology. It calls for, as Fodor and Piattelli-Palmarini (2010: 74) note, a constraint-based biology that questions "blind trial and error followed by natural selection" as a basis for biological growth and assumes instead that "It's vastly more plausible to suppose that the causes of these [biological] forms are to be found in the elaborate self-organizing interactions between several components that are indeed coded for genes (protein complexes, morphogenetic gradients, hormones, cell–cell inter-actions, and so on) and the strictures dictated by chemical and physical forces." Given Turing's Thesis, we should expect biological form and growth to be shaped by physical laws and structural design, an expectation supported by Deacon (2012: 68–69), who asserts that

Although the features that distinguish these different, specialized cell types depend on gene expression, the geometry of the developing embryo plays a critical role in determining which genes in which cells in which ways ... Many popular accounts of DNA ... ignore (that) the information ultimately embodied in the elaborate patterns of interaction among cells and how these affect which genes get expressed.

According to this line of argumentation, the evolution of organisms is not primarily governed by extrinsic forces, but rather is driven by the design properties internal to the organism in question. Or as Fodor and Piattelli-Palmarini (2010: 27) put it, "the whole process of development, from the fertilized egg to the adult, modulates the phenotypic effects of genotypic changes, and thus 'filters' the phenotypic options that ecological variables ever have a chance to select from." We accept the assumptions of constraint-based theories of biology and are committed to looking at the development of language in light of Turing's Thesis, investigating language as a biological system that emerges out of the interplay of internal, phenotypical constraints placed on the structural design of human language.

1.3   Minimalism and the design of the Faculty of Language

Minimalist inquiries into FL seek to formalize unified answers to questions 1–5 that also satisfy the constraints imposed by both evolutionary biology and conceptual necessity. These answers embrace "[t]he central idea ... that our human language capacity ... shows signs of optimal design and exquisite organization that indicate the inner workings of very simple and general computational (physical and mathematical) laws in a mental organ" (Boeckx 2006: 3). The challenge that Minimalism sets for itself, then, is to design an architecture for FL built on the principles of simplicity and economy.

Before moving forward we want to consider the plausibility of addressing the challenge above. Is this strong challenge one that can actually be met? Is it really possible to design an architecture for the Faculty of language that is grounded, in accordance with Minimalist assumptions, in both evolutionary biology and conceptual necessity? Kinsella (2009) thinks not. She contends that conceptual necessity in Minimalism is built on a notion of "perfection," in which "[t]he perfection of language is . . . understood to result from the simple uncluttered way that the system operates" (48), but such perfection simply "does not arise in nature as the result of gradual adaptive evolutionary processes" (60). Operational perfection of the sort advanced by Minimalism, as Kinsella rightly observes, runs afoul of evolutionary processes; that is, "perfection directly contradicts the bias for redundant, uneconomical systems, the trend for evolution to meliorize" (160). Kinsella makes a very important point: evolutionary processes are driven by contingencies not by conceptual necessity, and the structures that arise from adaptive processes are not conceptually necessary structures. So, if "language is a system that is grounded in biology" (91), it will not be a perfect system or even, as is often claimed about Minimalism, "a perfect solution to meeting the interface conditions" (57). Does this mean that the Minimalist challenge given above, as well as the Minimalist Program itself, should be abandoned as untenable? Kinsella thinks so; we think not. We think that the challenge only needs to be reformulated. While adaptive evolutionary processes might not yield optimal or perfect systems, they can yield optimal or perfect output. We certainly see optimal output in the petal-patterns of flowers and the structural symmetries of cells in honeycombs.[1] Given Kinsella's arguments, neither bees nor flowers have perfect designs. However, these imperfectly designed organisms can still produce perfect output. The same can be true of FL. That is, if the "perfection" of FL is in its output – in the fact that the linguistic structures produced by the CS of FL are necessarily usable by the performance systems – then FL, though an "imperfect" and adaptive system, can be grounded both in evolutionary biology and in conceptual necessity. But is the computational output of FL "perfect" in the sense of being necessarily usable by the performance systems?[2] It has been a long-held assumption in generative grammar that the computational output of the grammar is perfect – that, as Chomsky (1965) maintains, a grammar derives structural descriptions for all and only the sentences of a given language. Minimalism incorporates this assumption into its design of FL by having the CS meet (not feed) the interface conditions imposed by the performance systems. We, too, accept what we call the Strong Computational Thesis (SCT) (that the computational output of language is necessarily usable by its performance systems) as a working hypothesis, because denying the SCT opens the possibility of having an unknowable CS – one that in principle could generate unusable output that could not be tracked, identified, or studied. Given the SCT, language can be a biological system that is a perfect system grounded in conceptual necessity. This, however, would be true not only of the human language system, but of all animal communication systems. In other words, the perfection of the language system is not chauvinistically restricted to the human FL; rather, as Bickerton (2009) argues, all animal communication systems are designed to perfectly meet the communicative needs of the users. Of note, this notion of "perfection" applies to human protolanguage, which means that human language is not more perfect than human protolanguage – the former is merely an adaptive variant of the latter.

With the above discussion in mind, let's look at the Minimalist design for FL. Since its inception (see Chomsky 1995), the Minimalist Program has hypothesized that FL requires four independent (but connectable) subsystems: a Sensorimotor (SM) system, a Conceptual-Intentional (C-I) system, a Lexicon (LEX), and a computational system (CS). Broadly described, the SM system emits and receives linguistic signals; the C-I system interprets linguistic signals; LEX stores information about words; and CS generates complex linguistic structures from the words stored in LEX. Under standard Minimalist assumptions, the four subsystems of FL produce linguistic structures in the following way: lexical items (LIs) are placed in short-term memory (in a Numeration (NUM)); the LIs are brought into the CS and are structurally put together (via various syntactic operations to be discussed later); and these structures are sent to the external performance systems – SM and C-I – for phonetic and semantic-pragmatic interpretation. The architecture for FL, under these assumptions, looks like (6).

(6)

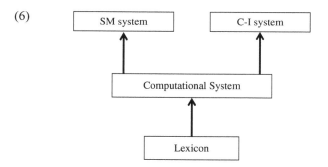

Of special note here, the performance systems in (6) are pre-linguistic systems that can "use" the linguistic structures produced by CS. These performance systems evolutionarily precede the linguistic systems (LEX and CS) and they are external to the linguistic systems. Because the performance systems are external to the linguistic system, linguistic structures produced by CS must be "transferred" to, or "shipped" off to, the performance systems for interpretation, as Chomsky (2005: 16) and Hornstein, Nunes, and Grohmann (2005: 46), among others, propose.

As we state above, the performance systems are pre-linguistic systems. They are ancestral systems that are millions of years old. The SM system, which is involved in the production and reception of gestures and/or acoustic signals, certainly pre-dates the evolution of homo sapiens; and the C-I system, which is responsible for the inferencing processes about the world, including our ability to project a Theory of Mind for others in which we can "read" their intentions from their actions, is so ancestral that it is something we share with other species of great apes.[3] Under Minimalist assumptions, the linguistic systems developed by humans use these older performance systems; however, they do so in compliance with established performance system conditions. That is, the linguistic system's "internal mechanisms and operations are not arbitrary, but a least-effort solution to minimal design specifications" (Ott 2009: 255). In slightly less technical language, this means that the linguistic system must be linked optimally and naturally with the performance systems it will utilize. Importantly, Chomsky (2000) argues that investigations into FL should be guided by the assumption that there is an optimal linkage between the linguistic system and the external performance systems – he calls this assumption the Strong Minimalist Thesis (SMT).[4]

Satisfying the SMT has spawned a rash of putatively necessary mechanisms for the linguistic system. The most widely embraced of these mechanisms is the Merge operation – an operation that "takes two elements, α and β, and combines them into a set $[\alpha, \beta]$" (Boeckx 2008a: 28); this operation is seen as conceptually necessary because it captures the compositional nature of human language. Although all versions of Minimalism accept some variation of the Merge operation, there is considerable disagreement about the properties of Merge. For one, Chomsky (2009: 29) and Ott (2009) propose that Merge is unbounded, allowing any two elements to merge together, as in (7a); on the other hand, some theorists such as Adger (2003, 2008) and Stroik (2009a) propose that Merge requires the two merged elements to have matching features, as in (7b).

(7)　a.　Merge $\{\alpha, \beta\} \rightarrow [\alpha\ \beta]$
　　　b.　Merge $\{\alpha[+F], \beta[+F]\} \rightarrow [\alpha\ \beta]$

For another, Chomsky (2005: 15) contends that Merge is the basic operation of FL, while Hornstein (2009) and Boeckx (2009) suggest that Merge is the product of two even more basic operations – Concatenate and Copy – that are not specific to FL.[5] Third, Chomsky (2005) argues that there are two flavors of Merge: External Merge, which introduces an LI into a syntactic derivation (SD), and Internal Merge,[6] which re-combines an element already in a syntactic derivation with the derivation; Hinzen (2009b), Stroik (2009a), and Putnam and Stroik (2009) argue, contra Chomsky, that Internal Merge is not a conceptually necessary operation.[7] And finally, there is a great deal of disagreement about the output of the Merge operations. Some theorists, such as Chomsky (2005) and Epstein and Seely (2006), permit the Merge operations to produce output that is not usable by the performance systems (output that "crashes" at the performance systems); others (for example Stroik (1999, 2009a), Frampton and Gutmann (2002), and Hinzen (2006)) contend that the CS must be crash-proof, sending only usable output to the performance systems.[8]

In addition to the Merge operation, some versions of Minimalism (see Chomsky 2000 and Boeckx 2008a, 2008b) have an Agree operation that allows one element (a Probe) to check the matching features of another element (a Goal). The Agree operation, which, as Boeckx (2008a: 77) states, "can take place at a distance," is used to explain the agreement relations between the main verb "appear" and the embedded subject "six very hungry children" in (8).

(8)   There appear to be six very hungry children sitting at the kitchen table.

Despite rather wide acceptance of the Agree operation, there is dispute about the properties of this operation. Some theorists, such as Lopez (2007), Hornstein (2009), Preminger (2009) and Sigurðsson (2006), accept the Agree operation, but they contend that this operation cannot apply at a distance; rather, it is restricted to local domains (Hornstein (2009: 126–130) offers a conceptual argument against long-distance Agree, claiming that this sort of Agree is unnecessary because it duplicates the Internal Merge operation). Stroik (2009a) takes an even more unsympathetic position on the Agree operation; for him, the only operation necessary in the CS is External Merge. Hence, he rejects the Agree operation.

One final CS operation proposed by various theorists is the Transfer operation, an operation that ships derivations, or portions of derivations, to the performance systems. Given that the CS is outside of the performance systems under standard Minimalist assumptions, it seems conceptually necessary that the output of the CS be sent along to the SM and C-I systems; hence, a Transfer operation would seem to be a conceptually necessary part of FL.[9] However, when does this operation apply? After each Merge operation applies, as Epstein and Seely (2002, 2006) and Boeckx (2008a) propose? After a phase head (C or v^*) is merged, as Chomsky (2001, 2005) and Ott (2009) propose? Or after the SD is complete, as Stroik (2009a) proposes?

As we can see, although there is some agreement about the CS operations in FL, there is also substantial disagreement (a matter that requires a conceptual resolution, under Galileo's Thesis). A similar situation arises with the Lexicon. Most theorists would agree with Tallerman's (2009: 181) claim that "The human mental lexicon is the repository of many tens of thousands of distinct vocabulary items, and of store information about their word classes and their selectional and subcategorizational requirements." And most theorists would agree that LIs are generally seen as carrying sets of phonetic, morphological, syntactic, and semantic features. However, Chomsky (2005: 18–19) claims that, in addition to the aforementioned features, phase heads (C and v^*) can carry "edge features," which "permit raising [of syntactic object in a derivation] to the phase edge without feature matching." And Reuland (2009: 211–212) asserts that linguistic signs (roughly, LIs) must include information not only about their form and their interpretation as individual concepts, but also formal instructions about their combinability into complex concepts.

Needless to say, the significant disagreement about what mechanisms are and what mechanisms are not actually constituents of FL leaves us with the pressing challenge of sorting through all the Minimalist proposals made about FL to determine which of them are conceptually necessary, that is, to determine which of them satisfy Turing's Thesis (and its constraints on structural design), as well as Galileo's Thesis (and its constraints on computations).

1.4   Re-shaping theory

Boeckx (2006) confidently claims that the Minimalist Program pursues a Galilean approach to FL, committed to the hypothesis that FL is perfectly designed. He states that

> minimalists endorse the belief (held by all major proponents of modern science, from Kepler to Einstein) that nature is the realization of the simplest conceivable mathematical ideas, and the idea that a theory should be more highly valued if it "gives us a sense that nothing could be changed . . . a sense of uniqueness . . . a sense that when we understand the final answer, we will see that it could not have been any other way" (Weinberg 2001: 39) (8–9).

Unfortunately for Minimalism, the pursuit of this Galilean vision has been restricted to finding "general properties of optimal, computationally efficient systems" (8) – i.e., it has been reduced to investigating the operations of the CS. Important as it is to locate all and only the conceptually necessary operations of CS, it is arguably even more important, in accordance with Turing's Thesis, to ascertain the simplest and most economical architecture (structure) of FL. After all, trying to determine the operations of CS without knowing the architectural design of FL misses the point that the operations must be design-appropriate; in other words, the operations are not architecture-independent. Any analysis of FL, then, that is committed to conceptual necessity must begin by finding the architectural principles of FL (by addressing Turing's Thesis).

Although Chomsky (1995) theorizes an architecture for FL (with four, independent subsystems organized as in (6)), few other minimalist analyses of FL have done so – not Bickerton (2009), Boeckx (2006, 2008a, 2008b, 2009), Brody (1995), Chomsky (2000, 2001, 2005, 2009), Collins (1997), Epstein et al. (1998), Epstein and Seely (2002, 2006), Hinzen (2006), Hornstein (2001, 2009), Lasnik (1999), Lopez (2007), Richards (2001), or Uriagereka (2002), among many others. All these analyses just mentioned accept (6), without any hesitation or concern, as the architecture of FL and build their various arguments, which are mainly about the CS, around this architecture. But how valid is this architecture (and, by extension, the many arguments that assume this architecture)? If we follow Hornstein's (2009: 10) assertion that "[t]he minimalist hypothesis is that FL is what one gets after adding just a little bit, a new circuit or two, to general principles of cognition and computation," then we should be suspicious about architecture (6). What is particularly alarming about (6), given Hornstein's remarks, is that this architecture is formed by adding not just a little bit of biological tinkering to the pre-linguistic C-I and SM systems, but by adding two new systems (CS and LEX) that are independent of the pre-linguistic systems. Since it would take considerable time to build new cognitive subsystems and the neural bridges required to connect the four subsystems (see Hornstein's (2009: 8–9) discussion of the evolutionary timetable for the development of language), it would seem highly improbable that architecture (6) could arise in the relatively short period it took for human language to evolve from human protolanguage.

There are three other significant problems with architecture (6). First and foremost, architecture (6) does not follow constraint-based assumptions about biological development; rather, it follows adaptationist assumptions. The design of (6) requires that a biological system (the computational system) be built to meet the interpretative needs of other "external" systems (the C-I and SM performance systems). That is, architecture (6) follows the assumptions of natural selection in that "both think of the structures they purport to explain as shaped primarily by processes of exogenous selection" (Fodor and Piattelli-Palmarini 2010: 153). That the CS in Chomsky's (1995, 2005) architecture of FL is designed to *optimally* meet the boundary conditions set by (and selected by) the external performance system makes it very clear that (6) rests on adaptationist assumptions. Given the arguments against adaptationism (and natural selection) that we have already presented in the Preface and in this chapter, we cannot help but have strong reservations about (6).

Second, as Hinzen (2009b: 128) argues, "there are no structured semantic representations beyond the ones that the syntax is inherently tuned to construct"; therefore, mapping syntactic representations to an independent semantic system (the C-I system) is redundant and not conceptually necessary. Relatedly, if the syntactic system and the semantic system are independent systems, one could not conceptually guarantee that the linguistic output of the syntax could be usable by the pre-linguistic C-I system. From these arguments, Hinzen concludes that "the outside systems [C-I systems] simply do not exist" (127). Importantly for our purposes, if Hinzen is correct, architecture (6) cannot be the appropriate architecture for FL.

The third problem with architecture (6) is that it misconstrues the relationship between the SM system and the C-I system. According to (6), there is no connection between these two independent systems, save through the CS that evolves much after the SM and C-I systems evolve.[10] This would mean that pre-linguistic hominids (and all non-hominids) would have no way to connect these two performance systems because they lack CS and LEX. However, if we look at the communication systems of a variety of animals (dolphins, bees, birds, dogs, whales, elephants, ants, apes), we can readily see that these animals both vocalize/gesture and interpret vocalizations/gesturings – see Bickerton (2009) and Fitch (2010) for extended, biolinguistic discussions of animal communication systems. That is, these animals do have interconnected SM and C-I systems. Positing that animals do have interconnected performance systems, though, is not a sufficiently constraint-based analysis; it lacks a conceptual warrant for the interconnection. In other words, what we have to understand is not that the animals do have interconnected performance systems, but that in order to communicate, these animals *must* have interconnected performance systems, which would explain why "animals [that] actually generate call sequences that appear random seem to be exceptional" (Fitch 2010: 185). Absent interconnected performance systems, there can be no communication system. We are now left with the problem of explaining why/how these performance systems are necessarily interconnected. Importantly, merely mapping information from one system to the other will not guarantee the necessity of the connectedness of these systems; it will just force us to explain why the mapping itself is necessary. Once we exclude mapping solutions to the interconnectedness problem, the only way we ensure that the performance systems are interconnected is to hypothesize that the systems are not independent systems, but overlapping ones. What this means is that each and every signal in a communication system, including FL, must carry, reminiscent of Saussure's (1915/1966) analysis of signs, both SM information and C-I information.[11]

From the preceding discussion, we can conclude that architecture (6) is not an appropriate or adequate architecture of FL. So, what is? Before we answer this question, we want to return to Hinzen's argument that we should scuttle the semantic component (the C-I system) because it only duplicates the work done by the syntax. We agree with Hinzen that a syntactic representation is a semantic representation and, therefore, that syntax cannot be seen as independent of the semantics. But this does not mean that the C-I system can be reduced to syntax. There are aspects of meaning – for example, the cognitive effects explained by

Relevance Theory (see Sperber and Wilson 1986 and Blakemore 2002) and by Theory of Mind (see Baron-Cohen 1995) – that are not grounded in syntax. To account for these types of meaning relations, we assume that it is necessary to have a C-I system. Granted, then, that we have both SM and C-I systems, that these systems overlap, and that this overlap contains each and every signal in the communication system, we conclude that the architecture of FL is (9).

(9)

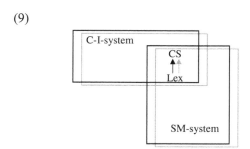

There are two interconnected relationships in (9) that merit special attention. First, both LEX and the CS in (9) – the subsystems that contain and/or derive every signal in FL – are subsumed within the SM–C-I overlap; and second, LEX and CS, which together comprise (FLN, also known as the Narrow Syntax), is a part of the union of the performances systems, which makes up the (FLB) that is involved in reading and interpreting the output of the Narrow Syntax. Interestingly, Chomsky's own assessment of the design of FL is congruent with our view that human language is positioned entirely within the external performance systems:

> The language is embedded in performance systems that enable its expressions to be used for articulating, interpreting, referring, inquiring, reflecting, and other actions. We can think of the SD (i.e., syntactic derivation) as a complex of instructions for these perform-ance systems, providing information relevant to their functions. While there is no clear sense to the idea that language is "designed for use" or "well adapted to its functions," we do expect to find connections between the properties of the language and the manner of its use. (Chomsky 1995:168).

Needless to say, Chomsky's model of FL presented in (6) clearly departs from his recognition that FL is embedded in the performance systems. We, on the other hand, strongly endorse the assumption that FL resides within the perform-ance systems.

Importantly, not only are there conceptual reasons for positing (9) as the design for FL, there are also empirical ones. As Wedeen et al. (2012) demon-strate, the brain is not a jumbled or tangled mass of separate neural networks; rather, it consists of interwoven neural fibers that criss-cross in a three-dimensional curved grid structure. This grid structure contains highly ordered neural overlaps. And, as Ramachandran argues, neural networks that intersect can share (or cross-activate) information, which happens in the case of, among other things, synesthesia: "The observations we have made so far broadly support the cross-activation theory and provide an elegant explanation of the different perceptions of ... synesthetes" (2011: 100). What we are proposing in (9) is a design for the Faculty of Language that is much in line with the neural overlap theories advocated by Wedeen et al. (2012) and Ramachandran (2011).

The consequences of building FL on the design principles expressed in architecture (9), and not on the design principles in architecture (6), are many. First, placing animal communicative systems within the performance systems will dramatically simplify answers to Darwin's Problem. Recall that Darwin's Problem is the twofold problem of explaining how language, complex as it is, could emerge in the human species at all and how modern human language could evolve from protolanguage (and do so in a relatively short period of time). If the communicative systems of all animals are located in their performance systems, as in (9), then no new (linguistic) systems will have to be built for the development of a protolanguage. This accords with Bickerton's view:

And if, under instruction, a whole range of species [dolphins, sea lions, and parrots] can learn some kind of protolanguage, this suggests that, in any species within that range, protolanguage is selection-limited, not variation-limited. In other words, no special changes, magic mutations, "language organs," or dedicated circuits were needed for language to start ... Just a large enough brain, a wide enough range of categories, and, most important, of all: the right selective pressure. (2009: 88)

Once protolanguage develops, the emergence of FL for modern human languages will likewise not require any special mechanisms outside the performance systems; rather, the narrow linguistic systems that comprise FL will be able to emerge out of the extant performance systems by, as Hornstein (2009: 10) asserts, "adding just a little bit, a new circuit or two, to general principles of cognition and computation." The architecture in (9), then, is the maximally simple architecture for FL, requiring no new, independent systems for FL to be constructed nor any special linking devices to align the narrow linguistic systems with the performance systems; this architecture directly incorporates the linguistic systems into the performance systems that will use the linguistic output. Constructed in this way, the architecture of FL proposed in (9) represents a truly minimalist account and, according to the principal grounds established by the SMT, is worthy of serious pursuit.

The second consequence of positing architecture (9) as the design for FL is that this architecture can explain Hinzen's (2009a) computational conundrum. As Hinzen argues, there is a logical problem with assuming, as does architecture (6), that FL is built on a pre-linguistic (and pre-combinatorial) C-I system and that FL subsequently adds a computational (syntactic) system, which generates output analyzed by the C-I system; he notes that a "circularity problem looms" in that "any attempt to explain language from the interface conditions imposed on it will have to figure out the nature of those conditions by looking at how narrow syntax satisfies those very conditions" (2009a:26). In other words, if the linguistic systems (evolutionarily) develop a combinatorial/computational dimension lacking in the C-I system, then the linguistic systems cannot be designed to meet the "needs" of the C-I system and, relatedly, the C-I system will not be equipped to process the computational output of the linguistic systems.[12] The conclusion that Hinzen draws from this is that "it must have been narrow syntax itself, in evolution, which helped to boost the dimensionality of the human mind and the thoughts or objects it can recursively generate: 'thought' wasn't multi-dimension before these specific computational operations of language ... evolved" (2009a: 31). Hinzen's solution to the computational conundrum that he observes, then, is to abandon the minimalist assumption that syntax evolves to satisfy the needs of the performance systems and to elevate the role that syntax plays, separate from the C-I system, in generating thought and meaning; what Hinzen does, in essence, is reduce structural meaning to syntactic form. There are, however, two reasons for not accepting Hinzen's solution. For one, as Saleemi (2009: 185–187) points out, citing examples such as (10) and (11), "the degrees of grammaticality and semantic coherence can be more or less independent of each other, depending on the extent of the intersection between the two, which is what we consider to be the meaning–syntax interface ..." (187). In other words, meaning cannot reduce to form.

(10)   Bleep tinged shoops.

(11)   Colorless green ideas sleep furiously.

The other reason for rejecting Hinzen's solution concerns Darwin's Problem. If, as Hinzen suggests, the CS is separate from, and independent of, the performance systems, the evolution of the faculty of language will require that a completely new system (the CS) be added to the performance systems. Building such a system, given the time constraints placed on the evolution of human language, seems implausible. The foregoing discussion leaves us in a position even more problematic than the one portrayed in Hinzen's conundrum: that is, the CS must have evolved combinatory properties not possessed, in prior fashion, by the C-I system (which must, somehow, still be able to compositionally "use" these novel structures generated by these properties) – all the while the CS must both emerge from the C-I system (as Hornstein argues) and be independent of the C-I system (as Saleemi argues). The problems just described, we would like to propose, can be resolved by architecture (9). In (9), the combinatory properties definitive of the CS are also properties of the C-I system (since the former system is contained in the latter system); of note, although this prohibits the C-I system from having combinatory properties that precede the combinatory properties of CS, it provides some explanation for how the C-I system could "use" the output of CS (which follows from the fact that the C-I system will inherit the combinatory properties from its computational subsystem and can use these properties to produce compositional semantics). Further, since the linguistic systems have properties of both the C-I and SM performance systems, not all the properties of the linguistic systems (LEX and CS) are exhaustively contained in either of the performance systems. As a result, the CS has a degree of independence from both the C-I and the SM systems. The architecture we posit for FL, then, resolves Hinzen's extended conundrum and it does so in a way that is compatible with Saleemi's suggestion that the form–meaning relationship can be adequately expressed only by "[redefining] the concept of form, resulting in an expansion of the [performance systems]" (2009: 185).[13]

Situating the linguistic systems in the intersection of the performance systems not only has an effect on how we address Darwin's Problem, but it also determines how best to answer Plato's Problem (how language is acquired) and Broca's Problem (how the knowledge of language is implemented in the brain) because it limits the properties of the linguistic systems. One such limitation concerns the information borne by the entries in LEX. Following Chomsky (1995), Epstein, Thráinsson, and Zwart (1996), Hornstein, Nunes, and Grohmann (2005), Müller (2010), Stroik (2009a,b), and Tallerman (2009), we assume that each LI in LEX consists of a set of features that collectively participate in structure building; we further assume, however, that since LEX resides in the intersection of the performance systems, the feature sets of LIs must be collections of performance system features (PSFs), which will include both C-I (semantic and pragmatic) features and SM (morphological and phonetic) features. Under this latter assumption, LIs will not possess any features that are not performance system features. In particular, LIs cannot have any features that are strictly formal/syntactic features, such as the edge features (or any form of Extended Projection Principle feature) of the type that Chomsky (2005) employs to activate and license syntax-internal operations (of the Internal Merge or Move sort).[14] All lexical features, then, must be inherently compatible with, and interpretable by, the performance systems. Given this constraint on lexical features, the function of syntactic operations cannot be, as Chomsky (1995) maintains, to check that all lexical features are legible at the performance systems (for Chomsky, having uninterpretable features show up at the C-I and SM interfaces would cause an SD to crash). Lexical features, under our analysis, do not have to be checked for C-I and/or SM interpretability or legibility since they are necessarily compatible with these systems. What this indicates is that checking the legitimacy of individual features plays no role in the linguistic system, suggesting that if features play any role in the linguistic system, this role must involve the legitimacy of how features group, rather than how they fare in isolation.[15] The theory of features we adopt, which bears some semblance to the function of "features" in unification grammars (especially with regard to the fact that certain features – namely, those features we identify as PSFs – appear to have a recursive nature), is Stroik's (2009a) theory, which proposes that each lexical feature not only is a performance system feature, it is also a concatenation feature that must pair with a matching feature to be (concatenatively) licit, as in (7b). Under this theory, which presupposes that the essence of FL is to create complex concepts from simple concepts (see Hinzen 2006), the mechanism at the heart of complex concept formation is the concatenation feature. It is the evolutionary development of such features, we surmise, that made human language possible.

In addition to constraining the contents of LIs, architecture (9) also delimits permissible operations in the CS. Since the CS is subsumed within the perform-ance systems, its operations must be performance-system-encapsulated, taking licit performance system input (starting with input from LEX) and generating licit performance system output, thereby satisfying the Strong Computational Thesis discussed previously, which requires computational output to be perfectly usable by the performance systems. Constrained in this way, the CS must be crash-proof (producing only usable output), as claimed by Stroik (1999, 2009a), Frampton and Gutmann (2002), Hinzen (2006), and Putnam and Stroik (2009). This means that the operations of CS will not include operations such as free External Merge – advocated by Chomsky (2005), Boeckx (2008b), and Ott (2009) – which freely merges two syntactic objects without regard for the usability of its output.[16] Nor will it include operations such as Internal Merge, an operation that copies con-stituents already in an SD and remerges/moves the copied material elsewhere in the derivation. This derivation-to-derivation operation, according to Hinzen (2009a), Kinsella (2009), and Stroik (2009a), is simply not conceptually neces-sary because its output includes a derivational repositioning (a movement) of syntactic objects that cannot be interpreted by the performance systems. Even though remerged syntactic objects can be interpreted in their "moved" positions, their structural repositionings (the movements) in and of themself cannot be interpreted. As a result, operations such as Internal Merge must be proscribed from the CS. Furthermore, the computational system will disallow Transfer-type operations. In his phase-theoretic version of Minimalism, Chomsky (2001, 2004, 2005) requires a Transfer operation to remove the TP and V complements of phase heads (C and $v*$) from the SD and move them to the performance systems for eventual interpretation. Given architecture (9), there is no need for such an operation. Moving structural material to the performance systems is simply not required since all structural output material is necessarily produced, and con-tained, in the performance systems.[17] The performance systems in (9) have no need to see or interpret the output of the CS until the computation of the syntactic derivation is complete. Hence, derivation-partial syntactic chunks (such as phases) and operations on syntactic chunks (such as Transfer and Internal Merge) are unnecessary. After expunging Free External Merge, Internal Merge, and Transfer from the set of permissible operations for being inconsistent with architecture (9), we would seem to be left with the External Merge operation. But is this operation consistent with architecture (9)? To be consistent with architecture (9), the External Merge operation would have to be inscribed in at least one of the performance systems; it would have to be a device that is not a special mechanism that subserves language alone. However, as Chomsky (2010: 53) observes, "Merge is not only a genetically determined property of language, but also unique to it." Given that the Merge operation is special to language and not general to the performance systems, it would not be a permissible operation over architecture (9). Hence, whatever the CS might look like, it will not include any of the operations – External Merge, Internal Merge, or Transfer – that standard Minimalism employs to derive syntactic structure.[18]

In the next section of this chapter, we investigate what the CS would look like within architecture (9); however, before doing so, we want to return to Kinsella's (2009: 36) essential question: "Is the minimalist language faculty evolvable?" Kinsella argues against the evolvability of a minimalist design for language built on (6), as do Bickerton (2009), Jackendoff (2010), and Lieberman (2010); but can the modern FL evolve within the design parameters of architecture (9)? It would seem so. Grounding (human) language firmly in the performance systems, as (9) does, secures it to an evolutionary biological base. The performance systems, which are interconnected with brain size and complexity, are biological systems that are prone to evolve; hence, all computations made by the performance systems, including the computations involving language, will evolve as the brain and its attendant performance systems evolve. Of special note, situating FL within (ancestral) performance systems also brings FL in line with many of the prevailing speculations about human language: that human language, or at least human protolanguage, is millions of years old (as Bickerton 2009, 2010 argues); that the iterative properties crucial to human language do not come from language-specific mechanisms, but are found in very old SM mechanisms for motor control (see Fitch 2010; Ramachandran 2011; Corballis 2002; 2010; and Lieberman 1998, 2006); that human protolanguage involves inferential communication and expressions of intentionality (see Searle 2010 and Sperber and Origi 2010); and that human language is not syntax-centered (see Jackendoff 2002, 2010).

1.5   A new direction for Minimalism

In this section, and throughout the remainder of this book, we will develop a (Minimalist) computation system for FL that not only satisfies the design constraints imposed by architecture (9), but also meets the compressed evolutionary time line Hornstein (2009) theorizes for the development of human language from protolanguage and does so parsimoniously (because, as Bickerton observes, "Evolution is minimalist. It doesn't do a lick more than it has to" (2009:17)). The challenge of developing such a CS, daunting as it is, is made all the more difficult by the fact that little guidance on how to proceed is available. Given that architecture (9) is a radical departure from previous architectures for FL and that architecture (9) sweeps away all the computation machinery currently being used in Minimalist-style syntactic derivations, there remains the scantest of trails to our destination.

We will begin our investigation of the CS of FL with two Minimalist assumptions. First, we assume that the two core structural facts a CS must explain are (i) how two discrete syntactic objects X and Y can be combined to form a third syntactic object Z, as in (12) and (ii) how a single syntactic object X in a given SD can appear in multiple structural relationships, as in (13).

(12)   see + Maggie → [see Maggie]

(13)   a. What did Homer give **what** to Bart on Monday morning?
       b. Otto was hired **Otto**.
       c. Marge seems **Marge** to be **the** happiest person in the room.

(In (13) the emboldened material denotes that the material is participating in a non-overtly expressed structural relationship.) The second assumption we make is that SDs are computed from the bottom up.

If we followed Chomsky (2005, 2009, 2010), we would explain (12) by appealing to the Merge operation as the operation able to link syntactic objects. However, as we have discussed previously, we must reject this explanation because it assumes that Merge is a language-specific operation. A more promising explanation can be found in Hornstein (2009) and in Boeckx (2009), both of whom assert that Merge is actually the combination of two general cognitive operations, Copy and Concatenate, where material is copied from LEX and concatenated with other material copied from LEX. This proposal, though appealing because it invokes operations that could be part of the performance systems, seems to undervalue and underexamine the Copy operation. To "copy X" is not merely a single act of making a facsimile. It is actually a complex three-part act: it involves (i) making a facsimile of X, (ii) leaving X in its original domain D1, and (iii) placing the facsimile in a new domain D2. So, to make a copy of a painting, one must reproduce the painting somewhere (on a canvas, on film, etc.), and to make a copy of a computer file, one must reproduce the file somewhere in the computer (at least in temporary memory). If the Copy operation is in fact a Copy-to-Domain operation, then there is no need for a Concatenate operation, which links material to a (structural) domain; this linking can be done by a Copy operation. The consequence of this analysis is that we can simplify Hornstein's and Boeckx's proposal, reducing Copy plus Concatenate to Copy-only. Under the Copy-only proposal, lexical material is copied from LEX to a working space in short-term memory called a Numeration (NUM) by a Copy-to-Numeration operation (CoN) and then this copied material is (second-order) copied, by a Copy-to-syntactic derivation operation (CoSD), from NUM to the syntactic derivation (SD), as needed (we will discuss this computational sequence in detail in the next three chapters).

The advantages of having a Copy-only CS are most pronounced when applied to displacement data, such as those in (13). For Chomsky (2005, 2009), displacement results from the application of an Internal Merge operation, which, for Chomsky, is merely a variant of the conceptually necessary Merge operation that links syntactic objects together.[19] The Internal Merge operation is the key operation in displacing syntactic objects; this operation is a derivation-to-derivation operation that copies material already in a derivation and places this copied material elsewhere in the derivation.[20] Although Internal Merge appears to be just another copy-type operation, it is a computationally complex operation, as Brody (1995) and Stroik (2009a) argue, in that it can apply only after another operation – a Backward Search operation through the SD – locates the syntactic object to be copied. It is also an ontologically expensive operation because it copies material in an SD that is already a second-order copy (LEX-to-NUM and NUM-to-SD), so it creates third-order copies, which themselves can undergo subsequent Internal Merge, creating fourth-order copies, and so on (with no end in sight to how many degrees of copy could eventually be produced). In a Copy-only CS, syntactic objects can reappear in an SD without searching backward through a derivation to locate a target (only NUM is searched); rather, they can reappear in the same way that they first appear, by copying them from NUM, but only under very constrained circumstances that we will discuss later. So, all appearances of a syntactic object X within a given SD are second-order copies of X from NUM to SD; no copies above second-order copies need be made. Of note, the CoSD operation not only inserts copies of material X contained in NUM into an SD, but also keeps X in NUM as part of what it means to "copy"; this allows for the possibility that X can be copied from NUM to the SD more than once.

What we are proposing, then, is that the CS of human language has only one general cognitive operation – Copy (to Domain), an operation that permits NUM to participate actively in SDs. Importantly, this computational design is easily subsumed within architecture (9). Since the CS consists of a single Copy operation that is used by both the C-I performance system and the SM performance system, the CS comfortably resides within the intersection of these systems; and since both LEX and all NUMs (which are always subsets of LEX) contain LIs that possess only information about form and meaning, information that arguably must be acquired through the performance systems, it must be the case that the lexical components of FL too, are contained within the performance systems.

Although the global design of the framework we are proposing and its CS are unique, this model does share some characteristics of the version of Minimalism developed by Stroik (1999, 2009a), called *Survive-minimalism* in Putnam (2007). Appealing to conceptual necessity and systemic simplicity, Stroik and Putnam argue that the CS can be reduced to two operations – Copy and External Merge – but only if lexical material "survives" in NUM and can be brought into an SD more than once. As with other versions of Minimalism, Survive-minimalism begins every derivation by taking LIs out of LEX and it builds linguistic structures (and conceptual categories) larger than words by utilizing the CS of FL. The CS makes copies of LIs stored in LEX, through the use of the free Copy operation, and places them in a short-term memory buffer called the Numeration (NUM) (see Chomsky 1995, Hornstein, Nunes, and Grohmann 2005 and Chapter 2 of this book for extended discussions of NUM). The copies of LIs in NUM are subsequently introduced into a structured SD, also located in short-term memory space, by External Merge (EM); it is the EM operation that forms complex structures (and concepts) from conceptually simple lexical items. Of special note, for Survive-minimalism, though not for other versions of Minimalism, the EM operation is actually a second-order Copy operation because in addition to merging lexical material into an SD, it also leaves a copy of the material that "survives" in NUM for later remerger into the derivation. That is, the EM operation in Survive-minimalism is the standard EM operation with a twist: it merges material from NUM to the SD, but it does not transfer the material directly from NUM to an SD – which would be tantamount to being a NUM-to-SD movement operation (standard Minimalism, as in Hornstein, Nunes, and Grohmann 2005, assumes that the material in NUM is actually "moved" to the SD without ever offering any justification for this sort of movement). Instead, EM in Survive-minimalism copies material in NUM (material that already consists of copies of LIs) and merges these second-order copies to derivational roots, doing so if and only if the attachment satisfies the feature-matching requirements imposed by the performance systems (as in (7b)). Importantly, this EM operation leaves the copied material extant in NUM; this material left behind can be said to **survive** in NUM if it has features that have not yet been checked/concatenated and this surviving material can be merged again at a subsequent point in the derivation.

The two operations in Survive-minimalism (Copy and EM) are formalized as in (14). Significantly, both the operations involve NUM: the Copy operation (14a) copies lexical material from LEX to a workspace in short-term memory (NUM) and the EM operation (14b) merges material in NUM to an SD. A bit more specifically, the Copy operation collects copied lexical material (α with a lexical Feature Matrix (FM) $<f_1 \ldots f_n>$ comprised of PSFs, including both semantic/pragmatic features and morphophonetic features) and the binary EM operation deploys this material, under feature-match requirements, to construct increasingly complex hierarchical structures of form (and of thought).

(14) a. Copy $\{\alpha, \text{NUM}\} \rightarrow [_{Num} \ldots \alpha \ldots]$
      b. EM: $\{\alpha < \ldots f_i \ldots>, \beta < \ldots f_i \ldots>\} \rightarrow [\alpha \ \beta]$

The fact that the EM operation not only accretes lexical material α to an SD but also retains the copied material in NUM is especially important because α could undergo EM again. This will occur in cases in which α has multiple lexical features $<f_1, \ldots, f_n>$, each of which must be appropriately concatenated in an SD for the derivation to be usable by the performance systems. Although each time α undergoes EM at least one of its features must be concatenated (and deactivated for any future use), there is no guarantee that all the features of α will be concatenated simultaneously. Hence, α may have to be copied into an SD more than once, and it must be available for the EM operation as long as it has features that survive (that are not deactivated). Stroik (1999, 2009a) argues that it is this remerging of lexical material from NUM to an SD that explains displacement phenomena, such as wh-constructions, passive constructions, and raising constructions (15a, b, c), respectively.

(15) a. What did Homer give to Bart on Monday morning?
      b. Otto was hired.
      c. Marge seems to be the happiest person in the room.

To see how this works, consider how (15b) would be derived from NUM {T, was, hired, Otto}. (Since our SD given below is merely illustrative, it will be only a partial derivation.) The first step in the derivation of (15b) is to bring the verb *hired* into the computational workspace. Since nothing is currently in the computational workspace, this means that the verb will be accreted to the null set, as in (16a), projecting the FM of the verb.

(16a) Merge {hired <passive, PATIENT thematic argument>, ø} → [hired]
       <passive, PATIENT thematic argument>

In (16a), we can see that the verb has (at least) two features: one feature for taking a PATIENT thematic argument, and one feature that identifies the verb as a passive participle. The second step is to Copy the DP *Otto* into the derivation. This DP can be brought into the SD because one of its features (its thematic role feature) can concatenate with the features of the verb, as in (16b).

(16b) Merge {Otto <Case, thematic role>, [hired] <passive, PATIENT
       thematic argument>} →[hired Otto] <passive>

Two things of importance happen in (16b): the verb projects its remaining feature <passive> and the DP *Otto* remains in NUM with one surviving feature <Case>. At this point in the derivation, the passive auxiliary verb *was* is copied into the derivation because it bears a passive feature of its own, together with a Tense feature.

(16c)   Merge {was <Tense, passive>, [hired Otto] <passive>} → [was [hired Otto]] <Tense>

The result of copying the auxiliary into the derivation is that the accreted SD projects the <Tense> feature of the auxiliary, which is concatenated with the <Tense> feature of T, as in (16d).

(16d)   Merge {T <Case, Tense>, [was [hired Otto]] <Tense>} → [T [was [hired Otto]]] <Case>

To deactivate the Case feature of the SD projected in (16d), the DP *Otto*, which has a surviving <Case> feature of its own, is remerged into the SD (see (16e)).

(16e)   Merge [Otto <Case>, [T [was [hired Otto]]] <Case>]→ [Otto [T [was [hired Otto]]]]

In the course of derivation (16a–16e), all the features of all the LIs have been concatenated and deactivated; consequently, the final derivation (16e) becomes a licit representation that is ready for interpretation by the performance systems.[21] Among other things, the C-I system will interpret (16e) as an event in which the DP *Otto* is the "logical object" of the verb; and the SM system will interpret (16e) as having the DP as its "grammatical subject."

We have given this long presentation on Survive-minimalism because it, of all versions of Minimalism, offers a computational design that can be adapted for architecture (9). The fact that Survive-minimalism dispenses with virtually all the special computational mechanisms of standard Minimalism and that it grounds LEX in the performance systems suggests that Survive-minimalism aligns somewhat congruently with architecture (9). This alignment, however, can be made exact: we propose that Survive-minimalism can be refitted to meet the design principles of (9) and can do so in an evolutionarily plausible way.

There are two modifications that must be made to Survive-minimalism to align it with (9). The first one is crucial, but relatively simple. Survive-minimalism must rid itself of its last vestige of standard Minimalism – the EM operation – and replace it with a variant of a general cognitive Copy operation. Since Survive-minimalism already has a Copy operation that freely copies material from LEX and places this material in NUM and since the EM operation in Survive-minimalism has a copy-function in it, it is possible to re-engineer the free Copy operation with a modicum of evolutionary tinkering so that it extends to structural domains. Adapting the free Copy operation formalized in (14a) to a specialized structural domain is a matter of changing the target domain.

(14a)   Copy $\{\alpha, \text{NUM}\} \rightarrow [_{\text{Num}} \ldots \alpha \ldots]$

The free Copy operation is a composite Copy operation that copies a lexical item α to a lexical domain (a NUM), with the consequence that the lexical domain is expanded but unchanged; that is, the free Copy operation adds LIs to a collection of LIs, producing a larger collection of LIs – as in a grocery list. In this way, the free Copy operation is not a structure-building operation. The Copy operation, however, can become a structure-building operation if we change composite Copy (of α) to part Copy (of the features of α), which would have become possible once humans could cognitively dissect lexical wholes into lexical items with subparts.[22] What the part Copy operation does is not copy LIs α to a collection of LIs; rather, it accretes lexical material by matching lexical features, as in (17).[23]

(17)   Copy $\{\alpha <f_i<f_n \ldots >>, [_{\text{SD1}} <f_i <f_m \ldots >>]\} \rightarrow [_{\text{SD2}} \alpha _{\text{SD1}}] <f_k \ldots >$, where $k = n$ or m (depending on which feature is higher rank – which we discuss later in this chapter)

In (17), the Copy-to-SD (CoSD) operation accretes lexical material to an SD, which not only expands the SD in the process but also changes its nature from SD $<_i>$ to SD $<\text{feature}_k>$ and, as a result, changes the accretion properties of each successive SD, thereby producing hierarchical syntactic relations (we discuss this in depth in Chapter 3). This difference explains why the free Copy operation in (14a) creates a linear collection of (conceptually simple) lexical material and the specialized Copy operation in (17) creates a structured collection of (conceptually complex) lexical material.

From an evolutionary standpoint, requiring only the Copy operation, Survive-minimalism is substantially leaner than the standard versions of Minimalism in Chomsky (2005), Hornstein, Nunes, and Grohmann (2005), Boeckx (2008b), and Hornstein (2009). While the former version of Minimalism requires a single general cognitive Copy operation, the latter versions of Minimalism require the External Merge EM operation, the Internal Merge (IM) operation, the Transfer operation, edge features, special domains (such as phases), crashes, and conditions that serve to identify the search-space for the IM operation (such as Attract Closest or Phase Impenetrability Condition).[24] By not having any of the complicated computational machinery necessary in standard Minimalism (the existence of which would need significant evolutionary explanation), Survive-minimalism does something that escapes standard Minimalism: it offers answers to Darwin's

Problem that are simple and plausible. In fact, if we look at FL through the lens of Survive-minimalism, we will see that the evolutionary distinctiveness of FL emerges out of its use of the Copy operation. For Survive-minimalism, the free Copy operation, which allows humans as well as some nonhuman animals to produce first-order representations, is not the distinctive mark of FL; rather, it is the specialized part Copy operation – which is a second (and higher)-order Copy operation (copying copies into SDs) – that generates the second-order (and higher) representations unique to FL. The specialized (and restricted) part Copy operation provides FL with what Hinzen identifies as its distinctive mark: "[FL's] distinctive mark is the way it breaks out of a given dimension of mental reality by projecting new categories upon merging two given syntactic objects, or by enacting categorial 'jumps' that give us a different kind of object to think about" (2009a:47). That is, it is the part Copy-to-SD operation that produces the additional dimensions of "mental reality" that Hinzen associates with FL.

It would seem that much of our search for a CS compatible with architecture (9) was done once we had reduced our combinatory operations to the Copy operation. Sadly, this is not the case. As we mention above, there are two modifications that must be made to Survive-minimalism, and the second one is the Hamletian rub. Although Stroik (2009a) and Putnam and Stroik (2009) argue for the conceptual necessity of Survive-minimalism, they do not offer a detailed analysis of how the Narrow Syntax works – that is, how NUM interacts with the CS. In their most recent work, Putnam and Stroik (2010) make inroads towards a strongly derivational theory of syntax based on core minimalist desiderata that explains how a derivation begins, proceeds, and (successfully) terminates. Although this work represents a significant step forward for the Survive-minimalist program, Putnam and Stroik's (2010) recent work is not fully compatible with the architecture of FL that we propose in (9). As a result, we must expand upon their previous work and demonstrate how these derivational events and procedures will transpire within (9). In the remainder of this book, we intend to provide such an analysis of the Narrow Syntax and its inter-workings, thereby providing an enriched version of Survive-minimalism.

We will analyze the Narrow Syntax by addressing three interrelated biolin-guistic challenges posed by Reuland, Boeckx, and Hinzen. These challenges roughly cover the entirety of the syntactic derivational process: how to begin the derivational process (Reuland's Challenge), how to sustain the derivational process (Boeckx's Challenge), and how to end the derivational process with usable output (Hinzen's Challenge). In the first challenge, Reuland (2009) posits that human protolanguage consists of a "collection of Saussurean signs" each of which consists of <f,i> pairs ("where f is a form in a medium (sound, gesture) and i its interpretation as a concept" (211)), but he argues that this sort of protolanguage could not, in and of itself, generate human language because it lacks the defining property of FL – recursivity/concatenativity

(211–212). Building a recursive language system from a collection of Saussurean signs, according to Reuland, requires expanding the linguistic sign from a form-meaning pair <f,i> to a form-meaning-concatenating triple <f,i,g> with "g as a formal instruction representing combinability" (212). For Reuland, SDs begin with linguistic signs (LIs), each of which has instructions for building syntactic structure. Although Reuland provides strong arguments for the necessity of having combinability instructions encoded into linguistic signs, he does not say much about these instructions. He leaves us, then, with the challenge of determining what g is, that is, of giving a precise definition of the formal instructions that allow LIs to combine. To complicate matters, if we assume that the content of each LI is a set of features interpretable by the performance systems and if we follow Reuland in assuming that g is a part of the content of LIs (linguistic signs), then Reuland's challenge becomes the challenge of defining g in terms of PSFs.

As with Reuland's Challenge, Boeckx's Challenge (2008a) also involves instructions about how to combine lexical material. Boeckx maintains that for SDs to be built efficiently "syntax must provide unambiguous instructions" (163) for combining syntactic objects, and he proposes that these instructions must allow syntactic objects to be readily identified for processing, which requires that "the extremities [edges] of syntactic objects must be clearly demarcated, and must be quickly reachable, by which I mean that once the beginning of a syntactic object is reached, its end should be nearby" (163). This proposal is formalized by Boeckx as the Quick Edge Detection requirement (18).

(18) Quick Edge Detection conjecture:
To ensure efficient, optimal mapping, processing decisions must be made as quickly as possible. Quick edge detection contributes significantly to mapping efficiency.

The challenge that Boeckx puts before us is to maximize the speed with which the edges of SDs can be determined – that is, to reduce as much as possible the search for these edges. Scholars such as Boeckx (2007) and Chomsky (2007, 2008, 2009, 2010) postulate that an axiom such as the Quick Edge Detection indicates that a featural component, namely, an edge-feature (EF), ensures that the computational system will continue to build unbound, cyclic structure. Although appealing on the grounds of sheer simplicity, the notion of EFs is problematic on several grounds. Most relevant for our current discussion, it is not immediately clear how features such as EFs would be acquired by children (see Putnam and Stroik 2009 and Stroik 2009a, b for a more detailed discussion of these issues). For us, Boeckx's Challenge and Reuland's Challenge are interrelated challenges, both of which bear on the instructions that drive the

CS. Responding to one of these challenges necessitates responding to the other as well.

Hinzen's Challenge, as we conceive of it, is to devise operations for the CS that are capable of deriving "multi-dimensional" thought (2009a: 31). Noting that the version of Chomsky's (2008) Merge-as-arithmetic successor function produces linear output, Hinzen argues that a Merge operation designed in this way would misconceive of language as being one-dimensional: "If Merge in language and Merge in arithmetic are species of operations, as per Chomsky's quote above, linguistic objects will be of the same mono-dimensionality as the natural numbers ... [and] our mind would be impoverished in a way it is factually not" (30). The conceptual complexity of human language, in Hinzen's view, is a function of its syntactic structure, so the CS must include operations able to "boost the dimensionality of the human mind" (31). The standard Merge operation cannot boost this dimensionality of the mind because it merely adds lexical material together creating material of the same type (as a result, the dimensionality of language remains unchanged). And, as Hinzen argues, supplementing Merge with a Label operation (which is the proposal made by Hornstein (2009) and Boeckx (2009)) still cannot boost the dimensionality of the CS, because providing the output of Merge with labels (which are, in themselves, lexical categories – D, N, V, C, etc.) makes the output (a label) the same as the input (labeled lexical items); hence, "hierarchy within syntax does not get off the ground" (33). To respond to Hinzen's Challenge means identifying operations in the CS that can yield hierarchy, recursion, and dimensionality.

In the remainder of this book, we offer a re-analysis of Survive-minimalism that resolves Reuland's Challenge, Boeckx's Challenge, and Hinzen's Challenge. Our reanalysis remains committed to the core assumptions of Survive-minimalism – the assumption that (9) is the global architecture of FL, the assumption that Copy is the only operation conceptually required in the CS of FL, and the assumption that NUM participates actively in SDs (all of these assumptions are essential, as we have previously argued, to answering Darwin's Problem). However, we introduce a substantial revision to Survive-minimalism by reconceiving the structure of LIs. This revision, we will show, will be crucial in responding to the aforementioned challenges.

Our revision of LIs proceeds as follows. Although we embrace Chomsky's (1995) claim that each LI consists of a set of features, we do not conceive of this set of features as being linear and unstructured $<f_1, \ldots, f_n>$. Instead, we follow Tallerman (2009) and Müller (2010) in assuming that features are hierarchically structured. We propose, in particular, that the lexical features of an LI are organized, within a Feature Matrix (FM), into subgroups of features based on whether the features are selecting-features or selected-features. Our inspiration for organizing features into groups of selected-features and groups of selecting-features comes from Chomsky (1965), who distinguishes SUBCATegory features (features selecting co-occurring lexical material) from CATegory features (features that define lexical material to be selected) (see also Collins 2002 for a similar proposal involving this feature inventory). Any given LI could have both SUBCAT features and CAT features; for example, the verb *admire* will have both a SUBCAT-D feature, which requires the verb to take a DP object argument, and a CAT-V feature, which identifies the LI as being a member of the Verb category. Notice, though, that these features are concatenated separately in a bottom-up SD: the SUBCAT-D feature will enter into a concatenating relation with some syntactic object bearing a CAT-D feature before the CAT-V feature enters into a relation with another syntactic object bearing a SUBCAT-V feature. That is, the SUBCAT features of an LI and its CAT feature are hierarchically organized, with the former entering an SD prior to the latter <SUBCAT-f <CAT-f>>. However, it is not only SUBCAT and CAT features that are hierarchically organized into selecting- and selected-features. As we will argue in Chapter 3, all remaining features (each of which is a PSF, such as a Case feature, a wh-feature, a focus feature, etc.) are either selecting or selected features that are structured so that all selecting PSFs must be placed in an SD before any selected PSFs are. This means that the FM for an LI has the following structure: <SUBCAT-f <selecting PSFs <CAT-f <selected PSFs>>>>.

Importantly, it is the FM itself that addresses Reuland's Challenge and Boeckx's Challenge. FMs provide hierarchical instructions about how SDs proceed (the core concern of both Reuland's Challenge and Boeckx's Challenge). Since LIs are defined by their FMs, combining lexical material is a matter of combining FMs to create/project another FM, which then continues the process of FM combination. Each FM, including each FM projected in an SD, will have a highest feature (an edge feature) and this EF determines which matching material the CoSD operation can enter into the derivation.[25] Once the EF of a syntactic derivation, say f_m in the FM $<f_m <f_n < \ldots >>>$, is concatenated/matched by some lexical material (LM) copied by CoSD from NUM, then the SD will have another FM – either $<f_n < \ldots >$ or, in case f_m is a CAT feature, the active FM of LM (we discuss this in depth in Chapter 3). In either case, copying lexical material to an SD changes the FM of the derivation, which will change the EF and its instruction on how the derivation must proceed. Notice that having CoSD operate over FMs will provide feature-based instructions for how to build syntactic structure (thereby meeting Reuland's Challenge) and it does this by making the edge of the SD, which consists of a single feature, readily and easily identifiable (thereby meeting Boeckx's Challenge). Furthermore, the FMs of SDs are projections/labels that are not static and do not replicate lexical category labels of the Hornstein-type. As a consequence, the output of the Copying operation constantly boosts the dimensionality of the syntax, and it generates new syntactic forms (and new thoughts) that are necessarily hierarchical and recursive – thereby meeting Hinzen's Challenge.

The foregoing discussion provides an indication of how Survive-minimalism can efficiently and successfully respond to some of the biolinguistic challenges that confront a linguistic system. In the rest of our book, we give a detailed analysis of the CS within Survive-minimalism and we show along the way that it is possible to elegantly solve Darwin's Problem and Hornstein's Challenge, while attending to Galileo's Thesis and Turing's Thesis, by endorsing Survive-minimalist assumptions.[26] Over the course of our analysis, we will theorize the Minimalist cognitive journey lexical material must take as it goes from LEX to the performance systems for interpretation. We will break up this analysis into three parts, reflecting the three stages of a syntactic derivation: its beginning, its growth, and its end. In the first part (Chapter 2 and Chapter 3), we develop a composite theory of LEX and the NUM. Chapter 2 ("The Structure of the Lexicon") proposes a composite theory of LEX, starting with a biolinguistic analysis of the protolexicon. Crucial to this analysis of LEX is defining LIs in terms of selecting-features and selected-features, all of which are hierarchically organized, in FMs, and connected to the performance systems. We argue that the development of category features and their inclusion in the FMs of LIs are the adaptations responsible for transforming structurally simplex protolanguage into recursive, desymbolic human language. Chapter 3 ("Constructing the Numeration") argues for the necessity of having a NUM (where LIs from LEX are placed in short-term memory so they can be used by the CS); and it argues that NUMs have four significant properties, the last three of which have not been discussed previously: NUMs consist of lexical material that is copied from LEX, they are assembled in piecemeal fashion during the course of an SD, their lexical material is targeted for selection (not blindly selected), and there is an ongoing connection between NUM and the CS throughout the compilation of an SD. The dynamic interaction between NUM and the CS, we show, makes human language possible. In the second part (Chapter 4 and Chapter 5), we provide a theory of syntactic relations, which incorporates FMs and the CoSD operation. Chapter 4 ("Copy and the computational system") constructs a theory of syntactic relations that uses only lexical features and the Copy operation to build syntactic structure. It argues for a crash-proof syntax that develops out of protolinguistic resources available in the performance systems, and that minimizes syntactic computations and simplifies language acquisition (this syntax avoids/eliminates syntactic movement and all of the complex, often language-specific, computational machinery required for movement, including the sorts of powerful look-back operations assumed by Chomsky, such as Internal Merge and Transfer). We show that Copy must be an operation from NUM to the SD (and not a derivation-internal operation, as advocated by Boeckx 2009 and Hornstein 2009). Having a domain-to-domain Copy operation provides a conceptually necessary mechanism for initiating, continuing, and terminating derivations, and a conceptually necessary mechanism for deriving displacement phenomena (without employing displacement operations). One substantial consequence of this analysis, which we discuss at length, is that derivations do not have to begin with predicates (which is biolinguistically appropriate given that the protolanguage need not have begun, and likely did not begin, with predicates and that children's acquisition of, and production of, language does not begin with predicates). Chapter 5 ("Some structural consequences for derivations") applies the computational analysis developed in the previous chapter to a broad range of grammatical constructions, including expletive constructions, conjunction constructions, and adjunction constructions, among other things. Of particular importance in this chapter is our reanalysis of conjunction constructions. As we demonstrate, our theory of syntactic relations predicts a startlingly new (and correct) structure for conjunction constructions that seems not to be replicable by other theories of grammar. The fact that Survive-minimalism alone can derive the structure required for conjunction constructions gives our theory of syntactic relations strong empirical support. In the third and final part (Chapter 6: "Observations on performance system interpretations"), we speculate, albeit briefly, about how the (crash-proof) derivational output from the computational system is interpreted by the performance systems, with particular attention paid to binding and scopal relations; and it offers a reanalysis of Pietroski's (2005) conjunctive semantics built around our reappraisal of conjunction structures. In our conclusion, we address Hornstein's (2009) Challenge, which is to explain how human language could have developed in a relatively short time span built on relatively minor evolutionary innovations. We argue that the language design proposed in Survive-minimalism, which situates the entire language system within pre-existing performance systems and which uses only pre-existing computational operations, provides plausible answers to Hornstein's Challenge because it requires only a relatively minor innovation (the development of category features) for complex human language to evolve from simplex protolanguage.

1.6   Final remarks

One potential concern about our proposal is that our simplification of the syntax of human language merely shifts much of the computational complexity commonly attributed to the Syntax to LEX. That is, our proposal could be construed as embedding the hierarchical relations associated with syntax in the hierarchically arranged FMs of LIs. This concern, however, misses our essential argument, which is that developments in LEX are responsible for what is identified as syntactic relations. Under our analysis, the emergent cognitive ability to dissect wholes into parts, which according to Bickerton (2009), Fitch (2010), and Searle (2010) is critical to the emergence of human language, gives us hierarchical lexical features, where the features are first-order parts of LIs and their hierarchical relations are second-order parts (the hierarchy is a part-of-part relationship). Once lexical features and their hierarchical relations evolve and the memory capabilities of our ancestors increase, it becomes possible to derive syntactic relations cost-free, with the use of a general cognitive Copy operation that is capable of accreting cognitive material (lexical features). What we are arguing, then, is that syntactic relations evolve from lexical adaptations; hence, the apparent computational overlap between LEX and what has formerly been called Syntax (note that in our analysis there is no Syntax component in the Faculty of Language). For us, Syntax is a free-rider (a "spandrel" in Gould and Lewontin's 1979 terminology) that grows out of lexical developments.

We would like to end this chapter by stating as overtly as possible exactly what the focus of this book *is* and what it *is not*. Our primary objective here is to investigate the overall design of FL (the challenge posed by Turing's Thesis) and the effects that the design has on the way that human language is computed; that is, our objective focuses directly on the structure of FL and only indirectly on the mechanisms (and mathematical laws) operating within the structure (the challenge posed by Galileo's Thesis). We are not investigating syntactic operations to see what they can tell us about the structural design of FL; rather we are investigating the structural design of FL to see what it can tell us about syntactic computations. In this we are following Einstein, who theorized the structure of space to explain gravitational laws, and not Newton, who theorized gravitational laws without regard for the space in which they operate.

2 The structure of the Lexicon

2.1 Introduction: compositional and relational problems

In this chapter and the next, we develop a composite theory of the Lexicon (LEX) and the Numeration (NUM), one that is in line with the proposed architecture of human language that we advance in the first chapter of this book. As we discuss here and in Chapter 3, placing both LEX and any NUM that is constructed from LEX within the Conceptual-Intentional (C-I) and Sensorimotor (SM) performance systems is critical to understanding what the protolexicon may have looked like and how it could have evolved into a modern human language that possesses not only a LEX but also a computational syntax. We argue in this chapter that LEX evolved as it did, as a system in which its individual lexical items are defined in terms of hierarchically organized features, because it is contained within the performance systems; and we argue in the next chapter that syntactic structure emerges out of hierarchical, feature-based relations determined by the lexical items (LIs) in a NUM. What we are proposing, in particular, is that the evolution of lexical features is responsible for the evolution of syntax.

Words are so basic to language that it would seem to be easy to discuss the nature of LEX. But this is simply not the case. LEX is actually a topic fraught with controversy. While there is little dispute over the existence of LEX or over the central role it plays as a "feeder" for syntactic operations, there is ample disagreement about what LIs in LEX look like internally (which we call *the compositional problem*) and about exactly how LEX is integrated into structure-building operations (which we call *the relational problem*). We will investigate the former problem in this chapter and the latter problem in the next chapter.

Since our analysis of LEX grows out of notions developed in the Minimalist Program, we will begin our analysis with a brief overview of Minimalist syntax, emphasizing the role that LEX plays in the syntactic/computational system. Following Chomsky (1995), most strands of Minimalism have assumed that an operation known as *Select* probes into LEX and pre-selects the LIs that will eventually be integrated in a syntactic derivation (SD).[1] These preselected LIs are placed in a NUM (at times called a Lexical Array), to be accessed when needed in the course of an SD. This approach to NUM-building was modified slightly with the introduction of phases into the theory (cf. Richards 1997; Uriagereka 1999; Chomsky 2000, 2001, 2005, 2008). According to Chomsky, phases, which are sub-units of an SD headed by $v*$ and C that are syntactically and semantically complete, raise the possibility of having lexical sub-arrays in NUM, consisting of all and only the LIs necessary to complete the construction of a phase (i.e., a sub-component of a derivation).

Once a NUM is built (whether all-at-once, or phase-by-phase), SDs in standard versions of Minimalism are mapped by the computational system (CS) from NUM (of LIs) to the C-I and SM interfaces, as in (1).[2] This mapping results from the cumulative application of two syntactic operations – External Merge (EM), which merges LIs in NUM into an SD, and Internal Merge (IM), which copies and remerges elements in SD to other positions in SD, as in (2).

(1)   CS: NUM → <C-I, SM>

(2)   a. EM: NUM → SD
      b. IM: SD → SD

The view of LEX and its interaction with the CS of human language briefly described above is widely held – see Collins (1997), Epstein et al. (1998), Lasnik (1999), Hornstein, Nunes, and Grohmann (2005), Epstein and Seely (2006), Hinzen (2006), Boeckx (2008a), Hornstein (2009), and many others.

Importantly, in Chomsky's (1995, 2004) version of Minimalism, every SD begins with the formation of a NUM – an array of LIs selected in pre-derivational blindness from LEX.[3] What is being selected though is not merely a collection of atomic LIs; rather what is being blindly selected are well defined subelements (called features) all of which play significant roles in the course of an SD. According to Chomsky (1995, 2005), Epstein, Thráinsson, and Zwart (1996), and Hornstein, Nunes, and Grohmann (2005), each LI in NUM consists of a set of lexical features $<f_1,\dots,f_n>$. They further assume that these features fall into three subsets: a semantic-feature set (SEM), a phonological-feature set (PHON), and a syntactic-feature set (SYN). The features in SEM and PHON are intrinsically compatible with the C-I and SM interfaces, respectively. The features in SYN – which include the Case of nouns – are said to be "formal" features that do not have to be compatible with either interface. To be appropriately interpreted at the interfaces, these "uninterpretable" formal features must be checked/valued and deleted before a derivation reaches the interfaces. The need to "interpret" or "value" features functions as the motivating force that drives the derivation.

With the LIs in NUM appropriately selected from LEX (in pre-derivational blindness), a syntactic computation will take place in which the LIs are merged into the SD. Of note, the Merge operation is a syntactic operation that involves two syntactic objects X and Y that have matching features, which become "checked" for interface legibility/compatibility in the course of Merge.[4] Through iterative applications of EM and IM, all the LIs in NUM must be incorporated into the SD and all the features of each LI must be checked and/or valued, or the derivation will "crash" and not be interpreted;[5] if all the features are appropriately checked, the derivation will be submitted to the interfaces for interpretation.

Stroik (2009b: 24) raises three concerns about this approach to derivations that we would like to emphasize at this stage of our discussion of LEX and of the relationship between NUM and the CS. First, although LEX in standard versions of Minimalism participates, through NUM, in SDs, it appears that LEX is extraneous to the performance systems. This seems to be the case due to the fact that the lexical features of LIs must be "checked" for interface compatibility with the performance systems; hence these LIs must potentially possess features that are exotic to (outside of and incompatible with) the performance systems. (For us, the term "interface" is a major misnomer for the biolinguistically plausible, derivationally simplistic version of the Minimalist Program that we are developing here; see note 2.) Second, in standard Minimalism, it is assumed that successful derivations can be built from the blindly selected LIs in NUM (or in sub-arrays), as can be seen in both Chomsky (1995, 2005) and Hornstein, Nunes, and Grohmann (2005). As we shall show in the next chapter, this is a dubious assumption that leads to a crash-rife syntax. And third, by designing derivations around the checking requirements on the features of individual LIs, standard Minimalism presents derivations, and their representational outputs, as the structured licensing of LIs. What this suggests is that the "interfaces" – or more aptly put the C-I and SM performance systems – give visibility to individual LIs and that the C-I and SM performance systems perhaps even sensitize their interpretations of syntactic representations to the individual LIs, rather than to the concatenated items formed by syntactic operations.

As we pointed out in the first chapter of this book, placing LEX outside of the C-I and SM performance systems is problematic on many grounds – especially in light of our evolutionary approach to the development of the CS of FL that we are pursuing here. We propose instead that LEX must be contained *within* the performance systems. Under our proposal, all LIs are "born interpretable," i.e., they possess no *un*interpretable or *un*valued variants that drive operations in an SD.[6] For us, the CS does not use the uninterpretable or unvalued features of (uninterpretable) LIs to build larger, interpretable structures; rather, it uses the interpretable features of (interpretable) lexical items to build larger, interpretable structures (see Sigurðsson 2006 for a similar view of features in the CS). But this discussion anticipates the *composition problem* – which is concerned with what the internal structure of LIs looks like.

While it is commonly assumed that LIs are composed of bundles of atomic features, it is often unclear what these features look like and how detailed their composition is. So how detailed does lexical information have to be? According to Borer (2003, 2004, 2005), whose analysis builds on the Distributed Morphology (DM) framework developed by Hale and Keyser (1993) and Marantz (1993) among others, LIs in LEX are void of all but the bare essential information, with much "lexical information" stored "at the interfaces." Under such a view, LIs are regarded as "√Roots" (a term first coined by Pesetsky 1995) that must merge with a light head (e.g., *n*, *v*, *a*, *p*, etc.) to receive semantic interpretation. The structural position of √Roots is of central importance in determining the argument and event structure of a predicate. (This strictly exoskeletal, neoconstructivist approach to phrase structure/syntactic relations has led to a relaxed stance on the motivation for Merge in the Narrow Syntax.) Although Borer's feature minimalization proposal has an intrinsic conceptual appeal, it rests on the conceptually unappealing assumption that LIs interface with, rather than reside in, the performance systems. Given our arguments that LEX must be contained in the performance systems, there is simply no way an LI can pick up any additional information stored at the "interfaces."[7] If, as we have argued, LIs and their features are born interpretable, then the sorts of mechanisms Borer enlists to make lexical items interpretable would lack conceptual necessity.[8]

Our view of lexical composition aligns more with the feature-rich approach to lexical composition advanced by Pollard and Sag (1994) in their Head-driven Phrase Structure Grammar (HPSG) and with Levin and Rappaport-Hovav's (1995 et seq.) projectionist view that lexical entries deterministically project onto syntactic positions according to universal linking principles than with Borer's constructivist assumption that meaning is built from feature-sparse LIs and from predicates that contain unordered lists of arguments. We will argue, in this chapter and in the next, that syntactic relations are formed, as Pollard and Sag claim, through processes of (recursive) feature-sharing that require both a feature-selector and a feature-selectee "to have their hands" involved in these processes. Where we crucially differ, however, from Pollard and Sag and from Levin and Rappaport-Hovav is in making Feature Matrices (FMs), and not heads or predicates, the mechanism that drives the formation of syntactic relations. As we will argue, what syntactic operators do is manipulate lexical FMs, regardless of whether these matrices are associated with heads-of-constructions (including predicate heads) or not.[9]

In this chapter we will provide a detailed discussion of the structure, composition, and function of LEX within Survive-minimalism. In Section 2.2, we take a biolinguistic view of LEX, investigating what a protolanguage must have looked like. We argue that the protolanguage must have consisted of LIs that possessed FMs with hierarchically arranged performance system features

(PSFs); and we argue that the modern LEX has emerged out of the protolexicon with the development of CATegory features. In Section 2.3, we consider how feature-impoverished vs. feature-loaded FMs must be. In this section we argue that the notion of √ROOT (as is generally accepted in DM) does not represent an ideal candidate for the featural composition of LIs in the LEX of the human language system, or in its protolexicon ancestor.

2.2   A biolinguistic interlude on lexical composition

Before analyzing the structure of LEX and the composition of lexical items, we want to make it clear that there are several intensely interesting issues surrounding the development (and the evolution) of LEX that we will not be addressing. We will not, for example, pursue questions about how long ago human proto-words first emerged, although we find the claims made by Bickerton (2009) and Fitch (2010) that these words might be at least two million years old quite fascinating. Nor will we have anything to say about the original function of proto-words, about whether these words originated as part of the food gathering process (as Bickerton 2009 contends) or as part of the sexual selection process (as Darwin 1871 and Fitch 2010 assert) or elsewhere. We also will not investigate the physical form of proto-words – were these words gestural forms involving the motor mirror cells possessed by our ancestors, as Arbib (2005) argues, or were they prosodic forms involving ancestral auditory mirror cells, as Fitch (2010) maintains? Both of these conjectures have some plausibility, as Fitch notes, because "Gestural origins hypotheses are ... consistent with comparative data from great apes, whose gestural capacities far outstrip their vocal learning abilities" (464) and because "The core hypothesis of musical protolanguage models is that (propositionally) meaningless song was once the main communication system of prelinguistic hominids" (506). Since it does not matter to our analysis which replication system (whether grounded in motor mirror cells or in auditory mirror cells) first provided the formal ability to re-create and proliferate proto-words, we will not take a position on this controversy. We do, however, find Ramachandran's (2011: 173) neural overlap analysis of gesture and prosody to be a promising resolution to the controversy:

Since the cortical areas concerned with the mouth and the hands are right next to each other, perhaps there is an actual spillover of signals from hands to mouth. As in synesthesia, there appears to be a built-in cross-activation between brain maps, except here it is between two motor maps rather than between sensory maps. We need a new name for this, so let's call it "synkinesia" (*syn* meaning "together" and *kinesia* meaning "movement") ... Synkinesia may have played a pivotal role in transforming an earlier gestural language (or protolanguage, if you prefer) of the hands into spoken language.

(We must admit that we find Ramachandran's analysis attractive because of its use of neural overlaps, which is consonant with our assumption that the design of the Faculty of Language (FL) requires overlapping cognitive systems.) And finally, we will accept, without comment or analysis, Jespersen's (1922) theory that the first proto-words were "holistic" (not having any internal structure) and that these words were decomposed into parts at a subsequent stage in the evolution of protolanguage. For us, it does not matter how or when lexical decompositions emerged, so we are willing to accept the assumption of proto-linguistic holism advocated not only by Jespersen, but also by Wray (2000), Searle (2010), and Fitch (2010). Although we believe all the aforementioned theories about protolanguage and about the protolexicon in particular are interesting and deserve to be investigated thoroughly, we find the questions posed by these theories to be orthogonal to our questions about the design of the Faculty of Language; hence, we give these theories but a passing nod, mentioning them only to provide a large grounding for our more focused discussion of LEX.

We will begin our biolinguistic analysis of LEX by considering the properties of a protolexicon as proposed by Tallerman (2009) and by Reuland (2009). For Tallerman, "a word-based lexicon evolved by building on ancient conceptual categories which are likely shared by many primates [and] . . . utilized what I will argue are pre-existing semantic organization, and built on the hierarchical struc-ture already in place in primate cognition" (2009: 181). Although the protolexicon will include "links between the store conceptual structure and lexical-semantic representations (semantic processing) [and] . . . links between a lexical-semantic representation and its sound or sign (phonological processing)" (183), it will not include any mechanisms to systematically link lexical items. Reuland (2009) presents a similar view of the protolexicon. He sees the protolexicon "as a collection of *Saussurean signs*" (211), in which each sign is a pairing of form and concept. These signs, however, lack any "formal instruction[s] representing combinability" (212).

For both Tallerman and Reuland, the protolexicon is pre-syntactic: LIs can carry and link information about form/sound and meaning/concept, but these LIs cannot combine together into any meaningful larger-than-word units. Under these assumptions, the development of human language requires two separate evolutionary leaps: (i) a lexical leap in which humans build a LEX upon the then-available resources in their cognitive systems and (ii) a combinatory (syntactic) leap which apparently emerges independently of the "semantic organization [and] . . . hierarchical structure already in place in primate cognition."[10]

We find this two-leap analysis of the evolution of human language to be problematic for several reasons. The first, and most blatant, problem with this analysis is that it leaves the CS (the syntax) of human language unexplained. If the CS is not built out of the available cognitive resources possessed by humans, where could it come from? And if it is built out of these resources, why must it develop separately from LEX? Second, the evidence that we have on primate attempts to acquire human language shows that primates can both acquire a small set of LIs and can link these LIs, albeit in a limited fashion. Premack (1976), for example, notes that a chimpanzee named Sarah could, among other things, classify properties such as "big" and "round" and combine these properties with objects, as in "round cracker"; and Gardner and Gardner (1969) observe that Washoe (a chimpanzee) could make thirty combinations of two–three words and she could coin new combinations, such as "water bird" to refer to *swan*, an object for which she had no term. Further, as Wallman (1992: 104) notes,

The testing of Kanzi's [a chimpanzee's] sentence comprehension, in summary, demonstrates that he is able to put together the object or objects and the action mentioned in the way that is appropriate given the properties of the objects involved, what he typically does with them, or both.

Fitch (2010: 168) summarizes the data we have about the language-learning abilities of great apes as follows:

From my perspective, Kanzi and other language-trained apes demonstrate an ability to acquire a sizeable lexicon, to use it in communicative interactions (though mostly, it must be admitted, to make requests for treats or tickles), and to produce and understand basic and non-random combinations of these lexical items.

Given that the linguistic abilities of primates are not limited to building a LEX, it is unlikely that our human ancestors, who arguably had cognitive resources beyond those of chimpanzees, would have had syntax-free protolanguages, which consisted merely of a protolexicon. Third, and most importantly, there is a conceptual reason for rejecting the dual-leap analysis of language evolution. That is, once humans had the cognitive ability to form the links necessary to build a protolexicon (an ability that requires humans to unite/combine/unify two types of dissimilar materials – phonetic material with conceptual material – that are arbitrarily and conventionally tied together), then they certainly had the cognitive ability to build a protosyntax (an ability that would require humans to unite/combine/unify lexical material with lexical material – two similar materials that would be linked cognitively and instrumentally, not arbitrarily and conventionally). What is at stake in building a LEX is the ability to create links, which is exactly what is at stake in building a syntactic structure. It would be bizarre and unexpected for our ancestors to possess a protolanguage that could build a productive protolexicon, but not any form of protosyntax, even a rudimentary form of this syntax. To look at this a bit more closely, notice that once a language has a LEX that includes property terms (*big*, *yellow*, *old*, etc.)

and quantifier terms (*one, two, all,* etc.), it will also have some form of syntax. Properties and quantifiers are properties and quantifiers of something; hence, these terms must be able to systematically connect with other LIs. Now given that chimpanzees, as Premack (1976) notes, can learn and use property terms such as "round" and "big" and quantifier terms such as "all," "none," "one," and "several," surely our protolanguage-speaking ancestors could too.

Having a productive LEX allows one to put words together in several ways. The easiest of these is word-list formation (which we adults practice with our very young, and cognitively nascent, children all the time). To form a word-list is a matter of using the Copy operation (see Chapter 1) to place LIs with (often) similar features into NUM and then using the Copy-to-LI (an early version of Copy-to-SD) to string these words together in a linear fashion – notice that the linearity is a natural by-product of putting lexical *sames* together with other lexical *sames* to derive expanded lexical *sames*. We create lexically matched word-lists for our children when we try to teach these children numbers, colors, and body parts, among other things. The second way to string words together is to unite LIs based on their shared (or intersective) performance systems features (PSFs), which are generally grounded in conceptual and/or perceptual categories, as Tallerman (2009) contends. When we combine *red* and *blood* to create *red blood*, or when we combine *two* and *cat(s)* to create *two cat(s)*, we do so by combining the intersective PSFs of the two LIs, one of which, say, possesses a *count* feature (the word *two* has this feature) and one of which selects that particular PSF by being *countable*, as is the case for *cat(s)*. It may even be possible to put together actions and objects using intersective PSFs, such as in combining the perceptual (olfactory) properties of the action *smell* with those of the object *meat* to form *smell meat*. Stringing words together in this fashion will derive non-linear structures because uniting these non-same LIs will create an output that differs from the inputs (note that young children can string together words in this way, as can some language-trained great apes).

Although it is possible to build syntactic structure by using intersective PSFs to feature-match (or feature-select) and connect lexical items, this sort of syntax will not be sufficiently robust to generate the two properties identified by Reuland (2009) as being most central to the faculty of human language: recursion and desymbolization. For Reuland, the essential properties of language are the unboundedness of its syntactic structures (*the recursive property*) and the dissociation of form and meaning (*the desymbolization property*). It is the latter property that "allows operations to apply blindly irrespective of meaning" (Reuland 2009: 218), with the consequence that "Desymbolization of language allows us to ignore common sense, play with expectations, say the impossible, express the inconceivable, escape from here and now, and create poetry ... [it] feeds into imagination and gives rise to the richness and diversity of human culture as we know it" (219).[11] Since PSFs such as animacy or countability are, as Tallerman suggests, connected to perceptual and conceptual categories, building structures by connecting PSFs will not produce a language in which form is divorced from perceptual and conceptual categories (i.e., *the desymbolization property* will not be met); and since PSFs are not inherently recursive features, it is not possible to combine them to produce unbounded conceptualization (so *the recursive property* will not be met).

From the foregoing discussion we can see that if LIs were comprised only of conceptually and perceptually grounded PSFs, human language would not have any recursion and desymbolization properties. This suggests that satisfying both the recursion and desymbolization properties of human language requires LIs to contain more information than just protolexical PSFs, which further suggests that this "other" information must be conceptually necessary for the two afore-mentioned properties of human language to arise. Of note, whatever the "novel" information happens to be, it must not only escape the recursive and desymbol-izing limitations that are imposed by conceptual and perceptual information, but it must, at the same time, be a special sort of lexical information – the kind of information that is able to integrate into the hierarchically structured FMs that define LIs (see Tallerman 2009 for arguments that the features of LIs are hierarchically structured). We follow Jackendoff (2002) in proposing that the "novel" information responsible for the development of human language involved lexical category (CAT) features (Noun, Verb, Adjective, etc.).[12] Unlike PSFs, CAT features are not grounded in perceptual and conceptual categories; that is, they are not inherently about the meaning of an LI or about its physical form. As such, these features are essentially desymbolic in nature. Further, if we assume that CAT features share the feature-match (or select) properties of the other features in an FM, then the CAT feature of one LI will be able to match with (or be selected by) a CAT-selecting-feature of another lexical item. Under this analysis, CAT-type features can appear twice in the feature matrix of any given LI-x: once as the CAT feature of the LI itself (all LIs will have a defining CAT feature) and once as a CAT-selecting-feature (known as a SUBCATegory feature) that identifies the CAT feature of the LI-y elements that LI-x can select. The fact that CAT-type features can show up twice in an FM makes this feature unlike any of the PSFs, all of which either possess a conceptual/perceptual feature or select that feature, but not both. Importantly, what emerges out of having multiple CAT-type features in FMs is recursion. If LI-x has a CAT feature that can be selected by the SUBCAT feature of LI-y, which has a CAT feature that can be selected by the SUBCAT feature of LI-z, which has a CAT feature that can be selected by the SUBCAT feature of LI-a, which . . ., then these possibly unbounded feature-matches will allow the LIs to connect with one another.

What we are proposing is that the protolexicon contained LIs, each of which is defined, as Tallerman (2009) argues, by a set of hierarchically structured features (we call this structure **a Feature Matrix** (FM)). These features partition into essential features that define the lexical item in question (these are selected-features) and contingent features that are associated with the LI (these are selecting-features). For example, the LI *cat(s)* would have a contingent countable-feature and the LI *two* would have a necessary count-feature; the former feature would select the latter feature to feature-connect the LIs, thereby creating *two cat(s)*. Since (contingent) selecting-features depend on (necessary) selected-features, the features would be hierarchically organized in an FM as follows: <selecting PSFs <selected PSFs>>. That is, the selected-features would be ranked lower in the FM than selecting-features would be (this makes evolutionary sense since the selected-features, which define the conceptual essence of an LI, are "older" than the selecting-features that extend, rather than define, an LI). Given the protolexicon described above, human protolanguage would consist of LIs and syntactic objects formed by matching selecting-features with selected-features. Although this protolanguage would have had a form of syntax, the syntax, as we have discussed previously, would not be recursive, and the protolanguage, even with some notion of syntax, would not have been desymbolic. The evolutionary leap that would have transformed protolanguage into (modern) human language is the development of lexical category features, CAT and SUBCAT. Since these "new" features are selected-features and selecting-features respectively, they would have been accreted into the FM as in (3), with the newest features being added on last.

(3)   <SUBCAT <selecting PSFs <CAT <selected PSFs>>>>

Once CAT-type features are integrated into FMs, the syntax operating over these FMs will be recursive and desymbolized – giving birth to human language.

2.3   The compositional problem: Just how much featural composition do lexical items need?

In the previous section we explored the (feature) composition of the human protolanguage/Lexicon that must have developed to arrive at the complex system of language that we have today. At this point in our investigation of LEX, we would like to reconsider the possibility, as hypothesized in current versions of DM, that the LIs in LEX consist of (highly) underspecified √Root-units, where these units "correspond to the non-grammatically definable part of a word" (Acquaviva 2008), and that morphosyntactic features, including CAT features, are added to √Roots in the course of SDs. There are (at least) two reasons to take seriously the DM proposal that LEX consists only of √Roots. First, from a biolinguistic perspective, the LIs in the protolanguage would have conceptual and perceptual features, but they would not have any syntactic or grammatical features; in other words, these LIs would be √ROOTS. Given that the LEX in the protolanguage contained only √ROOTS, it is conceivable that LEX in modern human language could continue to be a collection of √ROOTS. Second, if LEX has feature-rich LIs that bear grammatical features in addition to conceptual and perceptual features, then this LEX will be burdened with the (potential) disadvantage of housing a host of polysemous roots. To see this, consider the following data taken from Clark and Clark (1979):

(4) a. The factory horns *sirened* throughout the raid.
     b. The factory horns *sirened* midday and everyone broke for lunch.
     c. The police car *sirened* the Porsche to a stop.
     d. The police car *sirened* up to the accident site.
     e. The police car *sirened* the daylight out of me.

Borer (2004: 290–291) provides an analysis of the above data that raises the sorts of problems that emerge if LIs have fully specified feature matrices (FMs):

We note that if the syntax of the arguments and the event structures in (4a-e) are to be attributed to the properties of some verbal lexical entry *siren*, we would have to assume that there are five distinct entries for *siren*, the one in (4a) associated with an atelic agentive reading, and meaning "to emit a siren noise," the one in (4b) associated with a telic agentive (and theme?) meaning "to signal through emitting a siren noise," the one in (4c) associated with a telic agent-patient and meaning "to force by emitting a siren noise," the one in (4d) associated with telic-agentive, and subcategorizing a particle, meaning "to hurry while emitting a siren noise," and finally, in (4e), *siren* would be associated with a stative and an experiencer, and would mean "to frighten by way of emitting a siren noise." Of course, the common denominator here is the emission of a siren noise, which, indeed, appears to be the meaning of *to siren*, but it is entirely clear that in each of the (4a-e) the event denoted is modified by the emission of a sound, rather than determined by that emission. Thus at least in (4a-e), we must assume that the syntax of the event (and the syntax of the event's arguments) does not emerge from five different lexical items for *siren*. Rather, it is the syntax which determines the interpretation of the event and its arguments, as well as the specific nuance contributed to that interpretation by the vocabulary item *siren* which modifies that event.

To avoid the problem of having the overabundance of redundant lexical forms discussed by Borer, the DM framework advocates the existence of lexically impoverished LIs (for such proposals, see Hale and Keyser 1993, 2002; van Hout 1992, 1996, 2004; Marantz 1997, 2005; Ritter and Rosen 1996, 1998; and Borer 1994, 1998, 2003, 2004, 2005 and subsequent work). Under DM assumptions, underspecified LIs will enter the CS where they will pick up grammatical features from feature-bearing syntactic heads; as LIs proceed through an SD, the heads introduced will determine the argument structure and the event structure of the derivation, as well as some of the attendant syntactic features of the verbs/ predicates participating in the event structure. (A DM-analysis of the data in

(4) will list the root √SIREN as an unspecified unit in LEX whose argument structure will be determined by its event structure, which is regulated by the structural alignment of the root with its (optional) arguments.) Importantly, since there are features within the DM framework that emerge only syntactically, not all features will be listed as part of a lexical specification.

As described above, one of the central assumptions of the DM-framework is that syntax shapes semantics. In and of itself, this is not a very controversial assumption. Many theorists adopt equivalent assumptions: Hinzen (2009a: 42), for one, asserts that "The more plausible alternative is that the semantic objects in question are creatures of the syntax itself: Syntax was and is innovative for them"; and Reuland (2009: 222) takes a similar position when he argues that syntax precedes semantics, invoking the mantra "Create, interpret later." What is controversial about the DM framework, however, is its ancillary assumption that syntax shapes semantics from category-free (and grammatical-feature-impoverished) LIs. This latter assumption is not as widely embraced. Acquaviva (2008:4), among others, argues that "when the lack of category labels is taken seriously, and is not just a formal device to mask elements already interpreted as nouns or verbs, roots can be assigned no coherent meaning on their own, because meaning presupposes at least a categorization in semantic types, and this in turn presupposes a syntactic category."

Given that the assumptions underlying √ROOTS (and other proposals advocating lexical underspecification) are under serious debate, we want to look at the √ROOTS hypothesis a bit more, paying particular attention to its biolinguistic plausibility and its conceptual necessity. As we shall discuss below, our investigation of the √ROOTS hypothesis will demonstrate that this hypothesis is unsupportable.

We have noted previously that it is highly probable that LEX of the protolanguage would have, at some point in time, consisted entirely of √ROOTS. So, the DM framework has some initial biolinguistic plausibility. However, if we follow the DM assumptions about LEX – which would in essence have LEX in modern human language structured similarly to that of the protolanguage – then this plausibility quickly disappears. For the DM framework to offer a credible explanation for FL, the development of modern human language will require the construction of a CS that is completely divorced from, and unanticipated by, LEX. The syntactic features, the syntactic heads bearing grammatical features, and the syntactic operations conceptually necessary for a working syntax will not be found in the √ROOTS-rich LEX. Therefore, all of the syntactic machinery will have to be built from scratch. Needless to say, the amount of bioengineering needed to construct a CS from the bottom up far exceeds the modest re-engineering that Hornstein (2009) claims is required to account for the rapid evolutionary development of the modern human language faculty. Furthermore, if LEX is as separated from the syntax (the CS) as the DM framework assumes, then we are left with the puzzle of explaining why a CS would ever be built atop LEX in the first place. Where would the evolutionary pressure for innovating such a CS ever come from?

Not only does the lexical underspecification assumption of DM lack biolinguistic plausibility, it also lacks conceptual necessity. As we have previously noted in this chapter, the biggest (potential) conceptual advantage offered by the adoption of √Roots is the (significant) reduction of "redundant" polysemous LIs/√Roots in LEX. Although such an approach is in line with Hinzen's (and our) hypothesis that syntax builds semantics, it comes at a very significant cost – a cost which we feel is quite frankly too great and cannot be justified in favor of other simpler alternatives. As argued by Potts (2008), such an approach to argument/event structure leads to an enormous amount of overgeneration; as a result, there exists a vast, perhaps infinite, amount of material and structure created by the CS that the C-I and SM performance systems can do absolutely nothing with. This is more than just an unfortunate outcome, because, if we look closely, this problem can be found in nearly all the "minimalist" derivational approaches to syntax. Putnam's (2010) recent summary of this problem observes that approaches that accept the notion of an underspecified LEX (and, as a by-product, accept the notion of an underspecified √Root) require structure-building operations that are no longer "meaningful" but rather "simply occur" (such operations include Chomsky's 2004 "Merge-alpha" operation and later variations and adaptations of this operation); these operations apply licentiously, producing unusable derivational output that needs to be filtered out by the "external" interfaces. The resulting "snowball-effect" here should be obvious to the reader; having a LEX with underspecified √Roots leads to a lack of features carried by the √Root to be licensed/checked at the "interfaces," which leads to a relaxed stance on iterative structure-building operations such as Merge (and Copy), which, in turn, leads to the overgeneralization process noted in detail by Potts (2008), Stroik (2009a, 2009b), Putnam (2007, 2010), Putnam and Stroik (2009, 2010), and a host of others. In the words of Stroik (2009a, b), such a view of syntax is more than just "crash-tolerant," it is in fact "crash-driven." Our model of the grammar (as proposed in (9) from chapter 1) eliminates all of these formidable problems: with LEX situated within the C-I and SM performance systems there no longer are "external interfaces"; rather there are only the performance systems themselves, systems that are active participants in the derivation of, the valuing of, and the interpretation of syntactic structure. Given this view of the performance systems, there cannot feasibly be any "uninterpretable" structures produced by/within these systems (as a matter of fact, it is not possible to see how such structures would ever be produced in the protolanguage).

As we see it, a biolinguistic model of human language that posits underspecified √Roots in LEX cannot adequately/successfully address the "first cause" problem: although we agree that many aspects of semantic meaning are encoded in syntactic structure, it is not clear how these syntactico-semantic structures were generated (or established) in the first place. It is difficult to postulate that semantic interpretations based on structural relations appeared *ex nihilo*, which would seem to suggest by default that there is a little more "structure and meaning" associated with √ROOTS than commonly assumed in DM.

Given the foregoing arguments, it would seem then that the √ROOTS underspecification hypothesis is not supportable. What this means is that LEX will not be maximally efficient; that is, LEX will not consist of non-redundant √ROOTS. We propose, instead, that LEX will have feature-rich LIs, some of which will bear redundancies – as in the examples in (4), where the word *siren* could bear more than one set of features (the ability to have more than one set of features could be explained as an instance of *lexical respecification*, which would involve restructuring FMs). Of course, a consequence of this analysis is that we are saddled with a rather massive LEX that will require substantial storage needs for LIs and the FMs they contain. This problem, however, is merely a storage capacity problem, which we view as far less costly in processing terms than problematic production costs. As noted in Potts' (2008) review of Borer, syntactic systems that advocate versions of "free Merge" allow massive overgeneration of uninterpretable, unusable structures – these are the sorts of costs that must be avoided, especially if the ultimate goal of Minimalism is to eliminate any and all superfluous operations that generate potentially massive amounts of derivational output that neither the C-I nor SM performance systems could ever make use of.

Before closing this chapter, we would like to address the following question: just how *feature-loaded* were/are the LIs in the protolanguage/Lexicon? This is an important question to ask, especially if we are abandoning the concept of underspecified √ROOTS, because it raises a non-trivial question about whether or not there is an upper-bound restriction on the featural composition of LIs. A quick glance at some of the syntactic variation that exists between closely related predicates such as those in (5) – (9) suggests that developing a composite menu of lexical features will likely require a nuanced understanding of features that at present exceeds our ability to determine. (The data in (5)–(9) are taken from Pollard and Sag 1994: 105–106, examples (14)–(18).)

(5) a. Kim grew political.
     b. *Kim grew a success.
     c. *Kim grew sent more and more leaflets.
     d. *Kim grew doing all the work.
     e. Kim grew to like anchovies.

(6) a. Kim got political.
     b. *Kim got a success.
     c. Kim got sent more and more leaflets.
     d. *Kim got doing all the work.
     e. Kim got to like anchovies.

(7) a. Kim turned out political.
     b. Kim turned out a success.
     c. *Kim turned out sent more and more leaflets.
     d. *Kim turned out doing all the work.
     e. Kim turned out to like anchovies.

(8) a. Kim ended up political.
     b. Kim ended up a success.
     c. *Kim ended up sent more and more leaflets.
     d. Kim ended up doing all the work.
     e. *Kim ended up to like anchovies.

(9) a. Kim waxed political.
     b. *Kim waxed a success.
     c. *Kim waxed sent more and more leaflets.
     d. *Kim waxed doing all the work.
     e. *Kim waxed to like anchovies.

In (5)–(9), the verbs *grow, get, turn out, end up,* and *wax* are all closely related from a semantic point of view (i.e., all meaning something roughly equivalent to 'become'). Clearly, any analysis of these verbs on purely semantic grounds will most likely fail to deliver a descriptively adequate analysis of the subcategorization properties of these predicates. With that being said, a "purely syntactic" analysis of these structures, as would be suggested in the DM framework and in the work of linguists such as Borer, is also severely lacking (as demonstrated above). For example, as Pollard and Sag (1994: 106–7) ask, "why is it that all of these verbs that roughly mean 'become' except *wax* allow PP complements (of the appropriate type), while only *turn out, end up,* and *become* allow predicate complements? Similarly, what difference in meaning between *end up* and *turn out* could explain why only the former can license the presence of a present participial complement? Furthermore, why does *wax* allow only AP complements?" Clearly, we require a better understanding of the composition of LIs if we are going to provide a detailed analysis of the relationship between syntax and semantics.

What seems safe to assert, at this point, is that the composition of LIs must consist of features/representations that are richer than mere theta-roles (cf. Gruber 1965; Fillmore 1968). As argued by Levin and Rappaport (1986), the distinctions that can be gained from the application of theta-roles is simply too coarse-grained to provide a useful semantic representation of the sentence. The question is, how rich should the lexical features be? This matter is not yet settled. Some linguists accept Pustejovsky's (1991, 2004: 370) claim that what is needed is a nuanced lexical decomposition, which would include features shaped by "(1) a rich, recursive theory of semantic composition, (2) the notion of semantic well-formedness, and (3) an appeal to several levels of interpretation in the semantics."[13] On the other hand, there are other scholars such as Fodor and Lepore (2002), who argue against the fine lexical decompositions proposed by Pustejovsky. Although this question has not been resolved, the literature addressing it is extensive (see, for example, Davidson 1967; Higginbotham 1985; Krifka 1989; Parsons 1990; Pustejovsky 1991; Kratzer 1996; Ritter and Rosen 1998; Maienborn 2005; and Ramchand 2007, 2008). And the proposals are provocative. Take, for example, Ramchand's semantic representation of (10), which she gives in (11):

(10)   Jones butters the toast quickly with a tiny knife.

(11) $\exists e'' \ \exists e' \ e$ [buttering(e) & Agent(e, Jones) & Theme(e, the toast) & Constituitive-Event(e', e) & quickly(e') & Constituitive-Event(e'', e') & With(e'', a tiny knife)] (Ramchand 2007: 485, example (15))

Ramchand raises the possibility that there are multiple embedded events in (11):

the event of "buttering" that has Jones as its agent and "the toast" as its patient is a crucial subcomponent of a derived event e', which exists and which is defined by the additional property that the event is a quick event (i.e., performed quickly). The derived "quick event" e' is also a constitutive part of a third derived event e'', which is defined by the fact that it is an instance of e' that takes place with a tiny knife. The final, resulting predication is now the complex event e'', which is dependent upon the other embedded event descriptions.

And she proposes that the event structure is directly reflected in the syntactic structure, as in (12), with the above events possessing causative, processive, and resultative features:

(12) vP = [$init$P (causing projection) [$proc$P (process projection) [resP (result projection)]]]

Ramchand's analysis raises serious questions about the nature of events and their lexical-syntactic representations – including questions about what the upper-bound limit on such event-related projections would be (see Pylkännen 2002, 2008 and Taraldsen 2010, who raise similar questions), as well as questions about the necessity of having a hierarchical ordering in the lexical-syntactic representation of events, a topic that we discuss more fully in the next section.

2.4   Feature hierarchies

In our analysis of LEX, we propose not only that LIs consist of rich sets of features (as we discuss in the two previous sections), but also that LIs structure their features hierarchically. In this section, we will use arguments and evidence from Tallerman (2009), Müller (2010), and Ramchand (2007, 2008) to support our claim that LIs have hierarchically structured FMs.

We begin our analysis with Tallerman (2009: 184), who assumes that in the protolanguage, LIs possessed three types of information: conceptual information, lexical-semantic information, and phonological information (but no "syntactic information"). Of note, this information, according to Tallerman (2009: 188), emerged out of the developing hierarchical cognitive categories of our ancestors:

> prelinguistic knowledge in early hominins probably revolved around the following distinctions: hierarchical knowledge (e.g. subordinate/dominant, mother/self/daughter), categorial knowledge (e.g. edible/inedible, male/female, fertile/infertile), and gradational knowledge (e.g. harmful/harmless, light/dark, ripe/unripe, near/far) ... Hierarchical knowledge seems to be especially important, since it potentially gives structure to the whole lexicon, and may be exapted later on in evolution for handling the hierarchies found in other areas of the grammar (syntax in particular).[14]

In Tallerman's analysis, the evolution of our ancestors is connected to their cognitive growth, specifically their developing ability to hierarchicalize their experience (this is consonant with Conway and Christiansen's (2001) observation that nonhuman primates are extremely limited in their abilities to learn hierarchical behavior when compared with humans[15]), and this "hierarchical knowledge" becomes encoded in LEX of the protolanguage.

Tallerman's claim that lexical information is hierarchically structured is supported by Müller (2010), who argues that it is possible to account for "movement" barriers only if all syntactic operations are driven by lexical features and all lexical features are hierarchically ordered. Müller demonstrates, in particular, that Chomsky's (2001: 13) *Phase Impenetrability Condition*, which establishes structural limits on syntactic operations, can be accounted for within the context of a strongly/purely derivational system only if the features of LIs are crucially ordered. The key to this analysis is that all specifiers are extraction barriers and can only be a viable "escape hatch" if there exists another feature – either a "structure-building," a "trigger," or a "probe" feature – that forces the derivation to continue. In other words, once a LI has exhausted its feature inventory (in its FM), it will serve as an extraction domain, i.e., a barrier.[16] To briefly illustrate this point, consider the following examples in German and English (from Müller 2010):

(13)   a.   Ich denke [CP [VP das Buch gelesen]₂ hat keiner t₂]
             I think   the book read   has no-one
       b.   [CP Was]₁ denkst du [CP t'₁ hat keiner [VP t₁ gelesen]₂]?
             what think you   has no-one   read
       c.   *[DP Was]₁ denkst du [CP [VP t₁ gelesen]₂ hat keiner t₂]?
             what think you   read   has no-one

(14)   a.   Who₁ do you think that he will talk [PP2 to t₁]?
       b.   *Who₁ do you think that [PP2 to t₁] he will talk t₂?

As shown by Müller, a topicalized VP appears to always function as an extraction barrier blocking all instances of extraction out of VP in German (Postal 1972 makes a similar observation for topicalized PPs in English; see (14)). These effects are commonly referred to as *freezing effects*:

(15)   *Freezing Generalization* (from Rizzi 2006): A trace *t* may not be included in a moved XP (i.e., an XP that binds a trace) if the antecedent of *t* c-commands XP.

The Freezing Generalization defined in (15) is, however, problematic due to the fact that it does not explain how examples of remnant movement such as those below in (16) are possible. In (16), traces (or copies of "moved" constituents) appear within an XP that has been topicalized. Instances of remnant movement can therefore exhibit *anti-freezing effects*, where the antecedent eventually appears in a structural position lower than the trace included in the moved XP (data from Müller 2010):[17]

(16)   a.   [VP2 t₁ Zu lesen] hat [DP1 es]   keiner t₂   versucht.
                    to read has   it_ACC no-one_NOM tried
       b.   [VP2 t₁ Gelesen] hat der Fritz [DP1 das Buch] nicht.
                    read   has the Fritz_NOM the book_ACC not

The anti-freezing effects observed in the examples displaying remnant movement above can be explained away in a straightforward and parsimonious manner in the system that we propose here. If we assume that the hierarchical alignment and/or ordering of grammatical information represented in formal features on LIs function as the driving force behind the construction of human language, we can interpret scrambling as being licensed by the presence of a formal feature. Following Grewendorf and Sabel (1999), Sauerland (1999), and Putnam (2007), let us assume for now that scrambling in German is triggered by a feature, i.e., Σ, which is responsible for its distribution in the clausal structure (from Putnam 2007: 125):

(17)   *[VP2 den Kindern zu lesen] hat der Mann das Märchen versprochen.
           the children_DAT to read has the man_NOM the fairy tale_ACC promised

Once again, what is crucial here is the ordering of these lexical features in an FM. Müller proposes, in particular, the following feature hierarchy to account for the anti-freezing effects observed in (17):

(18) $\Sigma >> D^{18} >>$ top $>>$ wh $>>$

The sub-extraction of the scrambled items – *es* "it" in (16a) and *das Buch* "the book" in (16b) – is only possible due to the active scrambling feature on these LIs. Failure to "eject" LIs that bear a feature such as Σ/[Ref] will lead to a derivation that fails to be C-I and SM compatible (cf. (18)). It is the presence of a lexical feature – namely, Σ – that is responsible for the initial "movement" of the VP that will eventually undergo topicalization. That is, the ill-formedness of examples such as (17) follows from the presence and crucial ordering of the Σ-feature on a given LI.

Another argument in favor of structured feature hierarchies comes from Ramchand (2008). Ramchand observes that the light verb should be decomposed into three separate verbal projections, as in (12)

(12) vP = [*init*P (causing projection) [*proc*P (process projection) [*res*P (result projection)]]]

Having the "vP" consist of three sub-projections, each definable by a feature, allows *aktionsart* distinctions to be structurally expressed. One of the consequences of separating a process feature from a result feature is that atelic activity predicates (e.g., *play the piano*, *swim*, *run*, etc.)[19] can be differentiated from telic/bound result predicates (e.g., *open the door*) by these features, as in (19) and (20).

(19)   [*init*P John <play> [*proc*P John <play> the piano]]

(20)   [*init*P John <open> [*proc*P John <open> [*res*P <open> the door]]]

For our purposes, at least, what is interesting about Ramchand's analysis is not only the fact that events decompose into three features (and potentially more), but also that these features are crucially ordered syntactically and semantically. That is, as (20) states, the result feature is necessarily contained within a process feature that is necessarily contained within a causative feature; there can be no results without activities and no activities without causes.

2.5   Consequences

Given the arguments we have presented in this chapter, we conclude that LIs have grown out of the C-I and SM performance systems. They would have started as single units (with no formal or semantic sub-parts), as Jespersen (1922), Bickerton

(2009), Fitch (2010), and Searle (2010) claim. Then, as the performance systems (i.e., cognitive and motor abilities) of our ancestors developed, especially the ability to hierarchicalize information, these units would have been decomposed into conceptual and perceptual parts/features. That is, the LIs would have consisted of parts (PSFs) grounded in the lived experiences of our ancestors. These PSFs could have included property features (smell, color), quantity features, locative features, temporal features, focus features, reference features, among others. And these features would have been hierarchically structured, as Tallerman (2009) argues. We suggest that the crucial structuring mechanism was one that separated necessary features (that "selected" or identified a lexical item) that an LI must have from contingent, or associated, features (that are involved in "selecting" an LI) that an LI can have. For example, the LI *cat* would have <animate> as a selected-feature that identified a cat as an animal, but it could also have <color> as a selecting-feature that partitioned cats. (This selected–selecting distinction is important because it will be able to generate a protosyntax, as we will discuss in Chapter 4.) As our ancestors continued to evolve, we propose they were not only able to distinguish sub-parts of the physical world they experienced, but they were able to extend this ability to their developing linguistic world. In other words, they could find categories within language, too; they would have the ability to identify LIs by their lexical CATegory (noun, verb, etc.) and the SUBCATegories with which they are associated. Importantly, the former features are selected-features and the latter selecting-features. At this point in the evolution of language, our ancestors would have the following types of lexical features:

(21)   *Inventory of Concatenative Features*
    SUBCATegorial features – Features of an LI (e.g., [+ V], [+ N], and [+ P]) that identify the CATegories of the LI's co-occurring arguments.

    Performance system features (PSFs) – Morpho-syntactic and syntactico-semantic features, such as Topic features, Focus features, agreement features, and wh-features, among others, that have developed out of pre-linguistic cognitive and perceptual features. These features need to be exhaustively determined, but they may include property features, reference features, quantity features, and temporality features. We leave a precise determination of these features for future research.

    CATegorial features – The unique lexical-class feature of an LI that identifies the LI's syntactic category (e.g., [+ V], [+ N], and [+ P]).

As we will discuss in Chapter 4, once humans developed selecting and selected PSFs in the protolexicon, they would naturally have a protolanguage with a protosyntax, too; but once they developed CAT and SUBCAT features, they would have a full-fledged human language.

3   Constructing the Numeration

3.1   Introduction: Addressing the relational problem

In this chapter we give an in-depth analysis of what we call *the relational problem*, which concerns the relationship between the Lexicon/Numeration and the computational system (CS). Our proposal is that – contrary to 'mainstream' Minimalist assumptions that the Numeration (NUM) is exhaustively and blindly *selected* from the Lexicon (LEX) before a syntactic derivation is assembled by the CS – NUM is compiled in a piecemeal fashion throughout the course of a syntactic derivation, from lexical material taken out of LEX. We argue, in particular, that NUM is not merely a lexical depository in short-term memory that is used by, though separate from, the computational system; rather, it is a dynamic workspace that engages actively with its interconnected CS.

We will begin our discussion of the relational problem as we began our discussion of the compositional problem in Chapter 2: by situating our design of the Faculty of Language (FL) against that of standard Minimalism. In the two previous chapters, we have made the case that there are ample conceptual reasons for not accepting the design of FL posited in Chomsky (1995, 2005, 2009); in this chapter we make another case against the design assumptions of standard Minimalism, showing that this design for FL is computationally untenable. It is important to note that our arguments are not arguments against the Minimalist Program; on the contrary, we strongly endorse Chomsky's broad assumption that the CS builds syntactic structures from lexical material placed in a NUM and maps the completed structures to the Conceptual-Intentional (C-I) and Sensorimotor (SM) performance systems for interpretation (as in (1)). We do reject, however, the standard Minimalist assumption that NUM is extraneous to the CS and its lexical material is stockpiled oblivious to the needs of the CS.

(1)   CS: NUM $\rightarrow$ <C-I, SM>

We will argue that divorcing NUM from the CS is a serious design flaw, one that allows the CS to be so grossly inefficient that it rarely, if ever, will produce representations that are usable by the performance systems (this CS will be a "crash"-rife system). Our challenge, then, is to de-bug the design so that the CS is not overwhelmed by crashes. This will require that we provide a reanalysis of the interrelationships among LEX, NUM, and the CS. As should be expected at this point in our discussions, we will maintain that the optimal solution to the crash-problem is to situate LEX, NUM, and CS interactively within the C-I and SM performance systems, as in (2), which is the design for FL that we propose in Chapter 1.

(2)

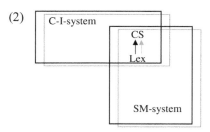

We develop our proposal as follows. In Section 3.2, we provide conceptual arguments against crash-tolerant designs of FL. In Section 3.3, we demonstrate that designs of FL that disconnect NUM from the CS produce large-scale crash problems that will make it virtually impossible for the CS to produce any usable output. We can avoid problems with large-scale crashes, as we show in Section 3.4, by adopting the computational model in (2), in which LEX, NUM, and CS are all integrated into the performance systems. Importantly, our integrative model also aligns NUM with CS by having NUM constructed derivationally (i.e., in a piecemeal fashion alongside a syntactic derivation). We argue, though, in Section 3.5, that NUM is not the only interactive, and integrative, workspace required to build syntactic derivation. Adopting a proposal made in Stroik (2009a) and further developed in Putnam (2007), Putnam and Stroik (2009), and te Velde (2009) among others, we argue that a NUM is actually a part of a larger workspace, called the *WorkBench* – a sub-derivational workspace where some syntactic constituents can be built prior to their introduction (or, in some cases, reintroduction) into a syntactic derivation.

3.2   Dealing with crashes

Given the central role that the notion of "crashes" plays in our analysis of the relationship between LEX/NUM and the CS, we feel that we should begin our analysis with an extended discussion of theories of grammars and theories of crashes.

A "generative grammar," as developed in Chomsky (1957), is a crash-proof grammar. What we mean by this is that a generative grammar is supposed to, in a maximally parsimonious way, compute syntactic structures for all and only the sentences in a Language L (as Searle 1972 states in his overview of Chomsky's early theories of grammar, "Such a theory came to be called a 'generative grammar' because of its aim of constructing a device that would generate all and only the sentences of a language" and would "provide a description of the grammatical structure of each" (19)). Of note, a generative grammar for any L will be able to derive only well-formed structures for the sentences in L; hence, generative grammars will necessarily be crash-proof because the grammar and L must be coextensive. (Had we continued to pursue Chomsky's notion of a generative grammar, Minimalist syntax would be a version of crash-proof syntax!) Despite the conceptual appeal of having a coextensive relationship between the computational power of a grammar and the sentences in a Language, the notion of a generative grammar was largely abandoned with the development of transformational grammars in the 1960s and 1970s. Transformational grammars, unlike generative grammars, defined a grammar in terms of its computational machinery, which included a system of second-order, transformational rules used to restructure syntactic structure. Importantly, the shift from generative grammar, with its commitment to a conceptual design of grammar, to transformational grammar, with its commitment to an operational design, removed the coextensivity relationship between grammar and Language, making it possible for grammars to produce syntactic structures other than those necessary for all and only the sentences in a Language. Since these (transformational) grammars could produce Language-extraneous structures (structures that would "crash" in Minimalist parlance), the grammars needed to have their expressive power constrained if they were to provide viable structural descriptions of the sentences of a Language. That is, transformational grammars had to incorporate mechanisms that could filter out "crashes." A wealth of filtering mechanisms have been posited over the last forty-five years – including Ross's (1967) constraints, Chomsky's A-over-A Principle, the various sub-theories in the Government and Binding Framework, and several generations of Minimalist filters, most recently the Phase Impenetrability Condition. As the foregoing discussion suggests, there is a relationship between "crashes" and grammar type. Generative grammars are crash-free grammars, while transformational grammars (including standard versions of Minimalism, which have second-order syntactic operations, such as Internal Merge, that can restructure syntactic structure and that have, if not constrained, the computational power to derive structures that crash) are crash-driven grammars. Since crashes result from the type of grammar assumed, crashes, in and of themselves, are not a conceptually necessary feature of grammar. So why should we have grammars with crashes? What is the conceptual advantage of granting grammars computational powers that must be rescinded? Taken as a Minimalist inquiry, the question about whether or not crash-inducing rules (and crashes themselves) are a conceptual necessity for grammar would seem rather easy to answer: avoid crashes. There is simply no readily apparent reason why a grammar *must* have computational machinery capable of generating unusable output that must be subsequently filtered or computational machinery that must be constrained. If this is correct, then the various crash-inducing mechanisms in Minimalist syntax – including blindly selecting NUM (even by phase) and both Chomky's (2004) free External Merge operation (which allows the Merge operation to combine any two elements α and β) and his Internal Merge operation – are not conceptually necessary and therefore should be expunged from the grammar.

However, before we bring our discussion of crashes and crash-inducing mechanisms to closure, let us consider the few arguments that have been offered recently to justify crashes. One of these arguments comes from Epstein (2007). According to Epstein, the syntactic operations in standard Minimalism – free External Merge and Internal Merge – are not operations that need to be computationally filtered, as in the Government and Binding (GB) framework, because their output is interpretatively filtered by the interfaces: "in contrast to the filters invoked in the GB system, the filtration in [Chomsky's 2004] system, will be achieved by natural, independently motivated demands imposed by the interpretative modules, the Bare Output Conditions (BOCs)" (33).[1] Epstein's claim, though, that the filtration system found in Chomsky (2004 and beyond) is an improvement and is radically different from the filters present in the GB system, is purely a matter of stipulation. To the best of our knowledge, the "filters" put forward in Chomsky's computational system (CS) for human language – usually in the form of (strong) phases and Transfer – are a reshaping of these earlier GB notions of "filter" along the lines of some form of economy (for example, consider Boeckx and Grohmann's 2007 comparison of the GB system's concept of "barrier" in Chomsky 1986 with the Minimalist concept of "phase"). Furthermore, even if computational output can be interpretatively filtered by the interfaces, this does not necessitate that the CS *must* submit syntactic structures to the interfaces that cannot be used by the interfaces and need to be disregarded by them. That is, having conditions on semantic interpretability does not justify having unconstrained syntactic operations.

A second argument in support of having a crash-inducing CS comes from Epstein and Seely (2006: Chapter 5), who maintain that crashes are in fact conceptually necessary for syntax to work at all. To see the gist of their arguments, consider the following sentence in (3) and a portion of its derivational history (given in (4)).

(3)   Rats eat cheese

(4)   a.   Step 1: *[$_{VP}$ [$_V$ eat] [$_{DP}$ cheese]]
      b.   Step 2: [$_{vP}$ rats v-eat [$_{VP}$ [$_V$ eat] [$_{DP}$ cheese]]]

Under Epstein and Seely's analysis, the VP constructed in Step 1 (see (4a)) violates Full Interpretation/θ-Criterion (Chomsky 1981) because the predicate *eat* does not discharge all of its θ-roles and thus when this VP undergoes Transfer to the interfaces, it will appear at the logical form (LF) interface with an uninterpretable feature, which should result in a "crash." This situation, however, is "repaired" in Step 2 (see (4b)) in which the subject/agent *rats* enters the derivation, allowing the second and final θ-feature of the predicate to be valued/discharged. The crash that arises in Step 1, then, is a necessary consequence of deriving the VP, but this crash is not fatal. What this line of argument suggests is that a CS must be able to produce output that can crash, although some of this "crashed" output will be repaired in subsequent derivational steps; hence, a CS cannot be crash-proof.

Epstein and Seely claim that one of the key issues preventing us from properly understanding and classifying these sorts of non-fatal crashes is our (erroneous) and continued reliance upon the GB characterization of the notion of "grammatical sentence," as formalized in (5) (taken from Epstein and Seely 2006: 179):

(5) a. All and only grammatical sentences have "well-formed" derivations.
     b. A derivation is well formed only if at every point in the derivation no principle is violated.

Epstein and Seely (2006: 179) argue that if the external interfaces associated with logical form (LF) and phonetic form (PF) must access/interpret every successive derivational step and if the criteria for well-formedness are as stated in (5), then "no well-formed derivations of grammatical sentences would ever be generable." Returning to example (3) and the derivational steps in (4), we can see that Step 1 is an example of non-fatal crash that is "repaired" by the addition of Step 2; in other words, it is not at Step 2, but rather, it is the combination of Step 1 and Step 2 that allows (3) to have a derivation that can be interpreted at the interface. The crucial point here is that what is "uninterpretable" is what is "shipped off" to "an external interface"; in other words, when considered as a whole, this system is perfectly fine.

Putnam (2010: 6–7) notes that Epstein and Seely's arguments for the conceptual necessity of crashes (and their notion that the inventory of crashes includes both "fatal" and "non-fatal" varieties) depends on the assumption that the CS allows multiple, iterative instances of a Transfer (or Spell-Out) mechanism that "ships" derivationally constructed materials to an "external" interface. If one assumes, following Chomsky (2000, 2001 et seq.), that all of the complements of every phase head Transfer to the interfaces, or if one assumes, following Epstein and Seely's (2002, 2006) notion of a level-free syntax, that the derivational output of every syntactic operation Transfers to the interfaces, then we are forced to envisage a CS that bifurcates the notion of "crash" into (at least) two different types: those that are "fatal" and those that are "non-fatal." However, as Putnam (2010: 7) observes,

> One of the potential problems with such a crash-tolerant model of syntax is that no good explanation exists as to why it is necessary to send all these unusable/uninterpretable structures to the interfaces. To put it bluntly, what are the interfaces supposed to do with these structures? These structures are – as far as I can tell – unusable and useless to the interfaces; the interfaces themselves cannot repair them because such repair can only occur in the computational system; and the interfaces cannot send these structures back to the derivation, mainly because these iterative applications of Transfer and Return operations would be circular/redundant in nature and accomplish nothing. In fact, it seems that the only reason the Narrow Syntax jettisons these structures is to ensure that they are not syntactically reusable (i.e., to limit the look-back domain of Internal Merge).

What emerges from this discussion is the recognition that standard versions of the Minimalist Program, including Epstein and Seely's version, lack a clear explanation for the conceptual necessity of Transferring these (as far as we can tell) unusable structures to the interfaces (see also Putnam and Stroik 2009 for similar arguments). If, as Putnam suggests, the Transfer operation lacks a conceptual warrant (and we believe it does), then Epstein's and Seely's Transfer-based arguments for crashes lose viability.

The case we are making here is that crashes are not conceptually necessary aspects of a CS for human language; rather, they are induced by the design of the CS. If the CS includes design elements such as a blindly selected NUM, a free Merge operation, an Internal Merge operation, or a Transfer operation, then this CS will necessarily induce crashes. Conversely, though, if crashes are not conceptually necessary components of the performance systems, then the design of human language should eschew any computational mechanism that necessarily induces crashes. We contend that crashes, which involve structures that are unusable by the performance systems, cannot conceivably be conceptually necessary components of these systems. If this is correct, then the design of human language must be radically different than the one proposed in standard versions of Minimalism – a conclusion very similar to the one we reached in Chapter 1.

3.3   Crashes and the Numeration

With our discussion of crashes in mind, let us consider the consequences of having the standard Minimalist version of NUM. According to Chomsky (1995, 2004), Hornstein, Nunes, and Grohmann (2005), and even Hinzen (2006), NUM must be exhaustively determined *before* a syntactic derivation, or even a portion of a derivation (such as Chomsky's "phase"), can begin. That is, lexical items (LIs) are brought into NUM, via a Select operation, from LEX prior to the computations of a syntactic derivation (SD). Furthermore, since these LIs are selected for NUM without look-ahead properties able to anticipate how a derivation might proceed, they must be selected in derivational blindness. This blind selection process, however, creates a mathematical complexity that undermines the commitment of Minimalism to a "minimal" design. Consider, for example, the effect that having a NUM with ten blindly (and randomly) selected LIs would have on syntactic computations, where NUM = {LI_1, ..., LI_{10}}. If we assume, as does Chomsky, that every LI_i in NUM must be eventually inserted into the SD, then from our NUM we could, in principle, generate 10! (3.6 million) structured strings of words from the LIs we select.[2]

Of these strings/concatenations, we must identify, within Chomsky's version of Minimalism, the usable strings (out of the 3.6 million that could be generated). This extensive search could be significantly reduced if some sort of feature-match requirement were placed on the iterative application of the Merge operation because a feature mismatch would terminate any given SDs, thereby expunging many of the computable 3.6 million structured strings. However, whether we have a feature-matching requirement imposed on the Merge operation or not, if we are to ensure that we can find usable SDs for the LIs in NUM, we must compute, at the very minimum, hundreds of structured strings, almost none of which will be usable by the performance systems.[3]

If we assume that LI selection is random and that it must take place under conditions of derivational blindness, the possibility of finding a single well-formed (usable) SD from the millions of derivations we could, in principle, compute from a NUM with ten LIs is infinitesimal (to see this, blindly select ten words from the Oxford English Dictionary and then try to find even one way of putting those words together as a sentence). If we follow this line of argumentation to its logical conclusion, we would observe that the situation just described suggests that the CS will spend (and waste) an enormous amount of processing time and effort producing huge numbers of derivational strings, virtually all of which will be unusable by the performance systems. For a more startling glimpse of this processing problem, consider what happens when we increase the size of NUM to twenty LIs. From such a NUM, we could generate 20! (over 1,000,000,000,000,000,000) structured strings of words, with little hope that any of them would be usable SDs (again, randomly select twenty words from the dictionary and look for ways to string them together as sentences). As before, we might not have to compute all 20! strings, but we will have to compute at least the first Merger ($20 \times 19 = 380$ strings) and we will have to continue computing any initially successful derivations. Hence, it is likely that we must compute thousands of derivations that will crash. And all these crashes will occur whether we eventually stumble upon an SD that could be interpretable, or not. (Notice, though, that having free Merge will place maximal stress on the computational system because the free Merge operation will generate all the mathematically possible strings and submit all of them to the performance systems for interpretation.)

Following proposals made by Nunes (2004), Chomsky (2004) attempts to simplify the search domain for constructing a NUM by making it phase based. Accordingly, the NUM is no longer a single set of LIs that will appear within an SD; rather, it is a set of subsets, where each subset contains a phase-head (C or v^*). Although each subset will have one element (the phase-head) that is possibly derivationally necessary and, consequently, each subset will contain an element that is arguably not selected in derivational blindness, the remainder of LIs in these subsets is selected, again, pre-derivationally. This attempt by Chomsky and others to implement a phase-based system that could reduce the computational load of CS is not successful. Given that these subsets (especially those with a v^* phase-head) could have ten or more LIs, the problems we discuss above do not disappear. As a consequence, Chomsky's (2004) proposal to construct NUM as a set of phase-selected sub-arrays will not substantially improve the likelihood of deriving interface interpretable SDs. Furthermore, having phase-selected sub-arrays introduces some new complexities into NUM because there will have to be selection mechanisms that ensure that each sub-array has one and only one phase-head in it (so the selection process cannot be completely random) and that the sub-arrays alternate C and v^* phase-heads (so the selection process cannot be blind).

In spite of the aforementioned limitations that a blindly, pre-derivationally selected NUM presents for a "minimalist" theory of syntax, most linguists working within this framework simply acknowledge this issue and offer little if any adjustments to improve the system. Take, for instance Hornstein, Nunes, and Grohmann (2005), who recognize that NUMs can be derivationally unco-operative, i.e., that there can be what they call "crazy" NUMs, such as those in (6), which will not have any convergent, interface-interpretable derivations built from them.

(6) a. NUM = {tree, of, buy}
     b. NUM = {with, about, Mary, John}
     c. NUM = {see, man, Infl}

Such "crazy" NUMs, however, do not appear to bother Hornstein, Nunes, and Grohmann. In their own words, "Since PF and LF already are responsible for filtering crashing derivations, there's no need to filter out the NUMs in (6), since derivations resulting from them will crash at LF and PF" (2005: 71). This casual attitude towards "crazy" NUMs misses, according to Stroik (2009b: 28), two very extraordinary facts about blindly selected NUMs: first, under the assumption that lexical items are selected for NUM blindly and without any look-ahead properties, selecting "crazy" NUMs will be the rule, not the exception. That is, it will generally be the case, even for NUMs with fewer than ten LIs in them, that for any given NUM, no convergent derivation will be able to be built from them. In other words, the derivations sent to the interfaces will almost always crash because they will come from "crazy" NUMs. Second, if, in some extremely rare circumstance, a NUM is not "crazy," it will still produce a substantial number of crashes. In fact, as we noted previously, if we have a NUM with ten LIs, we will have to compute hundreds of SDs for the LIs in NUM – perhaps as many as 3.6 million SDs – in our quest to find even one usable SD.

There is no doubt that standard versions of the Minimalist Program, which build NUM blindly, have a crash-rife syntax rather than a crash-proof syntax. The consequences of having a crash-rife syntax, it is important to note, are dire in processing terms because the C-I and SM performance systems will be fruitlessly working to interpret the almost-always-unusable output they receive from the CS. From this analysis we can see that constructing SDs out of blindly selected NUMs cannot help but be excessively costly as a computational system.

Given the problems with blindly selecting LIs for NUM, perhaps we should surrender our commitment to NUM and assume, instead, that the CS maps LIs directly from the LEX to the C-I and SM interfaces, thereby obviating the need for NUM.[4] There are, however, several reasons for having NUM: (i) Chomsky (1995: 236–238) argues that LIs in LEX lack formal features and that these features are accreted to LIs when they are mapped from LEX to NUM; (ii) as Hornstein, Nunes, and Grohmann (2005: 69–70) maintain, without NUM, the CS will not be able to determine, in principle, when a derivation terminates – that is, NUM sets computational boundaries for SDs (they note that "the computational system that builds syntactic structures doesn't work with the whole lexicon at a time, but with collections of lexical items" (2005: 71)); (iii) SDs involve computations in short-term memory, and NUM, rather than LEX, is the short-term memory storage for LIs used in a derivation; (iv) NUM restricts the LI domain of the External Merge operation; without NUM, this operation would have to sort through the LEX, which is a much more vast domain, and sorting through it would be costly in processing terms; and (v) if we surrender all Move-type syntactic operations, as Stroik (1999, 2009a) suggests, then, without NUM, it would be impossible to maintain a derivational account of displacement effects (which arise when a single syntactic constituent can appear in more than one structural position) – this occurs under Stroik's analysis because, absent Move-type operations such as Internal Merge, NUM provides the only domain from which any single LI could be multiply Merged into an SD (see (7)). Trying to multiply Merge an LI X from LEX will generate structures in which the LI X appears multiple times, but it will not generate displacement effects since each X will be a new X from LEX, so no single X will appear in more than one structural position.

(7) a. Merge {see, who} → see **who**
     b. Merge {Maggie, {see, who}} → Maggie see **who**
     c. Merge {will, {Maggie, {see, who}}} → will Maggie see **who**
     d. Remerge {who, {will, {Maggie, {see, who}}}} → who will Maggie
         see **who**

The emboldened wh-word in (7) indicates that this word has unchecked features and that, as a result, the LI continues to "survive" in NUM and can be Remerged into the SD to have its remaining features appropriately checked (we will discuss these computations in detail in the next chapter). In (7d), the wh-displacement occurs not because of a Move-type operation but because the wh-element in NUM can be merged into the SD more than once. Without NUM, this sort of multiple-merging of a single LI into an SD is not possible (see Stroik 1999, 2009a, 2009b and Putnam 2007 for extended discussions of the syntactic necessity of remerging LIs from the NUM to SD).

Let us assume, in the face of the foregoing arguments, that Minimalist syntax must have a NUM. However, as we have seen, if we are to have a syntax that is not prone to producing an egregious amount of unusable and uninterpretable derivational output ("crashes"), the lexical items in this NUM cannot be blindly and exhaustively selected prior to the onset of the SD. But this raises the question of whether or not any LIs in NUM can ever be selected independently of (i.e., blindly of and/or prior to) the derivation. Needless to say, once we allow even one derivationally independent LI to appear in NUM, there will be no principled way of ensuring that other such LIs are not selected for NUM, too. The consequence, then, of permitting any derivationally independent LIs in NUM is that we could have NUMs with all blindly selected LIs – which is exactly the sort of situation we must exclude. Therefore, it must be the case that no LIs in NUM can be selected derivationally blind. This suggests that the NUM is derivationally sighted, or derivationally built. In other words, all LIs enter NUM one at a time, as they are derivationally selected.

3.4   The Numeration in Survive-minimalism

As we have been arguing above, standard Minimalism is beset with conceptual and operational problems, some of which involve the construction of a NUM and the relationship NUM has with the CS. The latter problems arise primarily from two sources: (i) from positioning LEX and LIs outside both the performance systems and the CS and (ii) from selecting LIs for a NUM prior to the beginning of an SD. The design of Survive-minimalism, importantly, avoids NUM-related problems because it situates LEX, NUM, and the CS within the performance systems, as in (2), and because it integrates NUM-building into the CS.

In Survive-minimalism, the CS for the Faculty of Language does not function to structurally license LIs or their features for interface interpretation because LIs and their features are inherently performance system features and, as such, do not need to be licensed for interpretation; rather, the CS uses the features of LIs, which are already performance-system compatible, to derive performance-system-ready syntactic objects, which we will call concatenated items (CIs). From this perspective, the CS builds concatenated structures (by matching/merging features) and the performance systems interpret these concatenations. At issue for Survive-minimalism, then, is not the interface compatibility of LIs, but the performance system compatibility of CIs. In accordance with Hinzen's (2006: 250) suggestion that the CS constructs "complex concepts" from "simple ones," Survive-minimalism assumes that the CS functions to build and interpret complex concepts and complex forms (i.e., CIs), rather than to merely license strings of simple concepts (i.e., LIs). By conceiving of the Narrow Syntax in terms of the construction of CIs, Survive-minimalism requires a reanalysis of the standard approach to lexical features, especially SYN features. For Survive-minimalism, SYN features are not formal features that could be deleted or obviated in some way; rather, SYN features are concatenative (matching) features that are instrumental in the formation and interpretation of CIs – consequently, these features must be visible, and appropriately concatenated; this is another way of saying that all concatenative features, as well as all concatenations, must be visible both to the CS and to the C-I and SM performance systems. In fact, all SYN features must be intrinsically C-I/SM-interpretable, as are all SEM features and PHON features. (NB: It is important to note here that we are not limiting feature "interpretability" to the C-I module; rather, for our system what it means for a feature to be "interpretable" is that the feature can be read by at least one of the performance systems.) Since the LIs in LEX and NUM contain all and only C-I/SM-interpretable features, LEX and NUM are necessarily contained within what are considered to be traditionally the "external interfaces" (again, see (2) and our discussion of the design of FL in Chapter 1), and so are all the CIs derivationally constructed from LIs. The fact that LIs and CIs are composed of exactly the same materials (i.e., performance system features) suggests that LIs and CIs are varieties of the same thing: they are performance system items (PSIs). Of note, it bears to be repeated that although CIs show up at the C-I and SM performance systems for interpretation, we do not claim that the CS exists outside of the C-I and SM systems. Under this structural design, CS does not map interface-extraneous LIs in NUM onto the external interfaces; instead, according to Survive-minimalism, the CS maps performance system material onto "performance system" structures at every step in a derivation. In particular, it maps PSIs onto PSI*s, where the structure of any PSI* properly contains the structure of an PSI. We can represent this as in (8).

(8)   CS: PSI → PSI*, where PSI* contains PSI

Importantly, the computational design given in (8) places a significant constraint on the types of syntactic operations permissible in CS: in particular, since syntactic operations act within the domain of the performance systems, they must take well-formed performance input (starting with LIs) and derive well-formed performance system output PSI*. In other words, these operations, within the Survive-minimalist framework, cannot produce outputs that are *not* performance-system-compatible, or performance-system-interpretable. The design of Survive-minimalism, then, meets the design-threshold hypothesized by Frampton and Gutmann (2002: 93), who posit that the optimal computation system must be crash-proof in that "every derivation converges." Or, as Hinzen (2006: 249) states, "In an optimal system, an impossible meaning would never be produced, and syntax would be 'crash-proof' ... that is, the products of locally correct steps of a derivation are always well-formed, and meet interface conditions."

To ensure that the CS is rigorously crash-proof, producing only well-formed PSI* outputs, Survive-minimalism, as developed in Stroik (1999, 2009a, 2009b), Putnam (2007), and Putnam and Stroik (2009, 2010), rules out any look-back operations, such as Internal Merge (IM), that depend upon special filtering/economy mechanisms (e.g., Chomsky's Phase Impenetrability Condition or Attract Closest) to prevent these operations from looking too far back into an SD or from producing ill-formed PSIs. Since IM-type, look-back operations have the intrinsic capability of generating structures that cannot be interpreted by the performance systems (and, consequently, these operations must be constrained), they do not in and of themselves possess the restrictive, domain-encapsulated properties necessary to "meet performance system specifications": that is, they are not operations designed to function within the performance systems (most likely because they assume properties of "movement" that are not performance system properties in that movements themselves are not visible, or interpretable, by the performance systems).[5]

What is an intrinsic performance system property, however, is Copy (and concatenate); so the only types of syntactic operations allowable in Survive-minimalism are those syntactic operations (SynOp) that have the ability to copy and concatenate elements from LEX to NUM and from NUM to an SD, as in (9).

(9)   a. SynOp: LEX → NUM
      b. SynOp: NUM → SD

As we can see from (9), in Survive-minimalism, NUM plays a key role in SDs, as it does for Chomsky (1995), but it has very different properties than does NUM in standard Minimalism. The NUM in Survive-minimalism is not built blindly from LEX; its LIs are not selected all at once prior to the derivation; its LIs do not have uninterpretable features; and elements in NUM do not move into SD, thereby vacating NUM. Rather, NUM is built piecemeal throughout an SD, adding copies of LIs in LEX as needed; and these copies can be copied multiple times in an SD to satisfy the concatenative demands of PSI features (as we will discuss in the next chapter).

Although there are substantial design differences between Survive-minimalism and standard Minimalism, we will focus, in the remainder of this chapter, on only one key difference: the role that LEX and NUM play in an SD. We will argue here that, despite Chomsky's (1995, 2001, 2004) assumptions about NUM formation, the LIs in NUM cannot be selected (blindly) prior to the onset of an SD and LEX is not extraneous to the performance systems.

3.5 So where's the Lexicon?

One of the main presuppositions of standard Minimalism is that LEX, and therefore NUM, too, is somehow extraneous to the performance systems. We can observe this presupposition in Lasnik's (1999), Hornstein's (2001), and Chomsky's (1995, 2004) claims that a grammar maps lexical material from NUM to the interfaces, as if this mapping is from one domain to another quite different domain, and in their claims that syntactic operations make the features of LIs legible at the interfaces, which suggests that the features are not inherently interface-legible. Relatedly, Hornstein, Nunes, and Grohmann note that "natural languages, for yet unexplained reasons, have formal features that are legible neither at LF nor at PF" (2005: 328). Following Chomsky, they argue that the syntax "allows these illegible features to be appropriately deleted, allowing the interfaces to read the objects built by the computational system" (2005: 328).

Let us follow the standard Minimalist line of analysis and assume that some, perhaps even all, of the SYN features are extraneous to the "external interfaces" and are deleted in the course of a derivation to ensure that they do not show up at the "interfaces." If this is the case, then, as Stroik (2009a, 2009b) and Putnam and Stroik (2009, 2010) contend, it will be impossible for any such deleted formal feature (f_n) to be learned. Once the f_n feature of an LI is deleted in a derivation, it will not appear in the representation sent to the interfaces and it will not be part of the output sent through the SM mechanisms to other users of the language L. As a result, when children learn the language, they will not have any access to this feature. They also will not be able to enlist the C-I and SM performance systems in identifying this feature because the feature will not have any visibility in the performance systems. It would appear, therefore, that locating the feature f_n and attaching it to a given LI would not be a matter of the computational system of human language. Instead, this feature will have to be acquired in some ancillary fashion. We might have to posit an interface-independent parsing mechanism that can deduce the presence of the interface-invisible feature f_n and add it to the Feature Matrix (FM) of the appropriate LI. Going this route to explain interface-extraneous features is problematic, however. We would have to have a "crazy" grammar that allowed features to be added by one mechanism (perhaps the parser) and deleted by another mechanism (the CS) without ever allowing these features to appear at the only levels of representation (the interfaces) that matter for a grammar. Closeting and cloaking features as described above complicates the grammar in ways inconsistent with Minimalist commitments to conceptual/interface necessity, so we should strongly disprefer analyses that assume the existence of interface-extraneous features.

We can observe the problems of having performance-system-extraneous features closely if we take a look at the sorts of edge features that Chomsky (2001, 2004, and 2008) and others posit to manage syntactic movements/remergers. Faced with the need to limit the domain and range of syntactic movements, Chomsky assumes that various phrase heads (H) can have edge features, which permit a structurally defined set of constituents to move to the left edge of head phrases (HPs). These movements, driven by edge features, are short/intermediary movements of a constituent X that license other short movements of X and that cumulatively result in the long-distance movement of X; the edge features, in this way, serve as portals to subsequent movements. We can see these short, portaling movements in (10).

(10)   Who$_1$ does Smithers [t$_1$ believe [t$_1$ that Mr. Burns [t$_1$will hire t$_1$]]]

In (10), the LI *who* begins its derivational journey as the object of the verb *hire* and it moves leftward up the derivational structure in short steps, each of which is marked by the trace *t*. The movement of the LI *who* occurs because *v* heads and C heads have edge features that attract the wh-element in (10). (The edge features are a reconfiguration of the notion of "escape hatches" that has been present in most transformational grammars since the 1970s.) Importantly, these edge features, which are not interface interpretable features, delete once they merge appropriately with the wh-element. At the interfaces, the wh-element is interpreted in its highest structural position and in its lowest trace position, but nowhere else, because the edge features and their concatenations are not visible at the interfaces. So, given that these edge features do not show up at the "interfaces," how can these edge features of H be learned? As we argue above, these features cannot be learned from the interfaces, which suggests that, if they are learnable at all, they must be learned/acquired from some source other than the interfaces – say, the parser. However, a parser would discover the features associated with the intermediate trace positions of the wh-element in (10) only if it has to retrace the derivational history of a representation in reverse. And why would it do so? More so, how would it do so? To retrace the feature-driven derivational history of any sentence, a parser would have to know the features that motivated this history. Since all the edge features have been deleted in the derivation and do not appear at the interfaces, there is no way for the parser to know what these features might have been.[6] In other words, reversing feature-driven movements after the features have been eliminated would be as impossible as accurately back-tracking the journey of some animal after its tracks have been deleted. What this discussion seems to indicate, then, is that it is not possible to learn deletable, interface-extraneous features.

Perhaps what is most problematic in this account of extraction phenomena from a generative perspective is its lack of conceptual motivation. As we have discussed in the Preface and Chapter 1, and as laid out by Dawkins (2009), Fodor and Piattelli-Palmarini (2010), and Deacon (2012), the rules of biological systems operate on a strictly local basis, and they involve the exchange of structure-building information. Although Chomsky's edge features aid in proliferating structural notions of language, they need not be information enriching, which is problematic because, as we have just noted, all structure-building operations must increase the informational content of an emerging string.

If the analysis that we put forward in this book is correct, all lexical features must be interpretable by the performance systems. From this it follows that (i) no lexical features can be deleted in the course of a syntactic derivation because interpretable information cannot be excised; (ii) LEX, together with NUM, is contained within the performance systems since all their lexical material is performance system material; and (iii) given that all lexical features are intrinsically interpretable by the performance systems, syntactic operations, contra Chomsky, do not serve to check (or value) lexical features for interface (or performance system) legibility and the well-formedness of SDs is not dependent on feature legibility – rather, these operations licitly map performance system items (PSIs) onto larger performance system items (PSI*) by ensuring that all concatenations are linked together with matching performance system features. Under this view, a theory of the Faculty of Language is a theory of PSI* legibility and PSI* interpretations.

3.6   The necessity of a WorkBench

Thus far we have argued that LEX and NUM reside within the C-I and the SM performance systems. As part of this argument, we have proposed that NUM, which is interconnected with the CS, has three essential properties: (i) it is not blindly selected prior to the SD; (ii) it is constructed throughout the course of an SD; and (iii) it resides within the performance systems. Although we have spelled out a very specific design relationship between CS and NUM, this design is not quite complete. There remains part of the design that is missing. We can get some insight into the missing part of the design by investigating how the structure of the DP in (11a) is constructed (see (11b)).

(11) a. This woman
      b. [$_{DP}$ [$_D$ this] [$_{NP}$ woman]]

The structure in (11b), which follows Abney's (1987) hypothesis about the
structures of DPs, builds the DP in a very straightforward way: by merging the
noun *woman* with the determiner *this*. But now consider how the DP *this
woman* is built in the simple sentences in (12).

(12) a. *This woman* loves me.
      b. I gave *this woman* a present.

As the syntactic structure for (12a) is being built from the bottom up, the
derivation will reach the point at which the VP *loves me* has been constructed
and the DP *this woman* needs to be brought into the derivation. But how is this
to be done? The DP cannot be added to the VP one word at a time, the way that
(11b) is put together, without losing the structural connection between the
determiner and the noun. To protect the structural integrity of the DP, the DP
will have to be constructed in some additional workspace outside the SD and
then the entire DP will have to be copied into the SD. Stroik (2009a) calls this
additional sub-derivational workspace the *WorkBench* (WB) and he argues that
syntactic operators take as their domain the union of NUM and WB (i.e., NUM
∪ WB). Support for the proposal that the domain for syntactic operators is the
union of NUM and WB comes from te Velde's (2009) treatment of conjunction
constructions[7] and from an analysis of the left-branch constraint.

 Citing work by Munn (1987) and Johannessen (1998), te Velde observes that
conjunction constructions have both symmetric properties (as in (13)) and
asymmetric properties (as in (14)).

(13) a. Sam and his dog walked.$_{PAST}$ in the park and visited.$_{PAST}$ their
          friends.
      b. *Sam and his dog walked.$_{PAST}$ in the park and visit.$_{PRES}$ their
          friends.

(14) a. *Sam* and *his* dog went for a walk in the park. (Where italics indicate
          coreferentiality)
      b. **His* dog and *Sam* went for a walk in the park.

Te Velde (2009: 175) argues that standard Minimalism, with its commitment to
a pre-derivational construction of a NUM and to phase-to-interface Transfer,
cannot account for the data in (13) or in (14):

Earlier we noted that the matching of lexical features [in conjunction constructions] must
precede the narrow syntax in a phase-base model, if selection of the LIs proceeds as
Chomsky proposes. This type of selection eliminates the possibility of matching lexical
and syntactic elements globally. Syntactic features must be matched separately in the

narrow syntax, and for this matching, the relevant features must be present in the narrow syntax. But if the conjuncts are TPs or CPs, then multiple spell-out has eliminated the first TP or CP conjunct from the narrow syntax before the next one is derived and thus makes it impossible to match the required syntactic features before transfer to the interfaces, at which point unfulfilled feature matching for coordinate symmetry causes a crash.

On the other hand, as te Velde remarks,

[Survive-minimalism] uses an "on-demand" or dynamic selection process, in contrast to one-time selection, that does not require extraction of LIs from a lexical array or sub-array when they are merged. Rather, the LIs to be merged are selected directly from the lexicon. Furthermore, when merged, mapping algorithms are established for pronoun-antecedent relations and other long-distance relations that cannot be captured in a local feature-checking relation. Such mapping algorithms, along with dynamic selection, offer a means to first generate and then check coordinate symmetries (2009: 179).

Te Velde not only provides support for our conception of NUM, he also contends that WB plays a crucial role in accounting for conjunction data in German (the data in (15) are taken from te Velde 2009: 183).

(15)   Multiple conjoined TPs with a shared wh-element (copies in bold)
        Welches Buch hat Frank gern gelesen,
        which book has F gladly read,
        Peter nicht verstanden,
        Peter not understood
        Lars nicht gekauft . . . ?
        Lars not bought
        'Which book did Frank like reading, Peter not understand, Lars not buy. . . ?'
        [$_{CP}$ Welches.$_Q$ Buch.$_{ACC}$ [hat.$_{3SG}$ [$_{TP}$ Frank.$_{NOM}$ **hat**
        [**welches Buch** gern gelesen
        [$_{TP}$ Peter.$_{NOM}$ **hat**
        [**welches Buch** nicht verstanden
        [$_{TP}$ Lars.$_{NOM}$ **hat**
        [**welches Buch** nicht gekauft]]]]]]]]

As te Velde argues, the derivation he proposes in (15) is not permissible in a phase-based version of the Minimalist Program for at least two reasons: first, "it violates phase theory, which doesn't allow movement from one phasal unit to another without the use of the edge (Spec,CP in this case)" (2009: 184); and secondly, "it requires head movement for raising **hat** to the C^0 position" (2009: 184). (For an exhaustive discussion of this analysis, see te Velde 2009: 184.) However, a Survive-model can properly account for these data because this model has "a 'complex' derivational operation that merges the output of a simple derivation with the output of a preceding symmetric simple derivation" (184). That is, it is the ability to merge "the output of a simple derivation" (in WB) that allows conjunction structures to be built. We can see the role WB plays in deriving coordinate structure in the SD that te Velde gives (in (16)) for (15).

(16)   Sketch of the derivations required for (15)
    a. Derive *Welches Buch hat Frank gern gelesen* with the addition of WB merger for the DP *welches Buch*.
    b. Derive **Welches Buch hat** *Peter nicht verstanden* with **copies** of *welches Buch* and *hat* mapped to the CP domain via an algorithm.
    c. Conjoin the merged matrix clauses.
    d. Repeat (b) for the next conjunct **welches Buch hat** *Lars nicht gekauft*.
    e. Conjoin with the previous clauses.
    f. Elide at the left edge, eliminating the redundant CP domains.

Of note, without the use of WB in (16a), it would not be possible to derive a structure for (15).

Not only does WB play a central role in accounting for the conjunction data discussed above, but it also is crucial in explaining the Left Branch Constraint data in (17) taken from Kayne (1983) – note that these data demonstrate that it is not possible to extract from a left-branching constituent.

(17)   a. *[Which famous playwright] did [close friends of **which famous playwright**] become famous?
    b. *Who did [my talking to **who**] bother Hilary?
    c. *Who did you consider [friends of **who**] angry at Sandy?

As we have mentioned previously, WB is a sub-derivational workspace of an SD that is used to compute structurally complex left branch constituents, such as the bracketed constituent [friends of who] in (17c). Importantly, WB builds sub-derivations out of LIs placed piecemeal in a sub-Numeration – for (17c) the sub-Numeration would eventually be {who, of, friends}; then once the sub-derivation is complete, its structural output is copied into the syntactic derivation. So, at some point in deriving a structure for (17c), the syntactic derivation will be as in (18).

(18)   [[friends of who] angry at Sandy]

What is important to note about (18) is that although the LI **who** appears in the SD, it is not visible to/in the derivation. This LI is not in NUM for the SD (rather, it is in a sub-Numeration) and it has not, in and of itself, been selected for inclusion in the derivation (rather, the entire left-branch constituent has been selected). As a result, this LI is not active in the syntactic derivation and no computations or operations directly involving **who** can, therefore, take place in the SD. The ungrammaticality of (17c) arises as a consequence of the fact that the LI **who** (which should be invisible in the SD) is illicitly participating in a displacement operation. Similar analyses explain the ungrammaticality of (17a) and (17b).

Some support for our analysis comes from the data in (19). Crucially both (19a) and (19b) contain the constituent **[books about what]**; however, in (19a) this constituent is built from the bottom up in the syntactic derivation, but in (19b) the constituent is a left-branch constituent that must be built on WB and then brought into the SD as a composite constituent.

(19)   a.   Who wants [books about what]?
       b.   Who wants [books about what] to amaze college students?
       c.   Mary wants books about science; Bob wants books about cooking; etc.
       d.   Mary wants books about science to amaze college students; Bob wants books about cooking to amaze college students; etc.

There is an interesting difference between (19a) and (19b). In (19a), the question can receive multiple answers, such as those in (19c), in which each answer involves ordered pairs of <who, what>; in other words, (19a) allows the wh-elements in the SD to interact computationally. On the other hand, in (19b), the question cannot receive multiple answers, such as those in (19d). This suggests that the wh-elements in (19b), unlike those in (19a), do not interact computationally. Under our analysis, the essential interpretative difference between (19a) and (19b) that we have been discussing follows from the ways in which the **[books about what]** constituents are derived: in the former both wh-elements are introduced in the SD and can, therefore, engage in subsequent computational relations, but in the latter, the wh-element **what** is in the sub-Numeration of WB (and not NUM of the syntactic derivation) and it is not introduced directly into the SD and it cannot, therefore, participate in subsequent relations computed in the SD.

Even though "extraction" out of left-branch constituents in (17a–c) and in (19b) is not computationally possible, this does not mean that left-branch constituents cannot participate in subsequent syntactic operations that might take place in the course of a derivation; it only means that constituents contained within the left-branch constituents cannot participate in any such operations. Hence, while displacing the wh-elements contained within left-branch constituents is not permitted in (20a) and (21a), displacing the entire left-branch constituent is computationally permissible, as is demonstrated in (20b) and (21b).

(20)   a.   *Whom does it seem [to t] that Thelma left the party unhappy?
       b.   [To whom] does it seem t that Thelma left the party unhappy?

(21) a. *Whom did you mention [to t] that Sam was thinking of leaving the
          party?
      b. [To whom] did you mention t that Sam was thinking of leaving the
          party?

The examples in (20a) and (21a) cannot be derived because their wh-elements
contained with left-branch constituents are not visible in their SDs; on the other
hand, since the entire (bracketed) left-branch constituents are visible in (20b)
and (21b), there is nothing to prevent their displacements.

   Our arguments about WB are twofold. First, we have argued that structurally
complex left-branch constituents in a sentence must be built in a workspace
separate from the workspace of the syntactic derivation. Second, we have argued
that WB includes its own sub-Numeration and that while the structural output of
WB is accessible to the SD, the input to WB (its sub-Numeration) is not.

3.7   Final thoughts

This chapter, together with the previous chapter, addresses *the compositional*
and *relational problem*s for LEX and NUM in a biolinguistically plausible
grammar. Breaking rank with almost every other contemporary Minimalist
theory of natural language syntax, we propose here that NUM is built from
LEX in a derivational, piecemeal fashion and it is built throughout the course of
a syntactic derivation. In addition to NUM, certain syntactic objects must be
constructed in a separate WB, with its own separate sub-Numeration, prior to
their merger into an SD.

   Before we move on to the next chapter, where we look closely at the CS, we
would like to respond to K. A. Jayaseelan's (p.c.) concern that the relationships
we have explored in this chapter involving LEX, NUM, WB, and the SD create
a "catch-22" of sorts. According to Jayaseelan, the reason for pre-selecting a
NUM or a phase-defined Lexical Array (LA) (as proposed by Uriagereka 1999
and adopted by Chomsky 2000) is that it serves to reduce the burden on active
memory load during the course of an SD; so, having a derivationally compiled
NUM, as we propose, would seem to face the computational burden of keeping
the contents of NUM and of WB alive in the short-term memory. In other words,
our analysis of NUM carries a substantial memory load that must be borne
throughout the course of an SD. We acknowledge that our version of NUM
comes with a computational burden that standard versions of Minimalism do
not have; however, as we have argued in this chapter, having a blind (rather than
a sighted) NUM would require humans to expend enormous processing time
and energy computing syntactic structure without ever producing any usable
SDs. Such processing costs are incalculably greater than the costs of keeping the
contents of NUM alive in short-term memory.

Copy and the computational system

4.1   A biolinguistic reprise

In the first three chapters, we have argued that the evolutionary development of human language requires locating the linguistic systems of language – the Lexicon (LEX) and the computational system (CS) – within the performance systems themselves. We have also argued that the protolanguage included lexical items (LIs) that grew out of the hierarchically organized features/concepts in the performance systems and that this organization separated selected-features, which defined the essential performance system features/properties that a given LI must possess, from selecting-features, which defined (secondary) features/properties that an LI can, but need not, possess. Take, for example, the LI *cat*; it must have the defining feature <animate> but it can also, although it is not the case that it must, have the feature <colorable> (if humans were color blind, we mostly likely would not have this feature). The latter (inessential) performance system feature of the LI *cat* is a selecting-feature that can pair with an LI, say *gray*, possessing an equivalent selected-feature <color>, to form the hybrid concept/expression *gray cat*. The foregoing discussion suggests that not only would the LIs in the protolexicon have selected-features and selecting-features, but all these features would be organized in a Feature Matrix (FM) as <selecting-features <selected-features>>, with the former features being added to the latter features. That FMs would be organized in this way makes a great deal of evolutionary sense in that LI-defining selected-features had to be "older" than the "newer" selecting-features that build on them.

   The protolanguage, possessing LIs with both selected-features and selecting-features, would have had a limited syntax: LIs could have productively

We are grateful to the participants of the Exploring Crash-Proof Grammars Conference (held at Carson Newman College in March 2008) for their comments on early versions of the arguments advanced in this chapter. We would like to especially thank Omer Preminger, Elly van Gelderen, T. Daniel Seely, and Jan-Wouter Zwart for their insights and suggestions. This chapter is a revision of previous ideas of structure-building in Survive-minimalism developed in Stroik (2009a) and in Putnam and Stroik (2010).

combined by matching selecting-features with selected-features, as in the *gray cat* example above or perhaps even in examples such as *smell meat* (formed by matching the selected perceptual (olfactory) feature of the LI *smell* and the selecting perceptual (olfactory) feature of the LI *meat*).[1] Importantly, this feature-match ability to connect discrete LIs, however, is not an ability that has to be especially engineered for language, as are phrase structure rules (see Chomsky 1965) or the Merge/Concatenate operation (see Chomsky 1995, 2005, 2010). Rather, this ability, as we will discuss, utilizes our ancestral ability to Copy, which according to Corballis (2010), Ramachandran (2011), and Lieberman (1998, 2000, 2006, 2010), is located in our motor systems. And this ability appears to involve our "mirror systems." As Corballis (2010: 119) notes,

In the human brain, [the mirror system] also seems to mediate speech. In particular area F5 in the monkey brain includes some neurons, called mirror neurons, that respond both when the animal makes a grasping motion and when it watches another animal make the same movement. Area F5 is also thought to be the homolog of Broca's area in the human brain, leading Rizzolatti and Arbib (1998) to propose that speech grew out of manual gestures.

Corballis offers several additional arguments to support Rizzolatti and Arbib's proposal, pointing to, among other things, the role that gestures play in infants' development of language and in the acquisition of human language by nonhuman primates. For our purposes, what is interesting about Corballis' analysis is not his conclusion that "intentional communication began as a manual system" (Corballis 2010: 121), but his recognition that language grew out of a mirror system (a Copy-system). Now it may turn out that protolanguage developed out of our auditory mirror system, as Fitch (2010) argues, following Darwin's (1871) claim that protolanguage had a musical base used for sexual selection.[2] Or it might turn out that both the motor mirror system and the auditory mirror system were involved in evolving protolanguage, as Ramachandran (2011: 173) proposes: "If a manual gesture were being echoed by orofacial movements while the creature was simultaneously making emotional utterances, the net result would be what we call words . . . In short, ancient hominins had a built-in pre-existing mechanism for spontaneously translating gestures into words." The point is, though, that protolanguage appears to have emerged, in one way or another, out of our mirror systems.

The most obvious, and perhaps most significant, role that Copy plays in human language is in learning LIs. Without this ability to Copy, humans simply could not master a Lexicon (or have a language). After all, internalizing a new LI requires cognitively copying that item and storing it somewhere in the brain. But the Copy operation is not limited to building a Lexicon, it is also crucial for syntax. In fact, syntactic structure-building requires two types of Copy operations, both of which reproduce material in one domain and add it to another domain with similar properties (a mirror domain). For any LI to participate in structure-building, it (actually a copy of it) will first have to be placed in usable short-term memory (a Numeration). This placement-in-Numeration is accomplished by the Copy operation (Copy-to-Numeration, CoN, as we discuss in Chapter 1). CoN reproduces LIs in the Lexicon (LEX) and places the reproduced LIs into a lexical buffer, the Numeration (NUM), which is a mirror domain of LEX in that both are lexical domains. The CoN operation, in and of itself, is capable of stringing together words into word-lists, such as those with which we regale and amuse our children as we teach them language (*one, two, three, four*; or *ears, nose, eyes, teeth*; etc.) and those which we generate as types of shopping lists (*eggs, bread, milk, butter, bananas*, etc.). These word-lists are merely linearly produced word-domains selected from LEX and these lists are generally, though not restrictively so, built on the basis of some degree of semantic relatedness; these lists then involve word-match. To generate syntactic structure, however, necessitates another operation, one that projects LIs not to a linear word-domain, but to a structural domain. So how can this happen? We propose that the syntactic structure is incipient in, and a by-product of, the structure of words; that is, syntactic structure arises out of the fact that words decompose into hierarchically structured features. Syntactic structure, under our analysis, emerges not from putting "whole" words together, as happens in the formation of word-lists, but by putting together the hierarchically structured parts of words. What we propose in particular is that since every structural derivation begins with an LI – actually a copy of an LI in LEX – and since every LI is defined by its FM, structure-building from its outset will involve FM-building by accreting, in some feature-sensitive fashion, the FM of the first LI-1 placed in a derivation with the FM of a subsequent LI-2 placed in the derivation. But how do we get the lexical material copied into NUM, which is a temporary lexical storage, to be copied into the CS, where a syntactic derivation (SD) can be built out of this lexical material? The most operationally efficient way of doing this would be to use the same operation that introduced lexical material into NUM – that is, a Copy operation. Given that the Copy operation is a general cognitive operation that reproduces material in one domain and places the reproduced material in another similar domain, this operation should be able to copy material from NUM (one domain) and place it in an SD (another domain) if these two domains are appropriately similar. Importantly, as we will argue here, there are sufficient (and appropriate) similarities between the lexical material in NUM and SD so that it should be possible to copy material from NUM to SD. To see these similarities, we need to note that an SD, from the first LI placed in it, is exactly like any lexical material in NUM in that it is defined by, and it projects, a hierarchical FM $<f_i < \ldots >>$. The fact that lexical material and SDs are both defined by FMs is critical to building syntactic structure. The FM of an SD at each step in a derivation will have a hierarchically highest feature f_i that defines the SD and that serves as the "edge feature" (EF) for instructing a derivation on how to proceed. Building an SD only requires that the EF of the SD be met by copying material from NUM that feature-matches the EF of the SD. That is, a copy operation (which we will call Copy-to-syntactic derivation, CoSD) takes material from the NUM that is defined by its EF f_i and copies it to a domain (an SD) also defined by the EF f_i; this copying operation will derive a subsequent SD defined by another EF, as formalized in (I).

(I)   The Copy-to-Syntactic Derivation (CoSD) operation:
      Copy $\{\alpha <f_i<f_n \ldots >>, [_{SD1} <f_i <f_m \ldots >>]\} \rightarrow [_{SD2} \alpha\ SD1] <f_k \ldots >$,
      where k = n or m (depending on which feature is higher ranked).

The CoSD operation (I), then, is a unary operation that builds structure by copying syntactic objects to feature-matching SDs.

   Although the protolanguage will have had both the CoN and CoSD operations, its ability to build syntactic structure will have been severely restricted by the sorts of performance system features (PSFs) available in the protolanguage – these features, of course, will have evolved as cognitive abilities of our ancestors evolved. The conceptual and perceptual features most likely available in the protolanguage – such as animacy, referentiality, focus, secondary properties (color, number, size), etc. – are not inherently recursive features that can have both selected-feature and selecting-feature variants and they are also symbolic/meaningful features grounded experientially. As a result, the protolanguage will not be able to produce the unbounded and desymbolized syntactic structures typical of modern human language (see Reuland 2009 for a discussion of these two properties of human language). As we contend in Chapter 2, developing human language from protolanguage is a matter of adding CATegory features (V, N, P, Adj, etc) and SUBCATegory features to FMs – features that are desymbolic by nature and that function together recursively. This relatively tiny change, and this change alone, much in the spirit of Hornstein's (2009) claim that language evolution must be based on simple changes and much in the spirit of Bickerton's (2009: 17) observation that evolution "doesn't do a lick more than it has to," is sufficient to change protolanguage to human language.

   In the remainder of this chapter, we will show how the syntactic structures of human language follow from the interplay of the FMs of LIs and the Copy operation.

4.2   Preliminary remarks on syntax

Hornstein, Nunes, and Grohmann (2005: 7) note there are six "big facts" about the structural properties of human language that must be explained: (i) sentences are basic linguistic units; (ii) sentences are pairing of form (sounds/signs) and meaning; (iii) sentences are composed of smaller expressions (words and morphemes); (iv) these smaller units are composed into units with hierarchical structure; (v) sentences show displacement properties in the sense that expressions that appear in one position can be interpreted in another; and (vi) language is recursive, that is, there is no upper bound on length of sentences in any given natural language.[3] These "facts," the importance of which can be seen in (1) and (2), are essentially facts about structural construction ((i)–(iv) and (vi)) and about structural reconstruction ((v)).

(1)   a.   The working conditions at Mr. Burns' nuclear power plant are inhumane.
     b.   *Working$_1$ the t$_1$ conditions at Mr. Burns' nuclear power plant are inhumane?
     c.   *At$_1$ the working conditions t$_1$ Mr. Burns' nuclear power plant are inhumane?
     d.   Are$_1$ [the working conditions at Mr. Burns' nuclear power plant] t$_1$ inhumane?

Native speakers of English innately know a great deal about the structural relations in (1). They know, for example, that yes/no questions involve positioning auxiliaries such as *are* above the subject of the sentence – see (1d). They also know that grammatical strings are governed by some notion of structural dependency; that is, as examples (1b) and (1c) illustrate, native speakers of English know that the item/constituent [*the working conditions at Mr. Burns' nuclear power plant*] cannot be broken apart or freely re-arranged (at least not to form a grammatical yes/no question). Hence, the Faculty of Language (FL) must somehow have a design that respects and recognizes these structural dependencies. The examples provided in (1), then, argue strongly for some sort of primitive concatenating operation that can bring individual LIs together to form larger structurally defined units, culminating in the formation of sentences (in the process of iterated concatenations, all the construction "facts" should emerge). However, syntactic constituents are able to engage in more than one structural dependency, as (2) illustrates.

(2)   a.   What did Barney drink last night?
     b.   What$_i$ did Barney drink t_i last night?

Although the wh-item *what* in (2a) is pronounced only once (at the left periphery of the clause), it has multiple functions in the sentence (fact (vi)). As indicated by (2b), *what* is not only the wh-operator but also functions as the direct object of the verb *drink*. It appears, then, that there are two types of structural facts (constructive ones and reconstructive ones) that must be accounted for by any empirically adequate theory of syntax.

Generative theories of syntax – from Chomsky's (1965) Aspects model to Chomsky's (1981, 1986) Government and Binding model to Chomsky and Lasnik's (1993) version of the Principles and Parameters model – use phrase structure rules (including X-bar Theory) to explain constructive facts, and they use transformations (including the Move operation) to explain reconstructive facts. In all these models, the phrase structure rules and the displacement operations are treated as distinct and are placed in separate syntactic components. The phrase structure rules build structural representations (D-structures), which are operationally reconstructed by displacement operations into other (S-structure and LF) representations that could subsequently be interpreted. Importantly, such models are top-down output models; that is, they are representational models. They begin with the S(entence) node and proceed to define all the structural relations within the sentence as the output of phrase structure rules and transformational rules. By starting with sentences in their derivations, these models are not, in any real sense, construction models that build sentence structure; rather, they are *deconstruction* models that dissect given sentences and produce a series of representations for them.

In the Minimalist Program, Chomsky (1993, 1995) advocates a fundamental shift in generative syntax from a top-down representational theory of sentences to a bottom-up computational and derivational model that constructs sentences, instead of presupposing sentences (as happens in top-down theories that begin derivations with sentence nodes), and then deconstructing them into their parts. As a construction model of syntax, Chomsky's version of Minimalism has eliminated the top-down, output apparatus of previous generative models, including phrase structure rules, D-structure, and S-structure, and has replaced this framework with one that starts with LIs and builds sentence structures from them (this building process will explain "big facts" (i)–(iv) and (vi)). To construct syntactic structures, the Minimalist Program uses a binary, concatenative operation Merge, which is responsible for the generation of phrase structure relations, and in most cases also for the displacement of LIs in the Narrow Syntax (the Internal Merge operation has come to replace Move as the operation responsible for displacement – see Kitahara 1994, 1995, 1997; Epstein et al. 1998, Epstein and Seely 2002, 2006; Starke 2001; Chomsky 2004). Under this minimalist, derivation-based view of syntax, syntactic relations are properly established between a syntactic category α and a syntactic category β when they are united/concatenated, forging a sisterhood relationship (via Merge) between the two syntactic categories to form a newly formed syntactic object K, as in (3) below.

(3) $K = [\alpha, \beta]$

Although the Minimalist Program makes a substantial improvement over previous generative models in terms of parsimoniously explaining facts (i)–(vi), it is beset with two substantial problems: a design problem and a construction problem. The design problem is that Minimalism's move toward a derivational theory of syntax has not been successful in completely purging itself of all output/representational elements of previous syntactic models. In particular, Minimalism has continued to use displacement operations (Move, or more recently Internal Merge) to explain displacement phenomena (fact (v)). This design can establish constraints on displacement; however, it cannot, as Stroik (2009a) contends, explain displacement itself. As Stroik argues, appealing to *displacement operations* to account for *displacement data* allows Minimalism to define the structural conditions that license permissible displacements, but it says nothing about the nature of displacement. Furthermore, the consequence of having powerful displacement operations is that it becomes necessary to complicate the design of FL by adding (representational) filters and filter-sensitive domains to reduce the power of the displacement operations – filters such as the Phase Impenetrability Condition (Chomsky 2001), and filter-sensitive domains such as phases (Chomsky 2000 and subsequent work) or Prolific Domains (Grohmann 2000, 2003). Finally, as Brody (1995, 2002) has exhaustively maintained, any derivational model of syntax that uses look-back operations akin to Move and Internal Merge will unavoidably be at least "weakly representational" and, as a consequence, will have a non-economical, redundant design because derivational movements and representational chain-formations will duplicate one another. For Brody, a syntactic theory can be purely derivational if and only if the theory does not have look-back (chain-forming) operations. The foregoing arguments suggest that Minimalism needs to surrender not only the top-down apparatus of previous generative models, but also the look-back apparatus.

The second problem with Minimalism is a construction problem: current versions of Minimalism have no credible way to begin, to proceed through, or to end an SD. As detailed in Chomsky (1995, 2001), an SD starts with selecting lexical items (LIs) from LEX and placing them in a NUM, and it ends when all the LIs in NUM are merged into an SD (accounting for facts (i)–(iv) and (vi) in the process). The complication here is that the LIs must be (randomly) selected for NUM without any way to anticipate the eventual derivation. As we argue in Chapter 3, making NUM-selection the first step in an SD would be a processing catastrophe. Imagine randomly selecting ten words from LEX with the hope that these LIs will be merged together somehow to produce a sentence. Of the more than 3.6 million ways we could merge these ten LIs together it is unlikely that even one of the ways would end up with a well-formed sentence. A staggering amount of fruitless processing time would have to be spent trying to compute well-formed sentences. This seems unlikely. If, as Stroik (1999, 2009a), Frampton and Gutmann (2002), Hinzen (2006), and Putnam and Stroik (2009) maintain, derivations must be "crash-proof" (i.e., they must produce interface interpretable representations), then there is simply no way to begin an SD with an exhaustive NUM selection.[4] We are left, then, with the following questions about how to construct syntactic structures in Minimalism and, relatedly, how to account for facts (i)–(iv) and (vi):

A. How does an SD begin?
B. Based on the previous question, how does an SD proceed, i.e., how is iterative syntactic structure built in Survive-minimalism? What sort of syntactic, concatenative operations are involved? And what syntactic units project after each concatenation?
C. How does an SD end/terminate, and why does it end that way?
D. If the syntax is built on feature-geometries, as is assumed in Minimalism, what sort of feature typology exists and how do features decide answers to the questions given in A–C?

These questions can be answered, we will argue, if Minimalism is reconceived along the Survive-minimalism lines proposed by Stroik (1999, 2000, 2009a) and further developed in Chapter 1 of this book.

Before we discuss how Survive-minimalism answers the questions in (A)–(D), we will provide some additional background about the Survive model. Survive-minimalism is designed, in Stroik (1999, 2009a) and Putnam and Stroik (2009, 2010), to solve Brody's dilemma of explaining how to construct a grammar that can be both derivational and non-representational.[5] In early versions of Survive-minimalism (see in particular Stroik 1999 and Putnam 2007), Brody's dilemma is resolved by limiting allowable syntactic operations to two syntactic operations: Merge and Remerge. Importantly, both of these operations map elements from NUM into an SD; that is, neither operation is a look-back operation that maps from SD to SD and, as a consequence, SDs are non-representational, thereby avoiding the redundancy problems Brody attributes to Chomsky's version of derivational Minimalism. Within early Survive-minimalism, the Merge operation concatenates elements in NUM with constituents in an SD; and the Remerge operation re-concatenates, into SD, previously merged syntactic objects (SOs) that "survive" in NUM (or in the WorkBench), in accordance with the Survive Principle (see (4)), and that have active concatenative features that must still be checked (these features have "survived" previous applications of Merge).

(4) *Survive Principle* (based on Stroik 1999: 286)

If Y is a syntactic object (SO) in an XP headed by X, and Y has an unchecked feature [+ F] that is incompatible with the features of X, Y remains active in the Numeration.

As Stroik argues, in addition to circumventing Brody's dilemma, Survive-minimalism has several other theoretical advantages over more mainstream versions of Minimalism;[6] among these are (i) by having only strictly local operations, Survive-minimalism does not require any filtering/economy mechanisms to delimit over-powerful non-local operations and (ii) Survive-minimalism can account for displacement phenomena without resorting to displacement operations – hence, it can explain, and not merely presuppose, "displacement."

To date, Survive-minimalism has primarily wrestled with Brody's claim that a derivational syntax cannot be void of representational filters: it advances a model of derivational syntax that reduces its theoretical machinery to an active LEX/NUM, the Survive Principle, and two related Numeration-to-Derivation operations (Merge and Remerge) and that, as a consequence, is in fact void of representational filters. A detailed treatment of phrase structure rules and syntactic relations in general – although independently alluded to by Stroik (1999, 2009a) and Putnam (2007) – is, however, both lacking and required. Since all syntactic relations are generated by, and constrained by, the same local syntactic operations (Re)Merge in Survive-minimalism, the task at hand is to explain precisely how the iterative application of these operations builds licit syntactic relations through the course of an SD; that is, the task at hand is to answer questions (A)–(D). In this chapter, we examine how traditional "phrase structure rules" (and the syntactic relations they seek to explain) should be formulated in Survive-minimalism to answer the aforementioned questions.

Here we simplify Stroik's (2009a) version of Survive-minimalism and in the process extend it so that it offers an analysis of syntactic relations. As we argue in Chapter 1, we can replace both the Merge operation and the Survive Principle if we assume, as do Boeckx (2009) and Hornstein (2009), that the Copy operation (a general cognitive function visible in the mirror system that humans, and other great apes, share) plays a role in the computation of syntactic structure. The Faculty of Language, under this reanalysis of Survive-minimalism, evolutionarily develops from the interplay that the LEX/NUM has with the Copy operation, actually the Copy-to-Domain operation. What we propose, in particular, is that the Copy-to-Numeration (CoN) operation compiles a NUM of LIs in a piecemeal (though not blind) fashion throughout the course of an SD and that the Copy-to-syntactic derivation (CoSD) operation, which incorporates Adger's (2008) feature-linking requirement on syntactic operations as a way of defining structural domains, builds SDs. No other mechanisms are necessary for human language to emerge, or to have evolved. There is, however, one aspect of our proposal that deserves a bit more clarification – the role that features play in language. We have argued, in Chapter 2 and Chapter 3, that LIs have three types of hierarchically organized features: SUBCATegory features, PSFs, and CATegory features. Importantly, these features are concatenative features that must be checked via the syntactic operation CoSD and they must be checked in a well-defined order <SUBCAT <PSF-selecting <CAT <PSF-selected>>>>,[7] checking the less-embedded (higher-ranked) features before the more embedded features. Syntactic relations and syntactic structures ("big facts" (i)–(vi)), as we will demonstrate, arise as by-products of the feature requirements driving the CoSD operation in the following way: assuming a bottom-up analysis of syntax requires an SD to begin with an LI X that lacks a SUBCAT feature, or X will not be the bottom-most element in SD (and SD, then, would not be a bottom-up analysis); once X is introduced into SD, its FM (FM = <SUBCAT <PSF-selecting <CAT <PSF-selected>>>>) will feature-instruct SD how to proceed through to the completion of the derivation (thereby answering questions (A)–(D)).

We organize the remainder of this chapter as follows: in Section 4.3, we discuss the fundamental aspects of syntactic relations in a Survive-minimalist syntax. We pay particular attention to the ways in which the FMs of LIs interact with syntactic operations to shape syntactic relations; as we demonstrate, FMs dictate how an SD begins, proceeds, and terminates. The NUM, in our analysis, participates instrumentally in an SD because the LIs warehoused there may have features that require the LI to appear more than once in an SD. The fact that LIs "survive" in NUM, under our analysis, lies at the heart of all displacement phenomena. To support our Survive-analysis of syntactic relations, we provide, in Section 4.4, some detailed SDs. We conclude this chapter in Section 4.5, recapping the hypotheses and claims laid out in this chapter as well as speculating about consequences of our Survive-minimalist analysis of syntactic relations.

4.3   "Phrase structure rules": from Merge to Copy

As a starting point for our analysis, let us explore in more detail the theoretical notion of Merge from a Minimalist perspective. Merge is a binary operation (see (6)) that combines licit syntactic objects, as defined by Chomsky (1995: 243) in (5), to form other licit syntactic objects.

(5)   A syntactic object K is
   a. A selected lexical item (with sets of features) or
   b. K = {g, {a,b}}, where a,b are syntactic objects, and g is the label of K.
   c. Nothing else is a syntactic object.

(6)   Merge $\{\alpha,\beta\} \rightarrow [\gamma, [\alpha,\beta]]$

Of note, the Merge operation in (6) not only establishes sisterhood relations between α and β, it also defines a motherhood relation for γ that emerges from the interaction of the two syntactic categories that are being merged. Under the

Merge operation, something *must* project (a mother projection) to ensure that the derivation will continue.[8] But what is it exactly that projects and how does this projection determine the next step in an SD? Does one of the merged daughter constituents project as the mother (as Chomsky 1995 claims) or does a union of the two merged elements project (as Fortuny 2008 claims)?[9] In Survive-minimalism, neither Chomsky nor Fortuny could be correct because they both presuppose that a binary Merge operation is involved in building syntactic structure. Survive-minimalism uses the unary Copy operation, which, since it is not a binary operation, does not possess daughter or mother constituents, to add a syntactic object, such as an LI, to an SD. The Copy operation will add a syntactic object α to an SD-1 if and only if the FMs of these objects have a matching concatenative feature f (the matching feature should be the highest hierarchical feature available in each FM). Should α have the necessary feature-match for α to be copied into the feature domain of SD-1, it will combine with SD-1, concatenating and deactivating the matching features (which are now ready for interpretation) and forming a new syntactic domain SD-2 with its own FM that projects the highest ranking feature still alive/active in SD-1 or in α.[10] This newly formed syntactic domain SD-2, like all other syntactic objects, consists of, and projects, an FM possessing features that must be subsequently matched, via the CoSD operation, to ensure interpretability by the Conceptual-Intentional (C-I) and the Sensorimotor (SM) performance systems.

As described above, the Copy-to-SD operation accretes new material to a syntactic domain (a derivation) to beget yet another syntactic domain – which raises the question, "How could any such approach to syntactic derivations begin or end?" We observed, in the previous section, that the mainstream Minimalism advocated by Chomsky (1995), Adger (2008), and Hornstein, Nunes, and Grohmann (2005), among others, begins an SD by selecting LIs for a NUM (or for sub-arrays of a NUM) and ends when all the LIs in NUM have their features checked in the SD. We have already discussed reasons for rejecting this approach to SDs. What we did not note previously is that this approach requires multiple beginnings. If the NUM is the set {LI-1, . . ., LI-n}, then each and every LI-i is a potential first element selected for Merge in a derivation with LI-j. To determine which set of Mergers for NUM will produce convergent SDs, all possible sets of Mergers for each derivation-initial LI-i must be produced and evaluated for interface convergence. This will require one to generate up to n! sets of Mergers (i.e., derivations) for NUM {LI-1,. . .,LI-n} – a formidable task, indeed.

In Survive-minimalism, NUM is built one LI at a time, adding LIs if and only if they are feature-required by the SD. That is, a derivation begins with the selection of the first LI for NUM; and once the derivation begins, all the subsequent LIs are added to NUM to meet the concatenative requirements of the SD itself, as defined by the EF of the SD. In a bottom-up derivation, the first

LI in NUM (LI-1) must, however, have a very special property: it must be the most deeply embedded constituent in the derivation. It must, therefore, not have any potential nieces (sister constituents that could have daughter constituents) because any such nieces would be more deeply embedded in the derivation than LI-1 would be. This means that LI-1 cannot c-select (subcategorize for) a sister constituent Y. Although LI-1 cannot have any SUBCATegory features, it can have other syntactic (concatenative) features – CATegory features and perhaps PSFs, as listed in (7).

(7)   *Inventory of Concatenative Features*

   SUBCATegorial features – Features of an LI (e.g., [+ V], [+ N], and [+ P]) that identify the CATegories of the LI's co-occurring arguments; these features are checked, via the CoSD operation, by the CAT features of the LI's sisters.

   PSFs – Morpho-syntactic and syntactico-semantic concatenative features, such as Topic features, Focus features, property and agreement features, and wh-features, among others, that have developed out of pre-linguistic cognitive and perceptual features. These features need to be exhaustively determined, but they may include reference features, quantity features, and temporality features. We leave a precise determination of these features for future research.

   CATegorial features – The unique lexical-class feature of an LI that identifies the LI's syntactic category (e.g., [+ V], [+ N], and [+ P]); this concatenative feature is checked in via the CoSD operation with syntactic category X which has a matching SUBCAT feature.

The fact that the SUBCAT feature determines the eligibility of an LI to be LI-1 (the first LI placed in a NUM) suggests that the concatenative features of LIs are ordered for an SD; in particular, the first SUBCAT feature of an LI must be checked before its PSFs and its CAT feature are checked. If we conceive of feature matches as having a selecting feature and a selected feature and if we assume that "selecting" initiates the structural projection of an LI and "being selected" terminates the structural projection of an LI, then SUBCAT features should be checked before PSFs and before CAT features because SUBCAT features are pure selecting-features, while CAT features are pure selected-features and PSFs can be either selecting (as is the wh-feature of a C [+wh] complementizer) or selected (as is the wh-feature on a wh-DP such as *what*). Under these assumptions the FM of an LI should be structured in the following way: <SUBCAT <PSF-selecting <CAT <PSF-selected>>>>.

In previous versions of Survive-minimalism (see Stroik 1999, 2009a), SUBCAT and CAT features are handled by the Merge operation, and the PSFs are generally handled by the Remerge operation – note that the PSF-selected features of an LI, which must be checked in an SD at some point well after the LI's CAT feature is checked, force the LI to *survive* in NUM (in accordance with the *Survive Principle*). Furthermore, the LI will continue to *survive* in NUM until its PSF-selected-features are matched, via the Remerge operation, with the appropriate PSF-selecting-features. In early versions of Survive-minimalism, the concatenative operations Merge and Remerge continue to build feature-linked structures as long as the LIs added to NUM have selected-features <CAT <PSF-selected>>. An SD will terminate after an LI, typically a C(omplementizer), is added to NUM without having a CAT feature (alternatively, it could have an unselectable, performance system-ready CAT feature, CAT*). Allowing LIs to emerge from LEX with some version of a dormant CAT feature could explain how Bare Argument Ellipsis (BAE) constructions, such as *An eagle! [pointing]*, can be constructed syntactically without having to derive, then reduce, an underlying clause (see Merchant 2004 and Culicover and Jackendoff 2005 for arguments that BAE constructions do not involve ellipsis). If the Determiner *an* has a dormant CAT feature, the SD in which the LI *eagle* Merges with the LI *an* will terminate once the LIs Merge.

As we can see, Survive-minimalism, as formalized in Stroik (2009a), is a derivational theory of syntax that builds syntactic relations through feature-concatenation. Under Survive-minimalism, LIs are in essence nothing more than complex FMs and each of these features (e.g., SUBCAT, PSF, CAT) in an FM has to enter into Merge and Remerge relations in the course of a derivation (Narrow Syntax) to produce a string of concatenative items (CIs) that can be interpreted by the performance systems. In our present analysis of syntactic relations, we continue to follow Stroik's (1999, 2009a) basic design of the CS described above. That is, we assume that all syntactic operations build structure by mapping lexical material from a lexical domain (NUM) to a structural domain (an SD) and that no syntactic operation can relocate structural material by either remerging it from one structural location to another structural location (as does Chomsky's Internal Merge operation) or pruning it from the structure to move it to another cognitive domain (as does Chomsky's Transfer operation). The latter two operations are simply not conceptually necessary because structure-building operations that prune structure are by their very nature not building-type operations and operations that recycle structural material to build more structure, though conceptually feasible, are no more conceptually necessary than recycling glass is conceptually required for making more glass. Although we accept Stroik's basic design of the CS, we dramatically simplify Stroik's design by reducing his three syntactic mechanisms (Copy to Numeration, Merge/Remerge, and the Survive Principle) to a single mechanism (Copy). As we shall demonstrate, the Copy operation alone can derive all the syntactic relations permissible in human language.

4.4   Syntactic derivation, Survive-style

To show how our CS works, we will walk through a detailed derivation step-by-step. Let us consider, in particular, how our analysis can account for the syntactic structure of the following sentence (8).

(8)   Who will Lisa see?

We begin our analysis of (8) by taking stock of some of the proposals that we have already advocated. Recall that, under our analysis, the ways in which derivations begin, proceed, and terminate are dictated by the hierarchical FMs of LIs in NUM. Any given LI will have an FM with a CATegory feature, and can have an FM with SUBCATegory features, and with PSFs, such as wh-features, Case features, etc. All these features must be checked in the course of an SD to ensure that they are properly concatenated so that they can be interpreted by the performance systems. Of note, though, is the fact that these features in an FM are structured hierarchically, FM = <SUBCAT <selecting PSFs <CAT <selected PSFs>>>> and they must be checked in order (as we argue in Section 2.4 of Chapter 2, Müller 2010 also argues that lexical features are hierarchically ordered and must be checked in order). The selecting features of an LI – its SUBCAT features and any selecting PSFs, such as the Case feature of the light verb v or the Case feature on the Tense-head or the wh-feature of a C-head – must be checked before the selected-features are. Checking features in this order guarantees that an LI will not be selected for NUM or be copied into an SD unless it is required to match features already projected in the SD. That is, an LI with a SUBCAT feature f will enter a NUM and will be merged into the SD that is being built from this NUM if and only if there is an X being projected in SD that has a matching f-CAT feature. Since an LI Y with a SUBCAT feature is precluded from being selected for NUM unless the SD already has built an X constituent with a matching CAT feature, this means that Y cannot be the first element in the NUM of the SD. The first element in any NUM, as a result, must not have a SUBCAT feature.

We can see how this works if we return to the SD of the sentence in (8). The NUM for (8) begins with selecting the LI *who* from LEX and copying this LI from LEX into NUM; the LI is then recopied into SD. The fact that the FM for *who* has no SUBCAT feature – the FM for this LI is <CAT-D <WH>> (this FM states, in essence, that *who* is a DP with a wh-feature) – which makes *who* a suitable lexical selection to initiate an SD (see (9a)).[11] After *who* is placed from NUM into the SD, the SD projects the FM of this LI: <CAT-D <WH>>. Recall, though, that what is actually projected is the highest feature in the FM (<CAT-D>). For the projected feature to be interpreted structurally (rather than lexically), the feature must concatenate with a matching feature. Hence, it is now necessary to select an LI from LEX that has a matching SUBCAT-D feature.

Since the verb see has an FM (<SUBCAT-D <SUBCAT-D <CAT-V>>>)[12] that subcategorizes for two DP arguments, it has the appropriate SUBCAT-D feature to match the CAT feature of *who* and, therefore, can be added to NUM (= {see, who}) and copied into the SD, as in (9b).

(9) a. NUM = {who}: Copy {who <CAT-D <WH>>, SD-0} → **[who]** <CAT-D <WH>>

     b. NUM = {see, who}: Copy {see <SUBCAT-D <SUBCAT-D <CAT-V>>>, SD <CAT-D <WH>>} → [see **who**] <SUBCAT-D <CAT-V>>

(The emboldened syntactic object (SO) above indicates that this SO has unchecked features and that this SO continues to "survive" in NUM for subsequent Copy-to-SD.) At this juncture in the SD, three things happen. First, copying the verb's FM to the SD not only checks and deactivates the matching SUBCAT and CAT features (which ensures that the concatenated features form an interpretable concatenated item), but also projects the dominant FM – i.e., the FM with the highest ranking hierarchical feature. In this case the FM of the verb will project because its active <SUBCAT-D> (selecting) feature outranks the <WH> (selected) feature of *who*. Second, the LI *who* has had its selected CAT feature checked; however, it still has a selected <WH> feature that is unchecked and, as a result, this LI will "survive" (remain activated) in the NUM. Third, although the first SUBCAT feature in the verb's FM (<SUBCAT-D <SUBCAT-D <CAT-V>>>) has been checked in (9b), the remainder of the FM projects and must be checked. In particular, the next feature in the verb's hierarchical FM (i.e., the <SUBCAT-D> feature) both projects and must be checked next. To check this feature, we must add an LI to NUM with a <CAT-D> feature. The LI *Lisa* has the requisite feature: its FM is <CAT-D <CASE>>. Hence, *Lisa* will be copied from the NUM into the SD as in (9c).

(9c) NUM = {Lisa, see, **who**}: Copy {Lisa <CAT-D <CASE>>, SD <SUBCAT-D <CAT-V>>} → [**Lisa** [see **who**]] <CAT-V>

In (9c), the <CAT-D> feature of *Lisa* will be checked, though its <CASE> feature will not; consequently, this LI will also survive in NUM. Furthermore, the <CAT-V> feature of the verb will project because the active FM of the verb, which consists of a <CAT-V> (selecting) feature, outranks the <CASE> (selected) feature of *Lisa*. Checking the <CAT-V> feature being projected requires that an LI with a matching <SUBCAT-V> be added to NUM and merged into the SD. The modal *will* has this feature. However, it also has a <CASE-NOM-selecting> feature and, as one of its options, it has a selected Q(uestion)-feature, as well as its selected CAT-M feature. The modal will merge into the SD in the following way and with the following consequences.

(9d)   NUM = {will, **Lisa**, see, **who**}: Copy {will, SD <CAT-V>} [**will** [**Lisa** [see [**who**]]]] <CASE-NOM <CAT-M <Q>>>

As we can see, merging the modal into the derivation leaves the SD with a projecting <CASE-NOM-selecting> feature. This feature must be matched by some Y with a <CASE-selected> feature. Given that Y would have such a feature available if and only if its hierarchically higher features, including its SUBCAT and CAT features, have been checked previously in the SD, the appropriate Y must already be in NUM and must be available for recopying into the SD. The LI *Lisa* has the requisite available feature, so it will be recopied into the SD, as in (9e).

(9e)   NUM = {**will**, Lisa, see, **who**}: Copy {Lisa, SD <CASE-NOM <CAT-M <Q>>>} → [Lisa [**will** [**Lisa** [see **who**]]]] <CAT-M <Q>>

The projecting <CAT-M> feature of the modal now requires an LI with a <SUBCAT-M> feature to be added to NUM and copied into the SD. One LI with this SUBCAT feature is a C(omplementizer). Though there is a variety of C-heads, the sort we need here, as is indicated in (9e), is one with a Q-type feature, as well as a WH-selecting feature. Should we introduce any other C into NUM, the derivation will stall because the Q feature on the modal and the WH-feature on the wh-word will not be checked. So, let us assume that the C selected for NUM has a <SUBCAT-M <Q <WH>>> FM. Notice that this FM has no CAT features, which indicates that the NUM will not be able to add LIs and that the SD will terminate after all the projecting features are checked.

(9f)   NUM = {C, **will**, Lisa, see, **who**}: Copy {C, SD <CAT-M <Q>> } → [C [Lisa [**will** [**Lisa** [see [**who**]]]]]] <Q-selecting <WH-selecting>>

Although copying the C element into the SD checks the CAT-M feature of the modal, it leaves the <Q> feature of the modal unchecked; therefore the modal will survive in NUM and will be available for another Copy-to-SD operation. Since the projecting features <Q-selecting <WH-selecting>> that remain in the SD do not involve CAT or SUBCAT features, they must be checked by LIs already in NUM, as in (9g) and (9h).

(9g)   NUM = {C, **will**, Lisa, see, **who**}: Copy {will, SD <Q-selecting <WH-selecting>> → [will [C [Lisa [**will** [**Lisa** [see [**who**]]]]]]] <WH-selecting>

(9h)   NUM = {C, will, Lisa, see, **who**}: Copy {who, SD <WH-selecting>} → [who [will [C [Lisa [**will** [**Lisa** [see [**who**]]]]]]]]

The SD is now complete. All the concatenative features in all the FMs of all the LIs introduced into NUM have been appropriately checked; consequently, the SD in (9h) is now a structural representation that can be interpreted by the C-I and SM performance systems (note: since this representation is the output of LIs and derivational processes that are contained in the performance systems, it too is contained in the performance systems and will not have to undergo any Transfer operation to get to the interfaces – as it must in Chomsky 2005, 2009).

We want to stress at this point in the analysis the significant role that NUM plays in the SD provided above. Notice that by conceiving of NUM as a short-term workspace for the syntactic derivation, by building NUM under conditions of derivational necessity, and by positing an interactive relationship between NUM and the SD, we can design a CS for human language that is optimally simple and efficient, ontologically minimal (not requiring Movement-type rules or economy/minimality conditions or Transfer operations), and maximally crash-proof.

To see how our Survive-minimalist analysis of syntactic relations can handle a slightly more complex derivation than the one given in (9) above, let us consider how to derive sentence (10). (We will simplify the derivation somewhat by focusing on the roles that CAT and SUBCAT features play in the derivation and we will provide some visualization for our analysis by giving tree structures.)

(10)   Moe will give a beer to Homer.

The SD for (10) starts by selecting the LI *Homer* from LEX, placing a copy of this LI into NUM and subsequently recopying the LI from NUM into the SD. Since this LI has no SUBCAT feature (and, therefore, it will have no nieces that could be more deeply embedded in the syntactic structure than it is), it can be a legitimate LI-1 for the SD. The LI, however, does have a CAT-D feature, as do all LIs. To check its CAT-D feature, the LI *Homer* will have to concatenate with an LI-2 with a SUBCAT-D feature. An appropriate LI for this derivation initial concatenation is the preposition *to*, which can be copied from LEX and added to NUM. Once the preposition is in NUM, it can be copied to the SD and then concatenate with [D Homer] to yield the syntactic object in (11):

(11)   +P
          ⁀
        P_{to} DP_{Homer} ← Copy P to SD

Importantly, the preposition *to* has two features: a SUBCAT-D feature and a CAT-P feature. Copy enables the D features of the LI *Homer* and the LI *to* to be matched/deactivated. The CAT-P feature of the preposition *to*, however, is not valued at this point in the SD because the DP does not have any such feature in its own matrix that is identical to +P; hence this CAT feature is projected as the output of the Copy-to-SD operation, which will now drive how the derivation proceeds. We would like to emphasize at this point one of the radical theoretical departures of Survive-minimalism: rather than having the predicate, i.e. V, necessarily 'call the shots' and select its arguments from NUM, in the Survive framework developed here, it is possible for the syntactic category/ object in the position of the right-branch sister (traditionally referred to as the 'complement') to determine its subcategorizing head and not vice versa.[13] That is, the LI or SO argument bearing a CAT feature can enter an SD before the LI predicate with a matching SUBCAT feature. Although it might seem odd at first that syntactic constituents can appear in a derivation independent of a predicate, such a hypothesis is consistent with the sequence of LIs and predicates in L1 acquisition. In the single-word stage of language development, children acquire and use non-predicate LIs, regularly using one-word expressions referentially (at this stage in language acquisition, it is conceivable that LIs lack CAT and SUBCAT features altogether, which would explain how these LIs could be, in and of themselves, interpretable by the performance systems). Hence, children form SDs without prior appeal to a predicate. That is, at the single-word stage, children do not restrict their lexical acquisition to verbs or predicates; in fact, they do not even necessarily begin this acquisition by learning verbs first (or learning how to use words predicationally first). If we assume (as most versions of Minimalism do) that the driving engine of SD is the verb, then the afore-mentioned pattern of lexical acquisition would be quite unexpected. We should, under such an assumption, expect children to master verbs first and to sub-sequently build their two-word stage of development around these verbs. However, no such thing happens. Our naïve sense is that, in similar fashion, our species did not come into language by generating verbs first and then learning how to develop structure by merging other LIs with these verbs. Furthermore, as we have argued previously, NUM must be built piecemeal, rather than all at once, to avoid countless potential crash-situations, which, of course, is highly unwanted in a crash-proof syntactic theory like Survive-minimalism. Building NUM in a bottom-up fashion, as we have argued pre-viously, requires the first LI X in NUM to be the most deeply embedded constituent in an SD, which is possible only if X has no SUBCAT feature Y, or Y (and not X) will be the most deeply embedded constituent in the derivation. A verb (V) not having any SUBCAT features could potentially be the first X in NUM, but if V does have a SUBCAT feature (say, SUBCAT-D), then some Y with a CAT-D feature must precede V in an SD. So, whether a derivation begins with a predicate or not depends on the geometry of feature concatenation, not on the nature of predication itself.

Returning to (11), once the prepositional phrase is formed, it will project a CAT-P feature. Although there are several types of LIs (including some nouns and some adjectives) able to select a CAT-P feature, this prepositional phrase is selected by the verb V_{give}, which possesses, among other things, a SUBCAT-P feature. This results in the second feature concatenation of the derivation, as illustrated in (12).

(12)
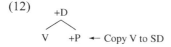

Similar to the initial instance of Copy-to-SD, the CAT-P feature of the right-branching sister feature-concatenates with an LI (*give*) possessing a SUBCAT-P feature. Since the LI *give* has two features that cannot be concatenated in (10) – a SUBCAT-D feature and a CAT-V feature – these features continue in the SD as the output of the Copy operation in (12). The fact that an LI, such as *give*, can possess more than one SUBCAT feature requires that we revise our previous analysis of an ordered FM. We have already established the order among SUBCAT-I, CAT and PSFs, but where does a subsequent SUBCAT feature (SUBCAT-2) fit in this order? A SUBCAT-2 feature for an LI cannot precede its SUBCAT-1 feature (for obvious reasons), nor can it antecede its CAT feature because the LI loses its ability to select features of other LIs once its (selected) CAT feature is checked. Consequently, a SUBCAT-2 feature must either come immediately before PSF-selecting features, or immediately after them. Given that SUBCAT-1 must concatenate with elements already in an SD and given that PSF-selecting features will concatenate with elements already in NUM, while CAT requires new material to be added to NUM and to the SD, it appears that SUBCAT-2, which also must introduce new material to NUM and the SD, feature-aligns with CAT. That is, the FM for an LI with two SUBCAT features will be (13):

(13)   FM: <SUBCAT-1 <PSF-selecting <SUBCAT-2 <CAT <PSF-selected>>>>>

Let us put (13) into perspective. Recall again that an SD must begin with an LI X that has no SUBCAT feature, though X will have a CAT feature and perhaps some PSF-selected features (<CAT-X <PSFs>>). Now the Copy-to-SD (CoSD) operation, which is a concatenate-feature operation, compels the CAT feature of X to be matched. This can happen only if X is merged with a Y that has a SUBCAT-X feature that matches the CAT-X feature of X; the LI Y, then, must have, at minimum, the FM: <SUBCAT-X <CAT-Y>>. The LI Y must now have its CAT-Y feature checked, which will require another LI to enter NUM and the SD. And so forth. This provides us with a much clearer vision of how an SD begins and how it (initially) proceeds. However, as (13) anticipates, an SD becomes complicated once an LI has PSF features. For example, if LI X has a PSF, say a wh-feature, then this feature, in accordance with the Copy operation itself (early versions of Survive-minimalism appealed to the Survive Principle*), will keep the LI active in NUM and available to be recopied into the derivation. For every subsequent LI Z brought into the derivation, should Z have PSF-selecting features, X will have to be recopied into the SD for potential concatenation. If Z does not have a compatible feature, X will continue to *survive* in NUM until it is copied to an SD with a compatible concatenative feature – at which point X is no longer active in NUM. Should X's wh-feature not find a compatible feature in the derivation, the derivation will stall and not be interpreted by the performance systems. All PSFs, then, are checked via the CoSD operation in the most economical way possible, by first using material already available in NUM before bringing new material into NUM. Notice, however, that the PSFs in (13) are ordered within an FM after the SUBCAT features: <SUBCAT-1 <PSFs <SUBCAT-2 <CAT>>>>. What this means is that an LI Y with FM (13) must be copied into an SD before its PSFs can participate in any syntactic operations; that is, the SUBCAT-1 feature of X must participate in syntactic operation before the selecting-PSFs can participate in any syntactic operations, which will themselves precede syntactic operations involving the SUBCAT-2 feature. Then, after all the SUBCAT features are checked, the CAT feature of X is checked, and, at this point, X stops projecting because it has become the argument of another LI. Even though X may stop projecting, it may show up again in SD because it may have selected-PSFs that have not yet been checked; that is to say X may "survive." There are, of course, other issues we must confront in any detailed treatment of the organization of an SD – especially with regard to directionality of the CoSD operation; however, we will postpone this discussion until Section 4.5.

Let us return to the next instance of feature concatenation in the derivation of sentence (10). This concatenation will involve the verb *give*, which has the following FM.

(14)   FM of V$_{give}$: <SUBCAT-P <SUBCAT-D <CAT-V <PSFs>>>>

(Note: the selected-PSF in (14) is the non-finite verb form <VForm> of the verb *give*.) The first SUBCAT feature (i.e., SUBCAT-P) has been matched and deactivated with the previous copy operation in (12). What is projected in the derivational step in (12) is the remaining FM <SUBCAT-D <CAT-V <PSFs>>>. It would appear that in the next feature concatenation the SUBCAT-D feature will be checked by [$_{DP}$ a beer], which will have a matching CAT-D feature. However, we encounter a minor complication here. The concatenation of the noun *beer* does not take place directly into the SD itself. According to the basic tenets of Survive-minimalism, it is not possible to concatenate this noun into the SD from NUM because it does not have an available CAT-D feature to Copy to the SUBCAT-D feature of the verb *give*. Instead, the DP *a beer* will have to be constructed elsewhere in a workspace separate from the SD prior to being brought into the derivation. The Copy-domain for an SD, then, is the union of NUM with this sub-derivational work-space. Stroik (2009a) defines this union as the WorkBench (WB) for the SD, the 'space' that includes all the materials used in constructing an SD (see Chapter 3 for an extended discussion of the WorkBench).

We can assume, at this point, that the DP [DP [D a] [NP beer]] is created in the WB before it is inserted in the SD. This instance of Copy in the WB is represented in (15).

(15)

+D

D_a NP_{beer} ← Copy of D to N

The noun *beer* possesses a CAT-N feature. The Copy operation concatenates the SUBCAT-N feature of the indefinite article with the CAT-N features of *beer*. Critically, the indefinite article *a* also has a CAT-D feature, which cannot be checked in (14); hence, this feature (and the syntactic structure it dominates) survives in the WB and can be copied from the WB to the SD. The constituent formed in (15) will now serve as the syntactic object able to satisfy the SUBCAT-D feature of V in the SD, as in (16).

(16)

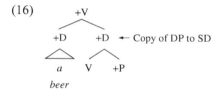

The concatenation of [DP [D a] [NP beer]] 'checks' the SUBCAT-D feature that is highest ranked in the FM of V_{give}. What remains to project are the <CAT-V <VForm>> features on V_{give}. Checking the CAT-V feature requires that a light verb *v* be copied to NUM from LEX and subsequently copied into the SD. Since the light verb has an FM with <SUBCAT-V <VForm <SUBCAT-D <CAT-*v*>>>> feature, it will be able to check the extant features of the verb *give*. These features, however, are checked in two steps. First, the concatenation of the light verb and the projected VP will check the CAT-V feature of *give*, but not its <VForm> feature. The consequence of this concatenation is that *give* will have a surviving <VForm> feature and, therefore, the copy of *give* originally brought into NUM will remain active in NUM. Second, what projects from this con-catenation are the features of the light verb: <VForm <SUBCAT-D <CAT-*v*>>>. This projected FM requires the <VForm> feature of the light verb to be checked next, which will take place when the LI *give* surviving in NUM is recopied into the SD. In fact, this recopy operation will check the [VForm] features of both the light verb and of the verb *give*, and in the checking process will eliminate all active features of *give*. Once the recopy operation applies, the <SUBCAT-D> <CAT-v>> features of the light verb will project, as in (17).

(17) +D
$$\diagup\diagdown$$
v +V ← Copy of v and V to SD
[Vform]

To complete what is traditionally known as the vP-shell, the projected SUBCAT-D feature requires an LI with a matching CAT-D feature. The DP *Moe* bears the CAT-D feature and can thus be copied to the SD once it is copied to NUM; this concatenation will project a +v feature – see (18). (Bear in mind here that the feature concatenation of *Moe* will check its CAT-D feature, but not its PSF-selected <Case> feature, which allows *Moe* to *survive* in NUM.)

(18)   [v]
$$\diagup\diagdown$$
DP$_{Moe}$ +D ← Copy of DP to SD

Among the LIs with SUBCAT-v features are modals, such as *will*. This modal, which has <SUBCAT-v <Case <CAT-M>>> features, can be copied to NUM and then be copied into the SD, checking the CAT-v feature of the vP. Once its SUBCAT feature is checked, the modal will project its <Case <CAT-M>> features, as in (19).

(19) <Case: Nom>
$$\diagup\diagdown$$
M   +v ← Copy of M to SD
$\diagup\diagdown$

To check the projected <Case> feature, the LI *Moe* will be re-copied from the NUM to concatenate its PSF-selected <Case> feature with the PSF-selecting <Case> feature of the modal. This feature concatenation, as shown in (20), will check the <Case> features and project a CAT-M feature.

(20)   +M
$$\diagup\diagdown$$
DP$_{Sam}$ M ← Recopy of DP$_{Homes}$, to SD

To complete the derivation, we require a functional head that can license the CAT-M feature. The most suitable candidate is C. Since this C will terminate the SD, it crucially does not possess any CAT features that will project and, as a consequence, require further iterative applications of the Copy operation to sustain the derivation. Thus the Copy operation in (21) successfully concludes the SD for (10) and presents a completed grammatical string (representation) ready for interpretation by the performance systems.

(21)   C

C   +T   ← Copy of C to SD, with Successful Completion of the SD

At the conclusion of this SD, sentence (10), repeated below, will have **Representation** (10*), where the completed derivation of a sentence becomes the **Representation** that is ready to be interpreted by the performance systems.

(10)   Moe will give a beer to Homer.

(10*)   **Representation** [C [Moe [will [**Moe** [give [v [a beer [**give** [to Homer]]]]]]]]]

This **Representation** is ready for interpretation because all the concatenative features of every LI have been appropriately checked. That is, none of the LIs in NUM will have any surviving features that are unchecked and uncheckable. Consequently, the completed **Representation** (10*) is properly processed, which guarantees that all the concatenations formed throughout the derivation are licit and able to be interpreted by the performance systems. Of special note about the **Representation** is that some of the LIs will appear more than once because they have features checked by more than one projecting SD; all appearances (i.e., copies) of any LI in a **Representation**, however, participate in interpretable syntactic relations and, therefore, they must all be visible to one of the performance systems. Since all the copies of any LI in the **Representation** must be interpreted by one of the performance systems, none of them can be deleted, although a performance system can ignore a given concatenated item if the concatenation involves features not recognized by that system. The re-concatenation of the LI *Moe* in the subject position of the sentence, for example, will be ignored by the C-I performance system because the Case-feature involved in this concatenation is not a C-I feature.

   Our analysis of syntactic relations in Survive-minimalism elucidates core aspects of syntactic theory that have in many previous versions of generative grammar been taken for granted. We now have an established notion of how an SD begins, how it proceeds, and how it successfully ends. An SD begins with the most deeply embedded constituent in the derivation (the bottom-most lexical item in the derivation, LI X), which requires that LI X have no SUBCAT-Y feature, or else some other lexical item LI Y (one that satisfies the SUBCAT feature of X) will necessarily be the most deeply embedded constituent in the derivation. The SD then builds structure by satisfying the feature requirements dictated by the geometry of whatever FM is being structurally projected, starting with the FM of LI X. The SD will continue to build syntactic structure until the FM being projected for an SD is exhausted (this will occur only if the SD does not project a CAT feature).

The two derivations provided above for (8) and for (10), although given slightly different analyses (one is focused on FM output and one on structural output), tell the same Survive-minimalist story: they both present the CS of human language as a mapping from LEX/NUM to an SD, using a general cognitive operation (the Copy operation) as the computational mechanism that brings lexical material into the SD. The output of this CS is a single, completed derivation, which becomes the representation interpreted by the C-I and the SM performance systems. As we have seen by looking at the representations for (8) and (10), all the syntactic relations within a derivation are built in a "crash-proof" way that guarantees their eventual interpretability and, moreover, they are built in a strictly local fashion – i.e., without the use of any movement or other displacement mechanisms. Even though we will be limiting, in this chapter, our Survive-minimalist analysis of syntax to the somewhat simple examples in (8) and (10), our analysis extends without any complications to more complex examples, such as those in (22) and (23), among a multitude of other examples.

(22)   Who does Smithers believe that Mr. Burns will hire?

(23)   I was persuaded that Moe will give a beer to Homer.

We will not analyze these sentences here only because of the length of their derivations; however, it should be clear to the reader, based on our discussions above, how these extended derivations would play out.

4.5   Consequences of our analysis of structure-building operations

There are two consequences of our analysis of syntactic relations that deserve special attention. The first of these has to do with the notion of "edges" and its corollary notion of "edge features." Chomsky (2001) first formulated an "edge" as in (24):

(24)   [$_{HP}$ ZP [H YP]]

According to (24), an "edge" of a phrase HP consists of all the lexical material in HP that is to the left of the head H; i.e., in (24), the edge of the HP would consist of the material in ZP. As we point out in Putnam and Stroik (2011: 392–393), this notion of "edge," unfortunately, is not a *derivational* one; but is, rather, a *representational* notion that is defined in a configurational relation to the head H. Notice that the ZP "edge" in [(24)] does not provide any derivational information about how structure-building will proceed once HP is constructed. In other words, this "edge" looks backwards at what has been constructed, providing only representational information about the already derived HP.

Although this view of structure-building often goes unchallenged, it is the anecdotal equivalent of putting your blinker on after you have already made a turn. For us, an edge should not be a representational edge with structural *hindsight*; rather, in an optimal system of structure-building, it should be a derivational edge that possesses structural *foresight*. Not only is Chomsky's notion of "edge" problematic, so too is his notion of "edge features" (EFs). According to Chomsky, EFs are contentless features that allow syntactic constituents to attach to the edges of constructions. These features, which are latter-day variants of the Extended Projection Principle (developed by Chomsky 1981), appear in the CS, but not in the performance systems, and they have only an operational function, that being to keep an SD building the additional structure needed to license some sort of "interpretive effect" at the "external interfaces" (as Chomsky 2001 argues). There are a couple of problems with this notion of edge features. For one, as Dawkins (2009) points out, the processes involved in building biological structures are self-assembly processes that require information exchange. What this suggests is that contentless edge features are simply not informationally rich enough to be able to participate in the biological computation of structure-building. This accords with arguments made by Putnam and Stroik (2011), Sheehan and Hinzen (2011), and Lohndal and Pietroski (2011) against contentless edge features. Another problem with Chomsky's analysis of edge features is that their function (to license interpretative effects) needs to anticipate what could happen at the interfaces, but it is not possible to determine these effects in advance, that is, in the course of a derivation.

Even though our analysis of SDs follows Chomsky in assuming that edges and edge features play prominent roles in structure building, we avoid all the problems that beset Chomsky's analysis. For us, an EF is not an extraneous, contentless feature; rather it is a contentful element of the FM defined for an SD – in fact it is the highest feature in the FM. Furthermore, under our analysis, an EF is/defines the edge of a derivation. It determines not what will eventually happen to the derivation (as it does for Chomsky), but how the derivation proceeds in its next step (of the computation). In this way, it serves as the instruction for self-assembly that Dawkins (2009) identifies as being central to the growth of biological structures.

The second consequence of our syntactic analysis concerns the directionality of the Copy-to-SD operation. If we inspect our analysis of (10) closely, we will notice that every application of the Copy operation involves left-Copy, where new material is introduced into the SD at the left periphery.

(10)   Moe will give a beer to Homer.

Should we embed (10) deeply into another clause, as in (25), we will find that building an SD for (25) will continue to use left-Copy operations. In other words, all the spinal heads used in deriving (25) – C-3, T-3, v-3, V-3, C-2, T-2, v-2, V-2, C-1, T-1, v-1, V-1 – will all be left-copied into a derivation after their complements are formed in the derivation; and all the nominal arguments will be left-copied into the derivation, too.

(25)   Barney wants you to tell me that Moe will give a beer to Homer.

The persistent use of left-Copy in SDs leads us to suspect that there might be a uniformity of directionality in the Copy operations, as formulated in (26), perhaps reflecting the left-position of the highest ranking features (the edges) in FMs.

(26)   *Copy's Uniformity of Directionality (CUD):* All Copy-to-SD operations are left-Copy operations.

Needless to say, the validity of CUD would require a great deal of empirical investigation before it could be accepted as a core derivational principle. However, CUD has substantial conceptual appeal. Having CUD simplifies the CS by reducing the number of potential syntactic operations from two operations (left-Copy and right-Copy) to a single operation (left-Copy). Without such simplification, the computational system could, in principle, have to generate all the left-right derivations and rule out all but one for interpretation. Consider, for example, the computations possible if NUM-X has four LIs {A, B, C, D} that will be introduced into NUM one LI at a time in order, which means that NUM-X starts out as {A}, then becomes {A, B} and {A, B, C}, and finally {A, B, C, D}. Given CUD, there is only one way to linearize a syntactic derivation from NUM-X: ABCD. On the other hand, if CUD is not a computational principle, then the CS could generate eight derivations from NUM-X, each of which would be structurally well formed, though not necessarily linearly well formed: DCBA, CBAD, DABC, ABCD, DBAC, BACD, DCAB, CABD. For a NUM with eight LIs, the CS could generate 128 derivations.[14] For a NUM with at least twenty LIs, such as the first sentence (up to the dash) in this chapter, there would be over a million possible structurally well-formed derivations; and for sentences with more than fifty LIs (such as the second sentence in this chapter), there would be over 250 trillion such derivations. It is easy to see that this progression of potentially well-formed SDs would complicate not only the CS (which would have to devote considerable effort to producing all these SDs), but also the performance systems (which would have to sort through them all, ruling out the vast majority of them). A CUD-less syntax, then, would tend to have all the computational inefficiencies of non-crash-proof systems. We could, of course, attempt to reduce the computations in other ways – such as placing lexical restrictions on the directionality of Copy. Under this approach, however, we would expect languages to exhibit a wide variety of mixed left-Copy and right-Copy phenomena and we would expect children to experiment with the directionality options of Copy operations until they learn the lexical constraint that needs to be imposed. Since we do not see these sorts of phenomena, there seems to be little motivation for assuming that the Copy operation is a lexically constrained operation. In the absence of evidence or argument to the contrary, we suggest that CUD is the optimal mechanism for reducing the computational permutations of Copy. But certainly much more investigation of these ordering phenomena is required.

In this chapter, we have sketched out the nature of "phrase"-level syntactic relations in Survive-minimalism. Following recent minimalist analyses, we assume that syntactic relations are derived by applications of a Copy operation and that syntactic features drive the Copy operation. Where we differ critically with other approaches to Minimalism is in our rejection of all non-local syntactic operations (such as Move or Internal Move), in our reformulation of NUM, and in our use of FMs in the CS. We argue that Survive-minimalism not only can account for all the constructive and reconstructive "big facts" discussed by Hornstein, Nunes, and Grohmann (2005), but that it does so in the optimal way. If our arguments are on the right track, as we believe they are, Survive-minimalism offers a design for FL that is crash-proof, label-free, and computationally efficient. It provides a derivational program for generative syntax that adheres strongly to the notion of conceptual necessity in its treatment of syntactic relations and constituent displacement.

5   Some structural consequences for derivations

5.1   Introduction

Our analysis, thus far, has focused on the conceptual consequences of applying Turing's Thesis and Galileo's Thesis to the design of the Faculty of Language (FL). We have argued that these theses require both the design of FL and the computational operations of FL, as we note in Chapter 1, to "meet thresholds of simplicity, generality, naturalness, and beauty, as well as of biological and conceptual necessity"; and we have made the case that Survive-minimalism satisfies Turing's Thesis and Galileo's Thesis in conceptually foundational ways. In Survive-minimalism, FL necessarily resides within the extant performance systems, and the computational system (CS) of FL uses extant cognitive operations (Copy operations) to build syntactic structure. Given our analysis of FL, what is special about human language is not its overall design, which is typical of all animal communication systems, or its computational operations, but its emergent Lexicon (LEX). It is the biolinguistic development of a feature-articulated LEX that yields human language; the syntactic complexity of human language, as we have demonstrated in the previous chapter, comes for free because it needs nothing more than LEX and an already available Copy operation. What this suggests is that the syntax of FL is merely a biological spandrel that emerges for free out of the evolution of LEX.

Although our conceptual arguments radically simplify the design of FL, we recognize that conceptual arguments by themselves, as Cox and Forshaw (2009: 12) point out, have limited scientific value: "If there is no observable consequence of an idea, then the idea is not necessary to understand the workings of the universe ..." That is, conceptual arguments must have empirical consequences. In this chapter, we show some of the consequences of Survive-minimalism for two historically recalcitrant constructions (adjunction constructions and conjunction constructions). We demonstrate that Survive-

We would like to thank an anonymous reviewer and Tim Osborne for providing a wealth of valuable comments on a previous draft of this chapter. These comments have been enormously helpful in revising the chapter.

minimalism provides structural explanations for the properties of these constructions that have previously eluded grammatical theories.

5.2   A thematic prelude

In the next section, we will give an analysis of adjunction constructions. Since much of our analysis requires a familiarity with thematic relations, we will begin our analysis with a Survive-minimalist account of these relations.

Lexical items such as *love* and *devour* are linguistic terms that function as predicates, that is, these terms not only take arguments but also define events. This means that to know a predicate, one must know both how many arguments the predicate takes (*love* and *devour* take two arguments, so they are binary or two-place predicates) and something about how the predicate and its arguments work together to represent an event. Gruber (1965) argues that the contributions that predicates and their arguments make to establishing eventhood can be assessed, in part, in terms of thematic relations, which define those ways that arguments participate in the predicated event. For example, the predicate *devour* is a two-place predicate in which one of its arguments is the Agent/doer of the devouring event and the other argument is the Patient/done-to of the devouring event; on the other hand, the predicate *love*, although also a two-place predicate, has arguments that make quite different thematic contributions than do the arguments of the predicate *devour* – the loving event does not have an Agent and a Patient argument, but an Experiencer (a being capable of having feelings) argument and a Theme (the content of the feelings) argument. Learning the meaning of a predicate, then, includes learning the thematic relations that the predicate assigns to (perhaps, imposes on) its arguments.[1] It is because we know what thematic relations the predicate *love* selects for its argument that we see sentence (1), taken from Chomsky (1965: 149), as being somewhat "deviant" (Chomsky's term).

(1)   Misery loves company. (where Misery is a concept, not a sentient object)

The fact that the argument *Misery* does not identify a thing capable of experiencing feelings makes it a peculiar subject-argument of the predicate *love*, which requires that we interpret this sentence metaphorically, by relaxing the thematic constraints placed on the loving-event.

From the above discussion, it is clear that thematic relations play an important role in defining and interpreting events, but we are interested in determining what, if anything, these relations have to do with computing syntactic structure. To investigate this question, we will return to a sentence we derived in the previous chapter, given here as (2). As you may recall, our derivation of (2) made use of the fact that the verb *give* has two SUBCAT features, a SUBCAT-P feature and a SUBCAT-D feature (the first of these features gets matched by the CAT-P feature of the prepositional head in the PP [PP [P to] [DP Homer]] and the second SUBCAT feature gets matched by the CAT-D feature of the determiner head in the DP [DP a [NP beer]]).

(2)   Moe will give a beer to Homer.

But let us problematize our analysis a little by considering what happens in a ditransitive construction where both internal arguments bear identical categorial features, as in (3).

(3)   Moe will give Homer a beer.

In (3), the verb *give* subcategorizes for two internal arguments; however, both of these arguments – *Homer* and *a beer* – have a CAT-D feature. Now if deriving a syntactic structure for (3) primarily depends on matching the SUBCAT of the verb with the CAT features of its arguments, as we have proposed in Chapter 4, then it should not matter how we bring these DP arguments into the derivation since they have equivalent CAT features. This seems problematic, though, since the DPs enter the derivation in a canonical order, as (4) suggests.

(4)   ??Moe will give a beer Homer.

Given that the DPs cannot be discriminated in terms of their CAT features, the ordering differences in (3) and (4) must come from other differences between the two DPs. Importantly, there is one difference between the DPs that appears relevant to their syntactic ordering – a difference involving thematic relations. That is, although these two DP arguments have the same CAT feature, they are assigned different theta roles in the sentence: the DP *Homer* is the Recipient (perhaps, Goal) of the giving-event and the DP *a beer* is the Patient (perhaps, Theme) of the giving-event. If we factor thematic relations into syntactic derivations (SDs), we can explain the differences in (3) and (4) in terms of the thematic ordering of the arguments: the Patient DP is brought into the SD before the Recipient DP. So it seems that thematic relations are expressed syntactically. And yet, something is troubling about this possibility. Should it actually be the case that thematic relations are involved in building syntactic structure, we would expect, under Survive-minimalist assumptions about the role feature-matching plays in SDs, to see thematic features (for Agent, Patient, Experiencer, Recipient, etc.) show up in FMs of the verbs and in the FMs of a verb's arguments, and to have the thematic features of the verb match those of its arguments (via the Copy-to-SD operation). This, however, does not happen. Even though the FM of a verb could have thematic features, the FMs of DPs do not. DPs are simply not lexically marked for specific theta roles. The DP *a beer*, for example, is not lexically marked to be a Patient argument, despite being assigned that role in (3); it could just as easily show up with any other theta role, including the Recipient role (see (5)).

(5)   Moe will give a beer an award.

Lacking a thematic feature, the DPs in (3) and (5) cannot enter into any checking relations that involve thematic features. What we can conclude from the foregoing discussion is that thematic relations do not show up as lexical features able to participate in syntactic computations. (This conclusion seems plausible in as much as theta roles serve to provide interpretative instructions to the Conceptual-Intentional (C-I) performance system, rather than concatenative instructions to the CS.)

So we are at an impasse. On the one hand, thematic relations (and their theta role equivalents) must participate in SDs to explain the differences between (3) and (4) and, on the other hand, thematic relations (expressed as thematic features in FMs) cannot participate in SDs without requiring DPs to possess lexically defined thematic features (which they do not have). To complicate matters further, getting out of this impasse may be but a temporary escape because there are other (equally problematic) observations about the relationship between thematic relations and SDs that also need to be explained. Chomsky (1981: 36), for one, has noted that syntactically expressed arguments and theta-roles (thematic relations) are in a one-to-one relationship, as stated in the Theta Criterion (6).

(6)   Theta Criterion: Each argument bears one and only one theta-role and each theta-role is assigned to one and only one argument.

The Theta Criterion requires that the predicate *admire* must have exactly two syntactically expressed arguments because it has two theta-roles – Theme and Experiencer. Having more than or fewer than two such arguments will produce ill-formed sentences (see (7)).

(7)   a.   *Marge admires.
      b.   *Marge admires the dog the piano. (where *the dog* and *the piano* are separate DPs)

A second observation about thematic relations comes from Hale and Keyser (1993, 2001), who argue that thematic relations do not show up in the syntactic component; rather, thematic relations show up only in the interpretative component as semantic roles that are read off of structural positions. And finally, Chomsky (1995: 228) makes an observation about the relationship between lexical information and SDs, formalized as the Inclusiveness Condition (8), that is highly relevant to thematic information.

(8) Inclusiveness Condition: Any structure formed by the computation is constituted of elements already present in the lexical items for N[umeration]; no new objects are added in the course of computation, apart from rearrangements of lexical properties.

According to the Inclusiveness Condition, the thematic properties of a predicate cannot be added to the predicate through the course of a derivation; instead, they must enter a derivation as lexical properties of the predicate.

How then do we meet all the (often) countervailing insights being offered about thematic relations/theta roles? How can these roles be part of syntactic computations and not part of them? We propose that there is a simple way out of the complex relationship between thematic roles/features and syntactic computations if we permit some multivalent features, including SUBCAT features, to possess sub-features, which we call coefficients, that select one of the options available for the features (this proposal is similar to what is found in attributive value matrices in Head-driven Phrase Structure Grammar, cf. Pollard and Sag 1994). The intuition here is that some features can be syntactically expressed in multiple forms, only one of which will be in play at any given time; the coefficient serves to select the structurally appropriate form.[2] Importantly, the SUBCAT-X feature is one of the multivalent features in need of a coefficient because the feature could show up with multiple thematic roles, as we have seen in our discussion of (3). Hence, to select the feature options appropriate for a given predicate, the SUBCAT feature of the predicate must do more than identify the categories of its arguments, it must also provide information about how the categories selected fulfill the needs of the predicated event; the latter information, we contend, can be expressed as a thematic coefficient in the SUBCAT feature. As an example of this, consider, again, the verb *give* in (3). The FM of this verb will not only identify its two SUBCAT features, it will also define the thematic roles imposed by the predicate on the SUBCAT features; these roles will be attached to the SUBCAT features as coefficients in the following way: <SUBCAT-D: RECIP <SUBCAT-D: PATIENT>>. The SUBCAT features state that the verb *give* must have two internal DP arguments, and they provide additional coefficient-instructions to the C-I performance system about how to interpret each DP – *Homer* and *a beer* – by assigning them the appropriate theta role in the giving event. Notice that if we have a theta role appear as a SUBCAT coefficient, we can still add a DP argument, using its CAT feature alone, to an SD without requiring that the DP already be theta-identified. That is, when the LI *a beer* enters the SD for (3), it will not have to come from LEX with any defined theta role. This is of particular relevance for our reanalysis of structure building because *a beer* will be added to the SD before the verb V_{give} will be (in the VP construction [[$_V$ give] [$_{DP}$ a beer]]). Not being able to anticipate the verb that will be added subsequently to the SD, the

DP *a beer* cannot possibly know what sort of theta role it must have. But this is a good thing because the fact that its FM does not identify any particular theta role for any given DP allows the DP to pick up whatever theta role the predicate assigns to it.

Although it makes a great deal of conceptual sense to assume that thematic relations/theta roles are sub-features (coefficients) of SUBCAT features, the reason for accepting this assumption is that it provides a way to explain all the countervailing claims about theta roles. To see this, let us consider these claims one at a time. First, do theta roles play a part in SDs? Specifically do theta roles contribute to the ordering concerns raised in (3) and (4)? As coefficients for SUBCAT features, theta roles provide the only information in the FM of the verb *give* able to discriminate the <SUBCAT-D> arguments of the verb at all; hence this information is crucial to deciding the order in which the arguments enter the SD for (3). Second, do theta roles contribute to syntactic computations themselves, as opposed to the orderings of the arguments? Since computations in Survive-minimalism are over features, and not coefficients of features, no coefficients, including thematic coefficients, participate in derivations. That is, the argument-predicate feature checking that takes place in the derivation of (3) involves the <CAT> features of the arguments and the <SUBCAT> features of the predicate; the coefficients of the SUBCAT features are not in play in these checking relations (this accords with Hale and Keyser's 1993, 2001 analysis of theta roles as having no syntactic visibility). Third, how can thematic coefficients explain Chomsky's (1981) Theta Criterion? If it is indeed the case, as we assume here, that SUBCAT features have thematic coefficients, as in <SUBCAT-X: theta role>, then this complex feature in and of itself explains the Theta Criterion because it establishes a one-to-one relation between syntactic arguments and theta roles. In other words, the Theta Criterion is a way of stating that a SUBCAT feature must be identified with a theta role (i.e., it must have a thematic coefficient). Fourth, are theta roles interpreted by the interpretative components of syntactic structures, as Hale and Keyser (1993, 2002) assert? It would seem so. Theta roles are carried into syntactic positions by SUBCAT features when these latter features are copied into an SD. The theta roles are then interpreted by the C-I performance system while this system is interpreting the structures submitted to it by the CS. And finally, are thematic features included among lexical features? Given that thematic features are part of SUBCAT features, these features are certainly contained in the FMs of LIs. Needless to say, this conclusion has conceptual appeal since thematic features are quintessential PSFs in that they are interpretative features, providing information about events; it makes sense then that LIs, which are a composite of performance system features (PSFs), would include thematic features among their PSFs.[3] From the foregoing discussion, we can see that our analysis of thematic coefficients has a great deal of appeal because it offers cogent explanations of seemingly contradictory observations about theta roles.

Of note, we can find some interesting support for our coefficient analysis of theta roles from sentences, such as (9), that are typically read metaphorically.

(9)   Apples love the sun.

These types of anthropomorphic metaphors assign thematic relations/semantic properties to DPs that do not ordinarily possess those relations/properties. That is, in the above metaphor, the DP *apples* does not inherently possess the Experiencer thematic relation/property that the verb *love* assigns to its subject. If a DP had to come into the Numeration (NUM) and into the SD with a theta role already in place and with this theta role primed to play a part in derivational operations, then we should expect anthropomorphic metaphors to produce thematic (semantic) clashes (as we see between the verb *love*, which requires an Experiencer subject argument, and the LI *apples*, which is not inherently an Experiencer) and we should expect these clashes to create derivational crashes (for an extended analysis of crashes, see Appendix A at the end of this chapter). However, if, as we have argued, theta roles are subcategorized coefficients, then theta roles will not participate in syntactic operations and they will not create syntactic crashes. Rather, the thematic (semantic) clashes that arise in examples such as (9) are resolved, and interpreted, by the C-I performance system.

And finally, additional support for our analysis of theta roles and thematic coefficients comes from expletives, which, in English, show up either as *there*-expletives (see (10a)) or as *it*-expletives (see (10b)).

(10)   a.   There is someone waiting outside in the rain.
          b.   It seems that Patty left the party two hours ago.

These expletives are of theoretical interest because they have very limited syntactic distribuitons. As Chomsky (1981) observes, expletives can appear in syntactic positions that are not assigned theta roles, as in (10a) and (10b), but they cannot appear in positions that are identified with specific theta roles, as in (11a-c).

(11)   a.   *Lisa loves there.
          b.   *There believes that Lisa is happy.
          c.   *It believes that Lisa is happy. (where *it* is an expletive)

Our approach to theta roles provides an interesting reanalysis of expletives. As we discuss above, theta roles are expressed as coefficients attached to CAT features identified within a SUBCAT matrix. An example of this can be seen in the FM of the verb *give* in (2): <SUBCAT-D: RECIP <SUBCAT-D: THEME>>. The connection between the CAT feature and the theta role, as we argue, is not accidental; rather it is necessary (as is expressed in Chomsky's 1981 Theta Criterion, which established a one-to-one correspondence between s-selected theta roles and c-selected CATegories). That is, a theta role is attached to each CAT feature within a SUBCAT matrix and each CAT feature in the matrix, in turn, must have a C-I interpretable coefficient (theta role). What this means for expletives is that if, as Chomsky (1981) proposes, expletives cannot have theta roles, then expletives cannot have CAT features either (if an expletive did have a CAT feature, say E, then for the expletive to be Copied into the SD, it would have to be selected by some syntactic object that had an FM with a <SUBCAT-E: Theta Role> selecting-feature, and this would require the expletive to have a theta role; hence, the expletive cannot have a CAT feature). Given the foregoing discussion, the FM of an expletive is much diminished: it will not have a CAT feature and, since an expletive is not an argument-taking LI, its FM will not have any SUBCAT features either. Absent CAT and SUBCAT features, the FM for an expletive reduces to PSFs. The consequence of having FMs with only PSFs is that expletives have limited opportunities to be copied into an SD: they cannot be copied into any positions involving CAT or SUBCAT features (hence, they cannot appear in "argument" positions, as is illustrated in (11a–c)), but they can appear in positions involving "pure agreement" features. This latter case shows up in (10a), where the expletive *there*, which has only a Case-feature, is copied to the SD of the T-projection [T [is someone waiting outside in the rain]] to have its Case-feature checked – note that the LI *someone* will be subsequently recopied into the derivation to ensure that its phi-features (Person and Number) and the phi-features of the T-projection are appropriately concatenated (we are following Belletti and Rizzi 1988 here in assuming that *someone* will have its Case-feature checked inside the *v*P). And in (10b), the expletive *it*, which has both Case-features and phi-features, is also copied to the SD of a T-projection to concatenate with the matching Case-features and phi-features of the T-projection.

Under our analysis, although the *there*-expletive and the *it*-expletive are similar in that neither of them has a CAT feature or a SUBCAT feature, they are dissimilar in that their FMs have differents PSFs: the former expletive has only a Case-feature, while the latter expletive has a Case-feature and phi-features. The fact that these expletives have different FMs with different PSFs means that they will not be interchangeable, as we can see in (12).

(12) a. *It is someone waiting outside.
      b. *There seems that Lisa left.

In (12a), the Case-feature and phi-features of the *it*-expletive will match the Case- and phi-features of the T-projection, leaving the phi-features of the LI *someone* unchecked and uncheckable; as a result, this LI remains perpetually active in NUM and the SD will stall (that is, it will not come to completion) because its NUM cannot ever be exhausted. In (12b), the Case-feature of the expletive will match the Case-feature of the T-projection; however, the phi-features of the T-projection are unchecked and uncheckable, which will, as in (12a), cause the SD to stall.

The fact that our Survive-analysis of syntactic relations, especially our treatment of theta roles, explains both why expletives exist (to enable PSFs to be interpretable to the external performance systems) and how they distribute (based on the types of PSFs they possess) provides some interesting support for our analysis.

5.3   Understanding adjuncts

Our analysis of thematic relations (and theta roles) has the added benefit of giving us a mechanism through which to explain the properties of one of the more poorly understood grammatical units – adjuncts (loosely defined, adjuncts are syntactic units that function as modifiers of other syntactic units). Adjuncts, which are illustrated by the italicized material in (13), are particularly trouble-some according to Hinzen because they "are mostly characterized *negatively:* basically they have never fitted into the apparatus of syntax that minimalism has tried to derive from 'virtual conceptual necessity.' They do not receive theta roles, and do not take part in the agreement system . . ." (2009b: 137).

(13)   a.   Bart leaves *tomorrow at 8 AM.*
        b.   Bart fell *under the table.*
        c.   Bart ran *hurriedly.*
        d.   Bart jogs *because he wants to.*
        e.   Bart slept *with a gun under his pillow.*

Identifying and explaining the properties of adjuncts is a daunting theoretical challenge because, as Hornstein (2009b: 105) observes, "Adjuncts are funny characters from a syntactic point of view . . . they appear to be simultaneously inside and outside a given syntactic tree." And Hinzen (2009a: 43) offers an even more stark assessment of adjuncts, noting that "there isn't much syntax to [them]." Not only do adjuncts appear to have rudimentary syntactic properties, they also have rudimentary semantic properties. That is, there is not much semantics to them either. As Hinzen claims, following Pietroski (2002, 2006) and Larson (2004), adjuncts are interpreted as simplex predicates: "Intuitively, *walking quickly* means that there is a walking [event e] and it is quick" (2009a: 44) – which can be formalized as in (14) (taken from Hinzen).

(14)   *walk quickly*: ($\exists$e) e is a walking and e is quick

The syntactic and semantic simplicity of adjuncts leads Hinzen to speculate that "adjuncts may well have existed in a protolanguage that had a simpler semantics than the semantics that plausibly depends on a more elaborate syntax that includes the argument-of relation, categories, A'-relations, etc." (2009a: 44).

We agree with many of the claims made above, especially Hinzen's claim that adjuncts "existed in a protolanguage." But the fact that adjuncts may have existed in the protolanguage tells us much more about the properties of adjuncts than Hinzen (or Hornstein) might admit. If adjuncts were part of the human protolanguage, then they would have also been part of a protosyntax, as we argued in Chapter 4, that allowed lexical elements to be concatenated if the FMs of the elements had intersective perceptual (performance system) features. Under these conditions, it would be possible to form the adjunction construction *gray cat* from the two LIs *gray* and *cat*, based on their shared properties of color; or it would be possible to form the adjunction construction *walk fast* from the LIs *walk* and *fast*, based on their shared properties of movement. Importantly, the expressions *gray cat* and *walk fast*, both of which include adjuncts, would be formed exactly the same way in the protolanguage as all other expressions were formed, by concatenating shared PSFs. There would not have been anything syntactically attenuated about, or abnormal about, adjuncts. We surmise that the same is true today, that is, despite the previously mentioned claims made by Hornstein and Hinzen, adjuncts behave syntactically exactly as do all other LIs – using their available features to build syntactic structure (we return to this point later in this section).

Not only have Hornstein and Hinzen underestimated the syntactic behavior of adjuncts, but they have also minimized the semantics of adjuncts by endorsing the neo-Davidsonian semantics advocated by Pietroski (2002, 2006) and Larson (2004). To see this, let us look a bit more closely at the adjuncts in (15a–e), paying particular attention to the semantic representation that a neo-Davidsonian analysis of adjuncts would generate – see (15a'–e').

(15) a. Bart leaves *tomorrow at 8 AM*.
      a'. ($\exists$e) e is a leaving and e is tomorrow at 8 AM
      b. Bart fell *under the table*.
      b'. ($\exists$e) e is a falling and e is under the table
      c. Bart ran *hurriedly*.
      c'. ($\exists$e) e is a running and e is hurried.
      d. Bart jogs *because he wants to*.
      d'. ($\exists$e) e is a jogging and e is because he wants to.
      e. Bart slept *with a gun under his pillow*.
      e'. ($\exists$e) e is a sleeping and e is with a gun under his pillow

It strikes us that the semantic representations given for the adjuncts in (15a–e) are not very satisfying, especially (15b'), (15d'), and (15e') – all of which are more than a little bizarre. If we follow Hinzen's analysis of (14), then we assert that in (15d) there is a jogging event and it *is* "because he wants to"; this assertion, however, does not make much sense. But then neither does the assertion that there is a falling event in (15b) and it *is* "under the table" or that there is a sleeping event in (15e) and it *is* "with a gun under his pillow"! The predicative *is*-adjunct just does not work in these examples. And even where the predicative *is*-adjunct seems to provide a tolerably appropriate predicate, it does so only because the *is*-adjunct predicate must be read as a *takes-place* relationship that involves time (in (15a')) or manner (in (15c')). What this line of analysis suggests is that the adjuncts in (15a–e) are not predicates. But if adjuncts are not predicates, what are they? We propose that the adjuncts in (15a–e) are participants in events, much akin to ways that the subject-arguments in (15a–e) are participants in events.[4] In other words, the adjuncts in (15a–e) participate in thematic relations with the verb-event. We contend then that the full interpretation of (15a) and (15d) are (15a") and (15d") respectively, in which the adjuncts are assigned thematic relations in the designated events.

(15)   **a"**   ∃e [e is a leaving & AGENT (Bart, e) & TEMPORAL (tomorrow at 8 AM, e)]

         d"   ∃e [e is a jogging & AGENT (Bart, e) & REASON (because he wants to, e)]

The fact that the representations in (15a") and (15d") provide readings for (15a) and (15d) that are semantically accurate in ways that the representations in (15a') and (15d') are not leads us to conclude that the former representations are to be preferred. As an example of this, notice that (15d") correctly represents the adjunct in (15d) as the reason for jogging; on the other hand, (15d') misrepresents the event of jogging as being "because he wanted to." If our interpretations of (15a) and (15d) are correct, the adjuncts in these examples are not predicates with event-arguments, but participants in the events, defined by their thematic roles.

Importantly, some interesting support for our thematic-relations analysis of adjuncts comes from the iterability of adjuncts, or the lack thereof. Hornstein (2009) asserts that one of the characteristics that separates adjuncts from arguments is that adjuncts (but not arguments) can be syntactically iterated (as in *a very, very, very old man*). Hornstein makes an important point about arguments – it does seem to be the case that arguments do not iterate, as reflected, in part, in the inability of a thematic role to be (iteratively) shared by multiple syntactic arguments (we can see this in (16), where the verb *admire* can assign its two thematic roles to two and only two syntactic arguments, in accordance with the

Theta Criterion; additional thematic assignations will produce ungrammatical constructions).

(16)   *Marge admires that woman the piano. (where *the woman* and *the piano* are separate DPs)

Hornstein's claims about adjuncts, however, are incorrect. Adjuncts do not behave differently than arguments do when it comes to iterativity.[5] In fact, the data in (17) demonstrate that the adjuncts in (15) exhibit the same resistance to iteration that we see for the arguments in (16). That is, as (17) demonstrates, if we add extra temporal, reason, or locative adjuncts to the examples in (16), we will produce ungrammatical constructions.

(17)   a.   *When will Bart leave tomorrow at 8 AM?
       b.   *Why does Bart jog because he wants to?
       c.   *Where did Bart fall where?

If adjuncts were as loosely connected to events as Hornstein (2009) and Hinzen (2009a,b) suggest and if they iterated as freely as Hornstein claims, then the tight constraints we see in (17) would be quite unexpected. Under our analysis, the inability of the adjuncts in (17) to iterate is fully expected because the adjuncts are assigned unique thematic roles that cannot, as they cannot in the Theta Criterion, be attached to more than one syntactic constituent.

Of note, though we find similarities between arguments-of-events and adjuncts (contra Hornstein and Hinzen), we do agree with Hornstein and Hinzen that there are substantial differences between arguments and adjuncts. For us, these differences are expressed in the structure of FMs. FMs, as you may recall, are hierarchically organized as in (18), with selecting-features higher ranked than selected-features and with CATegory/SUBCATegory features higher ranked than PSFs.

(18)   FM: <SUBCAT <selecting PSFs <CAT <selected PSFs>>>>

We have argued that the PSFs are grounded in the perceptual and cognitive (semantic) categories available in the protolanguage and that CAT-based features have developed as linguistic categories out of perceptual and cognitive categories. In this FM analysis, arguments are defined by, and show up as, CAT-based features; therefore, they are syntactically selected (by syntactic category) and they are critical to the recursive property of syntax (CAT features, as we have previously noted, provide the driving force for recursion). Adjuncts, on the other hand, are connected to pre-syntactic PSFs; as a result, they are semantically selected (not syntactically selected) and, consequently, orthogonal to the recursive property of syntax (i.e., adjuncts are not necessary for recursion to exist). Some significant grammatical properties follow from the aforementioned feature differences between arguments and adjuncts. For one, because arguments are CAT-selected, they are narrowly selected syntactically. We can see this if we consider verbs, such as *devour*, that subcategorize for a CAT-D object. As the data in (19) demonstrate, it is not permissible to have objects that do not have the requisite narrow syntactic CAT-D feature (see (19a–c)), and it is not permissible not to have an object.

(19) a. Bart devours good food.
      b. *Bart devours in the morning.
      c. *Bart devours when Lisa returns.
      d. *Bart devoured.

Since adjuncts are semantically selected, they are not syntactically circumscribed in the way that arguments are. That is, adjuncts, which satisfy a (temporal) PSF, can do so with a variety of syntactic categories, as (20) shows.

(20) a. Bart will leave tomorrow.
      b. Bart will leave in the morning.
      c. Bart will leave when Lisa returns.
      d. Bart will leave.

The semantic TEMPORAL feature of the verb can be satisfied by a nominal adjunct (as in (20a)), by a prepositional adjunct (as in (20b)), by a sentential adjunct (as in (20c)), or by nothing at all (as in (20d)).[6]

A second grammatical consequence of the feature differences between arguments and adjuncts involves their semantic interpretation. Because arguments satisfy syntactic CAT features, they cannot be interpreted in a straightforward way. They must be provided with a thematic coefficient (see our discussion of thematic roles in Section 5.2) to be interpreted. Hence, the DP *Homer* in (21), which has an intrinsic CAT-D feature but not an intrinsic PATIENT theta role feature, must be given the theta role by the verb (which has a <SUBCAT-D: PATIENT> feature) to be appropriately interpreted.

(21) Mr. Burns hired Homer after interviewing him.

So, arguments are category selected and semantically situated by the predicated event. The opposite is true of adjuncts: they are semantically selected and syntactically situated. If we look at the examples in (20), we will notice that all the adjuncts can satisfy the TEMPORAL PSF of the verb (verbs/events do occur in time, so verbs do have TEMPORAL PSFs) because all the adjuncts have intrinsic temporal features that can be semantically interpreted in a straightforward way. What the verbs do not select is the syntactic category of the TEMPORAL element, so the adjuncts in (20) can satisfy the TEMPORAL feature of the verb with a variety of syntactic categories – with a DP as in (20a), a PP as in (20b), or a CP as in (20c).

Even though arguments and adjuncts are selected by divergent types of features, when they are interpreted by the C-I performance system, the only features in play are semantico-pragmatic features, i.e., PSFs. This means that adjuncts will be read directly in terms of their PSFs and arguments will be read indirectly in terms of the thematic coefficients they pick up. We show this in (22).

(22) a. Mr. Burns hired Homer yesterday.
      b. ∃(e) (e is a hiring & AGENT (Mr. Burns, e) & PATIENT (Homer, e) & TEMPORAL (yesterday, e))

The verb *hire* in (22a) includes, within its FM, <SUBCAT-D: PATIENT <TEMPORAL>> features. These features are satisfied by *Homer* and *yesterday*, respectively. When the SD for (22a) is complete, it is conjunctively interpreted, as Pietroski (2002, 2006) maintains, by the C-I performance system; however, this interpretation incorporates all and only the PSFs used in the derivation, as is represented in (22b). Notice that, despite entering the SD in different ways, the arguments *Mr. Burns* and *Homer* and the adjunct *yesterday* are interpreted similarly: they are all interpreted in terms of their relationship to the event.

Our analysis of adjuncts squares nicely with Hinzen's (2009a) observations that adjuncts have virtually no syntax, that they are semantic in nature, and that they were likely present in the protolanguage, as well as with Hornstein's observation that adjuncts are quasi-syntactic objects. But we also account for properties of adjuncts that neither Hinzen nor Hornstein seem able to. One of the more interesting and theoretically challenging properties we can successfully explain involves the ability of adjuncts (but not arguments) to escape Principle C violations in constructions with displacement – this is illustrated in (23).[7]

(23) [which picture of Bart that Milhouse likes] did he buy? *Bart . . . he/OK Milhouse . . . he

To account for the argument/adjunct asymmetry in (23), theorists such as Lebeaux (1991, 1995), Chomsky (1993), and Fox (2003) propose that all arguments must be merged into the SD cyclically, while adjuncts have the option of being merged cyclically or non-cyclically. The early cyclical merge of arguments will guarantee that the DP *Bart* will be merged as part of the verbal object *which picture of Bart* and that the DP will be c-commanded by the pronoun when the pronoun merges into the SD (thereby creating a Principle C violation); and the late noncyclical merge of the adjunct *that Milhouse likes* will add this clause to the DP after the DP relocates into its surface position well above the subject position – consequently, the subject will not c-command the DP *Milhouse* when it comes into the derivation and, therefore, no Principle C violation involving this DP and the pronoun will arise. Despite having some obvious empirical advantages, this proposal faces serious problems. In particular, it is not clear how exactly adjuncts merge non-cyclically, nor is it clear why adjuncts should be permitted this prerogative or where this late merger could take place. We contend that these problems, though daunting for standard versions of Minimalism, dissolve under Survive-minimalist assumptions. Survive-minimalism has one key design feature that allows it to offer a natural explanation for the late-merger properties of adjuncts. That is, in Survive-minimalism, lexical material brought into an SD, and the syntactic objects built from this material, will continue to "survive" in NUM and its associated WorkBench (WB) area as long as this material has concatenative features that have not been checked. Given that the constructed DP argument *which picture of Bart* has an unchecked <WH> feature, this DP will survive in NUM and WB (we will call the combined NUM and WB the WorkSpace). Importantly, this WorkSpace is the only place where protolinguistic elements could combine before the development of SDs. It is an "old" space (the space where the protosyntax took place) in which adjuncts could combine with other lexical material to semantically enrich concepts; as protolinguistic remnants, adjuncts continue to possess the ability to combine non-syntactically, i.e., within the WorkSpace. This means that, while in the WorkSpace, the DP *which picture of Bart* can have an adjunct attached to it, forming the modified DP *which picture of Bart that Milhouse likes*. The modified DP will eventually be recopied into the SD for (23) to check the <WH> feature of the DP; however, this recopying will take place after (and structurally higher than) the merger of the subject pronoun. As a result, the pronoun will never c-command the modified DP, nor the DP *Milhouse* contained within it.

The argument/adjunct asymmetry in (23), then, follows from the design principles of Survive-minimalism. The fact that Survive-minimalism has a WorkSpace provides a place outside the SD (a non-cyclic place) in which modifiers can be added to syntactic objects (no other syntactic framework has an equivalent WorkSpace) and the fact that this WorkSpace is the space in which protolinguistic elements (especially adjuncts) could combine with other lexical material makes it the appropriate space for the late non-cyclical merger of adjuncts.

5.4   Coordinate structures

In the previous two sections, we have given reanalyses of thematic role assignments and of adjunction constructions built on Survive-minimalism assumptions. We have argued that, approaching thematic roles and adjuncts in terms of the FMs required within Survive-minimalism, we can account for the complex syntactic distribution and the semantic interpretation of adjuncts. In this section, we take on an even more daunting challenge – to explain the seemingly contradictory grammatical properties of conjunction constructions. Conjunction constructions, such as those in (24), have long been a puzzle for generative theories of grammar.

(24) a. Mary read a poem and a short story.
      b. Chris believes that Pat likes Sam and that Sue dislikes Bob.

The reason that these constructions have confounded previous attempts to analyze them is that they have two conflicting properties. On the one hand, coordination has a symmetrical property, which readily appears in lists, as is illustrated in (25).

(25) a. a,b,c,. . .,x,y, and z. (A child's recitation of the alphabet)
      b. $7.75, $8.00, $9.00, and $10.00 (store-clerk counting out change from a $10.00 bill on a $7.75 purchase)

It is the symmetrical property of conjunction constructions that supports a parallelist analysis of coordinate structure in which all the joined branches (X1 and X2) are structural sisters of the conjunction, as in (26). We can find this as the sort of multi-branch structure for conjunction constructions in both early generative analysis such as Bach (1964) and Chomsky (1965), and in more recent analyses, as in Takano (2004) and Johnson (2008).

(26) [X1 and X2]

On the other hand, as Munn (1993), te Velde (2009), and Zhang (2010), among others observe, conjunction constructions have asymmetrical properties, too. These properties can be seen in (27), where the DP *every man* and the pronoun *his* can co-refer in (27a) but not in (27b). (Read the italicized DPs as coreferential.)

(27) a. *Every man* and *his* dog left.
      b. **His* dog and *every man* left.

To account for the asymmetrical properties of conjunction constructions, Munn argues that these constructions require an asymmetrical structure; in particular, the left branches of the structure must be hierarchically superior to the right branches (see (24)).

(28) [X1 [and X2]]

Given (27), the left-branch DP *every man* will c-command the pronoun in the right-branch DP in (27a), but the pronoun in (27b) will not be c-commanded by the DP *every man*. These differing c-command relations will be responsible, in part, for the differing co-referentiality relations in (27a) and (27b).

However, as Stroik, Putnam, and Parafita (2008) point out, neither the symmetrical analysis of coordination in (26) nor the asymmetrical analysis of coordination in (28) can account for Principle C binding violations in conjunction constructions. That is, these two analyses cannot explain why binding relations involving the italicized pronoun in the first conjunct and the italicized DP in the second conjunct are prohibited in (29).

(29)   a. *Pat hugged *her* and kissed *Sue*.
       b. *I gave a book to *her* and to *Sue*'s father.
       c. *Chris hired *him* and Sam fired *Bob*'s mother.
       d. *Sue believes that Chris hired *him* and that Sam fired *Bob*'s mother.

If we assume that the conjoined XPs in (29a–d) have structure (26) or (28), then we should predict, under either analysis, that the pronouns contained within the left conjuncts should be too deeply embedded to c-command the DPs contained within the right conjuncts and, therefore, there should be no binding violations involving the italicized pronouns and the italicized DPs. This prediction, however, is incorrect, and, as a consequence, (26) and (28) must provide inaccurate structural representations of conjunction constructions.

From data such as those in (29), Stroik, Putnam, and Parafita conclude that, to account for the Principle C binding violations in conjunction constructions, every constituent in the left conjunct must c-command every constituent in the right conjunct.[8] They propose that the binding relations in (30a) are illicit because (30a) has structure (30b) in which the pronoun c-commands the italicized DP.

(30)   a. *a story about *him* and a poem about *Bob*
       b. [a [story [about [*him* [and a poem about *Bob*]]]]]

To test their proposal, Stroik, Putnam, and Parafita look at cross-linguistic Principle C binding data in conjunction constructions involving varying depths of embedding. What they discovered is that, as their proposal predicts, no matter how deeply embedded the pronoun in the left conjunct may be, it still induces a Principle C violation when co-indexed with a DP in the right conjunct (the data in (31) below are taken from their paper).[9]

(31)   a. *Mary read a poem to *him* and a short story to *Bob*.
           German
           **Maria hat ihm ein Gedicht und Bob eine Kurzgeschichte vorgelesen.*
           Swedish
           **Mary läste en dikt för honom, och en novell för Bob.*

Galician
María leulle un poema a él e un conto a Bob.
Japanese
Mary wa kare ni shi to Bob ni tanpen wo yonda.
Welsh
Darllenodd Mair gerdd iddo ef a stori fer i Bob.
Greek
I Meri tu egrapse ena piima ki ena diigima sto Bob.
Italian
Maria gli ha letto una poesia e un racconto a Bob.

b. *Mary gave money to *his* mother and to *Bob*'s father.
German
Maria hat seiner Mutter und Bobs Vater Geld gegeben.
Swedish
Mary gav pengar till hans mamma, och till Bobs pappa.
Galician
María deulle cartos á súa nai e ó pai de Bob.
Japanese
Mary wa kare no okaa-san to Bob no otoosan ni okane wo ageta.
Welsh
Rhoddodd Mair bres i'w fam ef ac i dad Bob.
Greek
I Meri edose khrimata sti mitera tu ki ston patera tu Bob.
Italian
Maria ha dato dei soldi a sua madre e al padre di Bob.

c. *Mary sent me a poem about *him* and a story about *Bob*.
German
Maria hat mir ein Gedicht über ihn und eine Geschichte über Bob geschickt.
Swedish
Mary skickade en dikt om honom och en berättelse om Bob.
Galician
María mandoume un poema sobre él e un conto sobre Bob.
Japanese
Mary wa kare no shi to Bob no monogatari wo watashi ni okutta.
Welsh
Anfonodd Mair gerdd i mi amdano fo, a stori am Bob
Greek
I Meri mu estile ena piima giafton ki mia istoria gia to Bob.
Italian
Maria mi ha mandato una poesia su di lui e una storia su Bob.

    d. *Mary believes that *he* likes Sue and that Sally hates *Bob*.
       German
       Maria glaubt, dass er Susi mag und dass Sally Bob hasst.
       Swedish
       Mary tror att han tycker om Sue, och att Sally hatar Bob.
       Galician
       María pensa que a él lle gusta Sue e que Sally odia a Bob.
       Japanese
       Kare wa Sue ga suki de Sally wa Bob ga daikirai dato
       Mary wa shinjiteiru.
       Welsh
       Mae Mair yn credu ei fod ef yn hoffi Sue ac fod Sally yn casau Bob.
       Greek
       I Meri pistevi oti aftos agapa ti Su ki oti i Sali misi to Bob.
       Italian
       Maria pensa che a lui paccia Sue e che Sally odi Bob.

    e. *Mary read a poem that *he* wrote and a short story that *Bob*'s mother wrote.
       German
       Maria hat ein Gedicht gelesen, das er geschrieben hat, und eine Kurzgeschichte, die Bobs Mutter geschrieben hat.
       Swedish
       Mary läste en dikt som han skrivit och en novell som Bobs mamma skrivit.
       Galician
       María leu un poema que él escribu e un conto que a escribiu a nai de Bob.
       Japanese
       Mary wa kare ga kaita shi to Bob no okaa-san ga kaita tanpen wo yonda.
       Welsh
       Darllenodd Mair gerdd a ysgrifennodd ef a stori fer ysgrifennodd Mam Bob.
       Greek
       I Meri diavase ena piima pu egrapse aftos ki ena diigima pu egrapse i mitera tu Bob
       Italian
       (?)Maria ha letto una poesía che lui ha scritto e un racconto che ha scritto la madre di Bob.

The data in (31) appear to corroborate the proposal made in (30b), which states that the asymmetry in coordinate structures is the following: everything in a left conjunct c-commands everything in a right conjunct and, conversely, nothing in a right conjunct c-commands anything in a left conjunct.

Interestingly, the surprising (Principle C) binding asymmetry noted above for the conjunct in (29), (30), and (31) is balanced with an equally surprising (Principle A) binding symmetry for the conjuncts in (32).

(32) a. *Mary likes *those men* and *each other*'s wives.
      b. *Mary likes *each other*'s wives and *those men*.
      c. *Those men* like Mary and *each other*'s wives.
      d. *Those men* like *each other*'s wives and Mary.
      e. *Mary wrote poems about *those men* and stories about *themselves*.
      f. *Those men* wrote poems about Mary and stories about *themselves*.

The data in (32) demonstrate that while subjects can c-command and bind anaphors in the right conjunct of a conjunction construction (as in (32c, d, f), nothing in the left conjunct can c-command and bind anything in the right conjunct (and vice versa).[10] Principle A data, then, indicate that there is a structural symmetry between the two conjuncts.

We are left with a seemingly pernicious contradiction about coordinate structures: on the one hand these structures require everything in a left conjunct to c-command everything in a right conjunct, as in (33a), and on the other hand, the structures also require nothing in the left conjunct to c-command anything in the right conjunct, as in (33b).

(33) a. $[_{XP1}$ A [B [C [and $[_{XP2}$ X [Y [Z]]]]]]]
      b. [[(and) XP1] [and XP2]] or [[and XP2] [(and) XP1]]

But how is it possible for two different structural representations to arise in the derivation of conjunction constructions? We believe that Lebeaux (2009) provides part of the answer to this question. According to Lebeaux, Binding Theory does not apply to a single representation; rather, Principle C applies throughout a derivation and Principle A applies to a single structure – an LF (logical form) representation.[11] Although Lebeaux's analysis of binding does not specify how structure (33a) or (33b) could be built – or why they would be built – this analysis does offer the possibility that the seemingly contradictory structural constraints placed on binding in conjunction constructions (see (33)) can both be met if the binding relations in conjunction constructions are checked in more than one place in an SD and if the derivation of conjunction constructions actually involves multiple structures. Satisfying these two conditions, however, will require some mechanism, not available within the current Minimalist framework, to generate structure (33a) and another mechanism, also not available in current Minimalism, to compel the right conjunct to reattach to the SD so that constituents in the left conjunct no longer c-command constituents in the right conjunct.[12]

Survive-minimalism, as we shall demonstrate, has the mechanisms that derive the structures in (29) and, as a result, it predicts all the data in (29),

(31), and (32). Before we show this, however, it is necessary to take a quick look at coordinate conjunctions themselves. These conjunctions, it is commonly believed, link together two constituents typically of the same type X to derive another constituent of type X.[13] Accordingly, a coordinate conjunction will link two PPs to derive a PP, as in (34). (Note: in (34) we are not assuming any particular internal structure for the conjunction construction.)

(34)   [$_{PP}$ [before Sue] and [after that man]]

Conceived of in this way, a coordinate conjunction has, in essence, a (traditionally based) FM that looks as follows: <SUBCAT-X <SUBCAT-X <CAT-X>>>. Although we can use this FM to derive coordinate structures such as (34), there are conceptual and empirical reasons for not accepting the traditional view of coordinate conjunctions as elements that category-combine an X category with another X category to form an X category (X + X = X). The conceptual problem with the traditional view of coordinate conjunctions is that although this additive view of conjunction works for building lists (such as, "a, b, c, . . ., x, y, and z" or "red, white, and blue"), it does not work for derivation-building because under this view structural input and structural output would be the same; therefore, the conjunction would not build any new derivational structure. We can see this in (34). Once the right conjunct is built, it will project a <CAT-P> feature; if the coordinate conjunct "adds" a left conjunct with a <CAT-P> to project a <CAT-P> feature, then the derivation will have merely looped from a <CAT-P> projection to <CAT-P> projection without building anything different in between. No derivational structure will have been built. A more poignant example of the structural vacuity of coordinate conjunctions can be observed in (35), where the conjoined subject [Sam and Chris], as left-branch material, must be built on the WB and then inserted into the derivation.

(35)   [Sam and Chris] left.

Since the conjoined material is not built in the SD for (35), it (in and of itself) does not participate in the SD. What the foregoing argument suggests is that coordinate structures of the type we see in (35) are not built in an SD. This means that a coordinate conjunction does not have a (traditional) projecting FM. Another conceptual reason for concluding that coordinate conjunctions lack a traditional, structure-building FM and, as a result, they do not participate in derivation-building is that all the features in the traditional FM of a coordinate conjunction are variable features that take their values from the features of the conjuncts; hence, the conjunctions do not have any features of their own to project. They are feature-vacuous elements that have no features to contribute to building a derivation.

Not only are there conceptual reasons for rejecting the traditional structure-building view of coordinate conjunctions, there are also empirical reasons. As we have already argued, if coordinate structures are built by conjoining two constituents, then, no matter how one combines these constituents, it will not be possible to explain the Principle C violations in (29).

(29)   a.   *Pat hugged *her* and kissed *Sue*.
      b.   *I gave a book to *her* and to *Sue*'s father.
      c.   *Chris hired *him* and Sam fired *Bob*'s mother.
      d.   *Sue believes that Chris hired *him* and that Sam fired *Bob*'s mother.

Adding two Xs together should produce a structure in which the elements in the left conjunct cannot c-command elements in the right conjunct; therefore, this additive analysis of coordinate structure should predict that the italicized pronouns and DPs in (29a–d) could be interpretatively bound to one another. Needless to say, this prediction is incorrect, as is the assumption responsible for the incorrect prediction – that coordinate conjunctions add two constituents together structurally. A second empirical argument against traditional views that coordinate conjunctions have structure-building properties comes from the conjunction extraction data in (36).

(36)   a.   *Who does Marge believe that Homer likes (who) and that Bart dislikes Lisa?
      b.   *Who does Marge believe that Homer likes Lisa and that Bart dislikes (who)?
      c.   Who does Marge believe that Homer likes (who) and that Bart dislikes (who)?

The data in (36a) and (36b) supposedly demonstrate that it is not possible to extract constituents out of only one of the conjuncts in a coordinate structure; however, as the data in (36c) putatively show, it is possible to extract out a constituent out of a conjunction if the constituent is contained within both conjuncts (this extraction is called across-the-board (ATB) extraction). If we assume that in conjunction constructions the conjuncts must be the same (i.e., must be symmetric), then the ungrammaticality of (36a) and (36b), as well as the grammaticality of (36c), reflects the fact that the conjuncts in (36a) and (36b) are not symmetric, while the conjuncts in (36c) are. That is, extraction out of a single conjunct creates non-symmetric (and ill-formed) conjuncts, while ATB extractions create symmetric (and well-formed) conjuncts. What needs to be explained, though, is how ATB extraction actually works. Importantly, all analyses of ATB extractions – including Nunes' (2005) sidewards analysis in which the wh-element first merges into the right conjunct and subsequently moves, sidewards, to the left conjunct before it moves into the Spec position of the matrix C, and Citko's (2005) parallel merge analysis in which the wh-element is shared by both conjuncts and moves from its shared position to the Spec position of the matrix C – require extraction out of the left conjunct, which is a left-branch construction that should prohibit extraction (see Ross 1967 and Kayne 1983 for arguments against left-branch extraction). Our original assumption that conjunction constructions involve combining (at least) two symmetric conjuncts then leaves us with the problem of left-branch extraction. This extraction problem becomes all the more acute when we consider the examples in (37).

(37) a. Someone was reading [[poetry to every child] and [fiction to many adults]].
     b. Who was reading [[poetry to which child] and [fiction to which adult]]?

To get the scopal reading for (37a) in which the quantified expressions *every child* and *many adults* have scope over the quantified subject *someone*, the quantified expressions will have to c-command the quantified subject, as May (1985), Beghelli (1997) and many others argue, at some point in the SD. For this to transpire, however, the quantified expressions will have to be extracted from their conjuncts to "raise" to a position structurally superior to the subject. Needless to say, such extraction is problematic for the traditional analysis of conjunction constructions because it necessitates both non-ATB extraction from the conjuncts and extraction from a left-branch construction (the left conjunct). A similar story emerges in (37b). According to Stroik (2009a), wh-in situ elements must appear in the Spec of CP; should this be the case, then the wh-in situ element in (37b) – *which child* and *which adult* – will have to be extracted from the conjuncts, creating problems akin to those in (37a).

   From the preceding arguments we conclude that coordinate conjunctions do not, as is generally assumed, build structure. This means that coordinate conjunctions do not put together two Xs to generate another X. Rather than simply build additive structure, coordinate conjunctions do something quite unexpected, something predicted by Survive-minimalism. Under the assumptions of Survive-minimalism, deriving a syntactic structure for the conjunction construction in (38) begins with copying the LI *Bob*, which is the most deeply embedded element in (38), from LEX into a NUM and subsequently into the SD, and then adding other LIs as required by the projected features of the SD.

(38) [a story about Sue and a poem about Bob]

From its initial LI *Bob*, the SD for (38) will proceed to build a structure for the right-conjunct, the DP [a poem for Bob]. This DP, importantly, will project an FM with a <CAT-D> feature, as well as some PSF selected-features. Once the

DP is constructed, it will be possible to continue building the SD if and only if some element is copied to the SD that matches the projected <CAT-D> feature. Since the coordinate conjunction *and* does not have a <SUBCAT-D> feature (or any other syntactic features, as we argued previously), copying it to the SD interrupts the SD because the conjunction does not check the <CAT-D> feature of the DP. The fact that the <CAT-D> feature of the DP is not checked requires that the DP "survive" in NUM, but it also suspends the SD as there is nothing in the SD left to project (the DP, which "survives" in NUM, cannot also project in the SD). What this means is that once the SD for (38) reaches (39), it will have to re-start the SD with a second "initial" LI *Sue*.

(39) [and DP]]

The derivation will bring the LIs *Sue, about, story,* and *a* into NUM and into the SD, adding this lexical material to (39), as in (40).

(40) [a [story [about [Sue [and a poem about Bob]]]]]

In (40), the left conjunct is not built to the side of the right conjunct, as is done in most analyses of coordinate structures; rather, the left conjunct is built on top of the right conjunct. Though it provides a startling (and certainly unorthodox) structure for (38), the derivation in (40) has two syntactic properties that will account for the many interpretative peculiarities of conjunction constructions: (i) every constituent in the left conjunct c-commands every constituent in the right conjunct and (ii) the right conjunct has features that are unchecked and remain active in NUM.

The first of the aforementioned properties plays an essential role in explaining the ungrammaticality of the examples in (29) and in (30a), repeated below.[14]

(29) a. *Pat hugged *her* and kissed *Sue*.
      b. *I gave a book to *her* and to *Sue*'s father.
      c. *Chris hired *him* and Sam fired *Bob*'s mother.
      d. *Sue believes that Chris hired *him* and that Sam fired *Bob*'s mother.

(30) a. *a story about *him* and a poem about *Bob*

In our left-conjunct-atop-right-conjunct analysis, the italicized pronouns in (29) and (30) will c-command the italicized Referential expressions, in violation of Binding Principle C. Hence, our analysis offers a straightforward account of the ungrammaticality of the examples in (29) and (30).

The second property noted above (i.e., that the right conjunct has an unchecked feature) will require this conjunct to be recopied into the SD. But what sort of copy operation is involved in this recopy of the right conjunct; that is, which of the two copy operations applies? Is it a list-copy (a copy-to-same operation, such as CoN) or structure-copy (a copy-to-match operation, such as CoSD)? This line of questioning arises because the right conjunct is in the unusual situation of having an unchecked CAT feature "survive" in NUM – normally, CAT features drive an SD, which means that they are automatically checked in the SD and they do not then survive in NUM. Troubling as these questions are, we can settle them if we consider examples such as (41).

(41)   Chris believes that Sue likes Bob and *that Chris hates him.*

Importantly if the italicized right conjunct in (41) could be recopied into the SD only if its <CAT-C> feature matched a constituent with a <SUBCAT-C> feature, then this conjunct would never be recopied into the SD because the sole constituent with the appropriate matching SUBCAT feature (the verb) would have its SUBCAT feature checked by the left conjunct at the point at which the verb is first copied into the SD. Given that there are no other constituents in (41) that have a <SUBCAT-C> feature available for the right conjunct in (41) to be structure-copied to the SD, we would expect, if structure-copy were required for the recopy of the right conjunct, that this conjunct would not have its CAT feature checked and that, as a result, (41) would be ungrammatical. The grammaticality of (41), then, suggests that structure-copy is not involved in the recopy of the right conjunct. This analysis leads to the conclusion that the right conjunct is list-copied into the SD.[15] If this is correct, the right conjunct will be recopied to the SD only if its features are the same as the projected FM of the SD. Applying the foregoing analysis to (40), the right conjunct *a poem about Bob*, which will have the same FM as the left conjunct, will be able to be list-copied to the left conjunct, deriving (43).

(42)   [a [story [about [Sue [and a poem about Bob]]]]]

(43)   [[a poem about Bob] [a [story [about [Sue [and a poem about Bob]]]]]]

At this point in the derivation, the two conjuncts are list-adjoined and this adjunction structure projects the shared features of the conjuncts.

Support for the above analysis comes from several sources. First, this analysis not only explains the ungrammaticality of the sentences (29), it also explains the grammaticality judgments in (32).

(32)   a.   *Mary likes *those men* and *each other*'s wives.
       b.   *Mary likes *each other*'s wives and *those men*.
       c.   *Those men* like Mary and *each other*'s wives.
       d.   *Those men* like *each other*'s wives and Mary.
       e.   *Mary wrote poems about *those men* and stories about *themselves*.
       f.   *Those men* wrote poems about Mary and stories about *themselves*.

As with (40), when the coordinate structures are initially built for (32a) and (32e), everything in the left conjuncts will c-command everything in the right conjuncts; hence, the italicized referential expressions in those examples should appropriately license the anaphors in the right conjuncts. We should then (mis) predict that (32a) and (32e) would be grammatical constructions. However, if, as Lebeaux (2009) proposes, Principle A (which licenses anaphors) applies to LF (logical form) representations and if the left conjunct shows up in the LF representation recopied to the right conjunct, as we see in (44a, b), then the anaphors are not duly licensed by any of the referential expressions available and the constructions are correctly predicted to be ungrammatical.

(44)   a. [[*each other*'s wives] [*those men* and *each other*'s wives]]
       b. [stories about *themselves*] [poems about *those men* and stories about *themselves*]]

A similar story applies to (32b). The ungrammaticality of (32b), which could be explained by the fact that the anaphor c-commands the italicized referential expression when the coordinate structure is first built, also follows from the inability of the italicized referential expression to c-command the anaphor even after the right conjunct is recopied into the SD (see (45)).

(45)   [[*those men*] [*each other*'s wives and **those men**]]

The reason that the referential expression in (45) does not c-command the anaphor is that the right conjunct is list-copied to the SD, rather than structure-copied; as a result, the recopied material does not engage in structural relations (including c-command relations) with the material to which it is attached.

A second support for our recopy analysis of coordinate structures comes from the grammaticality differences between (46), which exhibits a "weak" Principle C violation,[16] and (47a, b), which do not have a Principle C violation (the data in (46) and (47a) are taken from Progovac 1998).

(46)   ?**John* certainly likes *John's* wife.

(47)   a. *John* and *John's* wife are certainly invited.
       a'. **He* and *John's* wife are certainly invited.
       b. Pat hired *John* and *John's* wife.
       b'. **Pat hired *him* and *John's* wife.

Given the ungrammaticality of (46), in which a Principle C violation arises because the first italicized referential expression c-commands the second one, the well-formedness of the examples in (47a) and (47b) suggests that the italicized referential expression in the left conjunct does not c-command the italicized referential expression in the right conjunct. This "suggestion," however, seems at odds with the data in (47a) and (47b), which indicate that the pronouns in the left conjunct do c-command the referential expressions in the right conjunct. These data leave us with the challenge of explaining how the conjuncts in conjunction constructions can have contradictory c-command relations. Although no previous theory of coordinate structures has been able to meet this challenge, our Survive-minimalist analysis can. Under our analysis, the left conjuncts in (47a, a', b, b') all must be recopied (as list-copies) to the right conjunct; once this reattachment occurs, no material in either conjunct will c-command material in the other conjunct. If strong Principle C relations are, as Lebeaux (2009) maintains, determined everywhere in a derivation, then (47a') and (47b') will be ungrammatical because the pronouns in the left conjunct do indeed c-command the referential expression at some point in the derivation; however, if weak Principle C relations are determined, as are anaphor relations, at the representational stage (i.e., at the termination of the derivation), then the relations involving the italicized referential expressions in (47a) and (47b) will be determined after the left conjunct is recopied to the right conjunct, at which point neither of the referential expressions will c-command the other. Our argument, then, is that if weak Principle C relations are structurally assessed only after constituents dislocate (or are re-copied), then (47a) and (47b) should, under our analysis, be grammatical. So, are weak Principle C relations determined after structural dislocations occur? It seems that they are. To see this, consider the examples in (48).

(48)   a.   ?*_John_ likes those pictures of _John's_ mother best.
       b.   Which pictures of _John's_ mother does _John_ like best?

The fact that example (48b), which dislocates/fronts the wh-constituent from its object position in (48a), is not as degraded as (48a) demonstrates that relations involving referential expressions are determined after the dislocation/recopying takes place.

The third, and perhaps most important, support for our recopying analysis of coordinate structures comes from the data in (49).

(49)   a.   Pat gave money to the woman dancing with him and Bob.
       b.   *Pat thinks that Bill left and Sam.

Example (49a) is particularly interesting because it has two structural readings, but, surprisingly neither of these readings can escape a Principle C violation if _him_ and _Bob_ are co-referential. The two readings for (49a) are (i) that the woman is dancing with two people, one of which is Bob and (ii) that Pat gave money to two people, one of which is Bob. Although traditional approaches to conjunction constructions would have little trouble providing two different coordinate structures for the two readings (as in (50)), what they would find problematic is explaining why *him* and *Bob* cannot co-refer in either reading, especially in the reading associated with (50b).

(50) a. [a woman dancing with [him and Bob]]
      b. [[a woman dancing with him] and Bob]

The fact that the pronoun in (50b) does not c-command the referential expression *Bob* should lead to the erroneous conclusion that these two elements, if they are co-referential, would not produce a Principle C violation. Getting the two readings for (49a), then, is not a straightforward matter of lining up left and right conjuncts, as in (50); rather, getting the two readings for (49a) is complicated: it requires aligning the conjuncts in a way that can account for potential Principle C binding violations. Traditional approaches to conjunction constructions cannot explain how the structures responsible for readings for (49a) are related to the structures responsible for the potential Principle C violations. Survive-minimalism, however, can. As with our previous analyses of coordinate structures, the derivation for (49a) builds a coordinate structure on top of the right conjunct, as in (51).

(51) [a [woman [dancing [with [him [and Bob]]]]]]

In (51), the pronoun necessarily c-commands the referential expression *Bob*; hence they cannot co-refer without producing a Principle C violation. The derivational story for (49a), though, does not end here. Recall that once the conjunction is introduced into the derivation, the right conjunct *Bob* "survives" in NUM because its CAT feature is unchecked. To have its CAT feature checked, this syntactic object (SO) must be recopied, as a list-copy, into the SD, which can happen only if the SD projects features that match the unchecked features of the SO. Of note, in (51) there are two places in the derivation when the derivation will project features that exactly match the CAT-D feature of the SO *Bob*, once when the pronoun is copied into the derivation (at this point the derivation will project the features of the pronoun, including its CAT-D feature) and once when the DP *a woman dancing with him* is constructed (at this point the derivation will project the features of this phrase, including a CAT-D feature). Now the SO *Bob* must be list-copied into the derivation to have its features checked; however, since this recopying is not performed by a structure-copy operation, it will not have to satisfy the locality conditions of the CoSD operation. That is, the SO *Bob* will be able to be list-copied to any available matching domains/projections – in this case, to either the pronoun or the aforementioned DP – during the course of the derivation (it is also possible that the SO could be list-copied to all the available feature-matching domains/projections). It is the nature of the list-copy operation, then, that allows the right conjunct in (49a) to be interpreted in multiple syntactic positions. Should no matching domain come available for a right conjunct throughout the course of a derivation, then the features of the right conjunct would continue to survive in NUM and the derivation would stall (i.e., it would not be submitted for interpretation). This happens in (49b), repeated below.

(49b)   *Pat thinks that Bill left and Sam.

As with (49a), adding a conjunction to the right conjunct in (49b) will force the derivation to pause and leave the right conjunct active in NUM. The derivation that is built upon the paused derivation, however, constructs the structures in (52), none of which projects a CAT-D feature.

(52)   a.   left
       b.   [Bill left]
       c.   [that Bill left]
       d.   [thinks [that Bill left]]
       e.   [Pat [thinks [that Bill left]]]

Since the SO *Sam* does not feature-match any of the structures in (52), it cannot be list-copied into the derivation. As a result, the features of this SO can never be checked, and the illegitimate/ungrammatical derivation will stall.

As we can see, Survive-minimalism offers an analysis of conjunction constructions that differs substantially from all previous analyses. At the heart of the Survive analysis is the recognition that the primary syntactic consequence of bringing a coordinate conjunction into an SD is not to add/connect material, but to pause the derivation and restart it. The additive properties of these conjunctions are secondary properties that arise as a by-product of the derivational pause and the associated stranding of the right-conjunct material; that is, a feature-matching left conjunct must be added to the derivation to ensure that the features of the right conjunct can be checked. If a right conjunct lacks features that need to be checked, then under the Survive-analysis, there will be no need to add a left conjunct. We can test this prediction by looking at matrix sentences – the only syntactic constructions that have all their features checked, so they do not have any features to strand. Consider the following examples.

(53)   a.   And where do you think you are going?
       b.   And that's that.
       c.   And then went down to the ship, Set keel to breaker . . . (Beginning of Ezra Pound's *The Cantos*)
       d.   And I'm off.

There are few limits on the (matrix) sentences that we can begin with a coordinate conjunction and that have no need for a left conjunct. These sorts of data provide strong confirmation of our Survive analysis.

Conjunction constructions are central to all languages. The fact that all syntactic frameworks find conjunction data troubling for their theories tells us something quite illuminating about these frameworks. *And* the fact that Survive-minimalism can handle conjunction data in a straightforward fashion is also telling.

5.5   Conclusion

This chapter has explored what the general design principles that underlie Survive-minimalism can tell us about two of the more intractable grammatical constructions – adjunction constructions and conjunction constructions. Looking at these constructions through a Survive lens has allowed us to see them in a new light. Conjunction constructions, in particular, appear radically different under a Survive-minimalist analysis than under any other grammatical analysis. That conjunction constructions, under a Survive-minimalist analysis, involve structural pauses and derivational restarts is certainly an odd and unexpected way to conceive of these conjunctions. However, the uncanny ability of this analysis to (uniquely) account for the seemingly contradictory properties of conjunction constructions speaks to the theoretical strengths of Survive-minimalism.

Appendix: features, crashes, and derivations

Stroik (1999, 2009a), Putnam (2007), and Putnam and Stroik (2009, 2010) argue that Survive-minimalism has a crash-proof design. Directed by the specifications of LI FMs, an SD in Survive-minimalism begins with the first LI placed in NUM and continues to build syntactic structure, via feature-matching Copy operations, until all concatenative features of all the LIs in NUM are appropriately checked for performance system interpretability. Should at any point in an SD a feature become both unchecked and inactive in NUM, the SD will immediately stall and abort before it ever is submitted to the performance systems for interpretation. Survive-minimalism is designed to produce a single derivation for any given NUM, and this derivation takes on representation status only if, and when, it is complete and ready for performance system interpretation. To the extent that the derivational mechanisms employed by Survive-minimalism are set up to license only interpretable representations, Survive-minimalism is a crash-proof syntax.

The computational advantages that Survive-minimalism has over "standard" models of Minimalism are striking. Most models of Minimalism will over-generate syntactic structure and produce what Chomsky (1995) calls "crashes." Such crashes arise when the syntactic operations derive structures that are uninterpretable by the C-I and/or SM performance systems. Not only do standard Minimalist models generate crashes, they also generate, according to Epstein and Seely (2006), some "non-fatal crashes." Epstein and Seely argue that there are some derivational steps that are deficient and should produce crashes, but these deficiencies can be corrected subsequently, so the crashes they produce are "non-fatal." We can see one of these derivational deficiencies in the initial merger of *[[$_V$ give] [$_{DP}$ a beer]] for sentence (3) (repeated below as (54)), which we analyzed earlier in this chapter.

(54)   Moe will give Homer a beer.

A derivational "deficiency" arises in (54) because the verb *give* (V_{give}) possesses two internal theta roles – one for the argument *a beer* (Patient) and another for the argument *Homer* (Recipient) – and in a level-free derivational approach that assumes concatenated syntactic units are interface legible, the initial merger of *[$_{VP}$ [$_V$ give] [$_{DP}$ a beer]] does not allow V_{give} to exhaust all of its theta roles; hence this merger should produce a crash. This "crash," however, is short lived and "non-fatal" with the merger of the argument *Moe* in the next derivational step. But does this merger really resolve the apparent crash? Doesn't the merger merely derive another derivationally deficient structure [[Moe] [[give] [a beer]]]? Are the interfaces any more prepared to interpret [Chris give apples] than they are to interpret [give a beer]? It seems, in fact, that Epstein and Seely's level-free derivational syntax cannot escape "non-fatal crashes" until the derivation terminates – this is the case because, until the derivation terminates, there is always some missing structural information that will create (at the very least) a non-fatal crash. If this is so, what does it mean to assert that concatenated syntactic units are interface legible when all these units, save the final one, crash or non-fatally crash? Clearly, interface legibility is not established piecemeal, and models of Minimalism which assume such legibility should be dispreferred.

Crashes, both fatal and non-fatal, are costly.[17] Grammars that produce them allow the syntax to derive and present syntactic structures to the performance systems that cannot be interpreted there. Allowing these crashes doubly drains our CS – first by taking processing time to derive (uninterpretable) syntactic structures, and then by taking processing time, when they are submitted to the performance systems for interpretation, to decide that the structures are uninterpretable. As Hinzen (2006: 249) observes about unproductive processing: "In an optimal system [of human language], an impossible meaning would never be produced and syntax would be crash-proof." Survive-minimalism is the one derivational model of the CS of human language that is crash-proof.

As we mention above, Survive-minimalism does not generate structures that crash. Classic "crashed" constructions such as super-raising (see (55)) simply cannot be derived in this framework.

(55)   *Chris seems that it was fired (Chris).

In (55), the DP-object of the embedded verb *fired* shows up as the subject of the matrix sentence, "raising" over the embedded expletive subject. Although the raising construction in (55) has some initial plausibility (in that the features of the raised DP <CAT-D <CASE>> can be arguably checked by the embedded verb and by the matrix Tense head, respectively), Survive-minimalism categorically disallows the aforementioned feature checking. Given the way syntactic structures are built in Survive-minimalism, a derivation for (55) would begin with copying *Chris* (with FM <CAT-D <CASE>>) in NUM and then in the SD; subsequently the verb *fired* would be copied into the SD, as in (56a).

(56a)   [fired [Chris]]

Since the passivized verb cannot check the Case feature of the DP *Chris*, this DP, with its still active Case feature, will "survive" in NUM. Once the SD reaches the point where the Tense element has been copied into the SD and is projecting a Case feature <CASE: NOMINATIVE> (as in (56b)), the DP *Chris*, which has an active matching Case feature, will immediately be copied from NUM into the SD. In other words, the SD will necessarily reach derivation (56c).

(56)   b. [T [was [fired [Chris]]]]
      c. [Chris [T [was [fired [Chris]]]]]

There is no way for the derivation at derivational point (56b) to search LEX for an expletive to satisfy the Case requirement of the T head (as would be necessary to derive (55)), overlooking the active features in NUM. Under Survive-minimalist assumptions, the search-first domain for building an SD is NUM, since searching the materials already gathered for the SD requires much less processing effort than going back to LEX to find an LI with the requisite features, then copying that LI to NUM and then copying the LI from NUM to the SD. The consequence of requiring the DP *Chris* to be recopied into the SD at derivational point (56c) is that this DP will have all of its concatenative features duly checked; hence, the DP will not survive in NUM and will not be eligible to participate in other structure-building operations, so this DP could never reach the matrix subject position, as in (55). Should (56c) undergo further structure building, it could eventually derive the well-formed sentence (57), but it could not derive the ill-formed string (55).

(57)   It seems that Chris was fired.

In a related sense, Survive-minimalism will not allow a syntactic structure to be built for sentences, such as (58a) and (58b), that have a super-raised wh-element in them.

(58)   a. *What should Pat know when Sam fixed (when) (what)
       b. *When should Pat know what Sam fixed (when) (what)

In the SDs for (58a) and (58b), the wh-elements will both "survive" in NUM after they are first copied into the derivations because they have selected <WH> features that cannot be checked by the embedded verb *fixed* and, therefore, the wh-elements remain active in NUM. When the derivation reaches (59), the C-head, which will have a selecting <WH> feature, must be matched by a constituent with a selected <WH> feature. Both of the wh-elements in NUM have the necessary <WH> feature; consequently, both wh-elements must be copied to the SD.

(59)   [T [Sam fixed (when) (what)]]

Copying the wh-elements into the SD will deactivate the <WH> features of these elements; however, the C head can check only one of the <WH> features. This means that one of the wh-elements will have a deactivated, but an unchecked and uncheckable, feature. At this point, the derivation aborts/stalls because it can never be interpretation-ready for the performance systems. No SD for (58a) or for (58b), then, is possible in Survive-minimalism.

All other constructions that are said to "crash" at the performance systems in standard Minimalism (see Chomsky 1995) receive a similar Survive-analysis to the ones provided in (54) and (55) (many of these constructions are discussed in Stroik 2009a). That is, these "crashes" never occur in Survive-minimalism because they cannot compute an SD that reaches the performance systems for interpretation. As far as Survive-minimalism is concerned, we really cannot speak of these errors as "crashes" (although in the traditional terminology of Frampton and Gutmann (2002), Survive-minimalism is indeed "crash-proof"); instead they should be understood as "stalls." In other words, for any given derivation, if a successful concatenative union cannot result from a Copy-to-syntactic derivation operation operation (CoSD), the derivation will be abandoned.

6   Observations on performance
       system interpretations

6.1   Introduction

We have set out in this book to identify the optimal design principles for the
Faculty of Language (FL) and to develop an evolvable Narrow Syntax consonant with this design. Over the previous five chapters, we have argued that the
optimal design for FL is one in which the Lexicon/Numeration and the computational system (CS) must reside within the Conceptual-Intentional (C-I) and
Sensorimotor (SM) performance systems, as in (1).

(1)

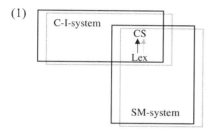

The consequences of this design are that the lexical items (LIs) in the Lexicon
(LEX) will possess only performance system features and that the CS will use
only performance system operations (namely, Copy operations). From performance system input (features), the CS will necessarily produce usable performance system output, which means that the final output of any syntactic
derivation (SD) is a representation able to be interpreted by the performance
systems. At this point, then, our task is essentially complete: we have developed
a structural and computational design for FL that is grounded in the performance systems and that exhibits both a conceptually necessary connection
between the CS and the performance system and a plausible evolutionary
connection between them. Although we have finished our core argument, we
want to extend our analysis a bit farther by pursuing the question of how the
performance systems interpret the syntactic representations submitted to them.

Before we take a look at the performance systems and their interpretative
processes, we would like to return to a topic we have addressed, albeit briefly, in

other places in this book: crashes. In Survive-minimalism, there are no crashes – i.e., no unusable derivations are submitted to the performance systems for interpretation. We would like to point out here, however, that although Survive-minimalism is crash-proof, it can still derive structures that are not performance-system-ready and must be aborted. Take, for example, the following string in (2).

(2)   *Why Sam is leaving?
      (as a matrix clause in an adult grammar)

The ungrammaticality of (2) arises from the fact that the <WH> feature of the wh-element cannot be checked by a matching feature in the matrix CP because this CP lacks a C-head with a <WH> feature. It is simply not possible to compute a derivation for (2) in which all the concatenative features available for the derivation are appropriately checked; derivations for (2), then, will be incomplete and, as a result, they will abort. That is, no derivation for (2) will be submitted for interpretation. Similar sorts of situations show up in all the examples in (3).

(3)   a.   *What does Pat know whether Chris fixed?
      b.   *What did Pat tell Chris where to put?
      c.   *Who does Pat think that left?
      d.   *What did who read?
           (as a multiple-wh question)

In Survive-minimalism, the island effects in (3a) and (3b), the *that*-trace effect in (3c), and the superiority effect in (3d) follow from the presence of uncheckable <WH> features (see Stroik 2009a for a detailed Survive-minimalist analysis of data such as those in (3)). Since it is not possible to generate syntactic derivations (SDs) for (3a–d) in which each and every concatenative feature is checked, all derivations for (3a–d) will necessarily be incomplete and unusable, and they will not be submitted to the performance systems for interpretation. We will not say anything more about such examples or about other types of aborted derivations, but again see Stroik (2009a) for an exhaustive discussion of these derivations.

What we *will* do in this chapter, though, is outline an interpretative analysis of the syntactic representations that are derivationally complete, focusing on the contributions that syntactic structure makes to interpretations. Our analysis will consider both C-I interpretations and SM interpretations, and it will extend to cases involving binding relations and scopal relations. But our analysis will be partial, not treating interpretative issues that are not structural in nature – including the role that cognitive effects (as in Relevance Theory) play in interpretation or the role that intentionality plays (see Theory of Mind) or the role that referential values and truth conditions play in interpretation. That is, we will not offer a composite theory of how the performance systems interpret representation; such a theory would require a book-length investigation in its own right. Our goal here is modest and suggestive, seeking to identify some of the processes involved in the structural interpretation of syntactic representations.

6.2   Interpreting syntactic representations

Let us begin our analysis by asking a terribly complex question: what happens when a syntactic representation (a well-formed and complete derivation) is submitted to the performance systems for interpretation? And by giving a terribly simple answer to the question: the performance systems, at the very least, must interpret all LIs in the representation and all the syntactic relations in which the LIs appear. For a sentence such as (4), this means that the C-I performance system must provide a semantic interpretation for each LI in its Numeration (NUM) {Pat, hire, Chris, will} and for all the SDs (5a–d) that are built from the LIs in NUM, culminating in the syntactic representation (5e).

(4)   Chris will hire Pat.

(5)   a. [Pat]
      b. [hire [Pat]]
      c. [Chris [hire [Pat]]]
      d. [will [Chris [hire [Pat]]]]
      e. [Chris [will [Chris [hire [Pat]]]]]

In Survive-minimalism, interpreting LIs is straightforward because LIs are learned and stored with their interpretable performance system features in place. Hence, the fact that *Pat* and *Chris* are semantically interpreted as individuals and the fact that *hire* denotes an event and *will* denotes a temporal operator are all facts that are determined by the C-I system independent of structural relations that these LIs eventually become part of. No special prepping operations have to ready these LIs for their semantic interpretations. The semantic interpretations of the SDs in (5a–d), on the other hand, have to be computed. This computation, in Survive-minimalism, will be determined by the features that are concatenated. Since (5a) adds the LI *Pat* to a null-SD, the semantic value/interpretation of (5a) is just the semantic interpretation of *Pat* ($\|$Pat$\|$), as in (6a); since (5b) and (5c) are both SDs that involve the feature <SUBCAT-D: theta role>, the semantic interpretations of these two SDs will be determined by the theta role, as in (6b) and (6c) respectively; and since the SD in (5d) involves a <SUBCAT-*v*: TEMPORAL> feature, this SD will be interpreted as in (6d).

(6) a. ||Pat|| = p (an individual)
     b. ||hire Pat|| = PATIENT (hire, p)
     c. ||Chris hire Pat|| = AGENT (hire, c), where ||Chris|| = c (an individual)
     d. ||will Chris hire Pat|| = FUTURE (hire)

Importantly, the semantic interpretations we see in (6) result from the structural interplay of lexical features with one another, as built by the CoSD operation. That is, structural meaning is compiled.

   But is structural meaning restricted to LIs and the syntactic relations in which they appear? Or are there other syntactic objects that must be interpreted by the performance systems? There is one other syntactic object posited in the Minimalist program (see Chomsky 1995) and its Government and Binding predecessor (see Chomsky 1981) that might be visible to the performance systems for interpretation: derivational chains that link together the multiple appearances of lexical material. However, do derivational chains actually exist (that is, does the CS form such chains)? And if so, what sorts of mechanisms might be needed to interpret the interconnections among the multiple appearances of lexical material that form chains? To answer these questions, let us consider the chains formed in the derivation of (7) – which we can see in (8) (NB: the material in bold typeface indicates a copy).

(7)   What does Chris seem to have stolen?

(8)   what does Chris seem to **Chris** have stolen **what**

In (8), there are putatively two derivationally formed chains involving DPs: a wh-chain (what, **what**) and a DP-chain (Chris, **Chris**). These chains, if they are legitimate syntactic objects, will have to be interpreted by the performance systems, but doing so is no easy task. The problem with interpreting chains is that they have a complex bundle of properties, which we can readily observe in Haegeman's (1994) description of the properties of DP-chains, also known as A(rgument)-chains:

(9)   Properties of A-chains
      a. Moved element is always a DP/NP
      b. Movement is obligatory.
      c. The landing site of movement is an empty position.
      d. The landing site is an A-position.
      e. The landing site is an NP-position.
      f. The landing site of movement is a position to which no theta-role is assigned. Let us call this a θ' (theta-bar) position by analogy with an A'-position.
      g. The landing site of the movement is a position to which case is assigned.

h. The site from which the element is moved is an NP-position to which no case is assigned.
i. Movement leaves a trace.
j. The trace is co-indexed with the moved element, the antecedent, with which it forms a chain. Because the head of the chain is an A-position, the chain created by NP-movement is called an A-chain.
k. The chain is assigned one theta role.
l. The theta role is assigned to the lowest position of the chain: the foot of the chain.
m. The chain is case-marked once.
n. Case is assigned to the highest position of the chain: the head of the chain.

(Although Haegeman's above description of A-chain properties is grounded in Government and Binding assumptions about licit syntactic movement, these properties (or analogs thereof) largely persist within standard Minimalism, which remains committed to some version of derivation-internal syntactic displacement.) What we will argue here is that A-chains with the properties in (9a–n) are problematic for at least three reasons. First, only two of the properties in (9) – namely (9l) and (9n) – actually involve potential interaction with the performance systems, and, therefore, only these two properties are conceptually necessary; all other properties should be dispensed with.[1] If this is the case, then an A-chain will have only two properties and only two links: a foot-link that has its CAT feature (and its thematic coefficient) interpreted by the C-I performance system and a head-link that has its Case feature interpreted by the SM performance system. The fact that each performance system sees/interprets only a single link suggests that the chain itself has no visibility to the performance systems, which further suggests that chains, too, should be dispensed with. Second, A-chains are designed to oversee the legitimacy of derivation-internal displacement (formerly known as syntactic movement) – if we look closely at properties (9a–j) above, we will notice that they are not interpretative properties; rather, they are licensing properties that seek to define the conditions for licit syntactic movements. However, the performance systems do not see/interpret displacements, hence neither displacements nor the chains that legitimate (or license) them are conceptually necessary. And third, as Brody (1995, 2002) contends, syntactic chains duplicate the interpretative chains formed by the performance systems. Consequently, syntactic/derivational-chains are redundant and unnecessary. The three arguments we have just given all seem to lead to the same conclusion: chains, if they exist at all, are not syntactic objects and they play no role in the structural interpretation of syntactic representations.

Whereas standard Minimalism is concerned with interpreting LIs and syntactic chains (both of which, as we have just argued, are untenable),

Survive-minimalism interprets concatenations. In Survive-minimalism, the CS builds (interpretable) concatenated items from (interpretable) LIs by matching (interpretable) lexical features, resulting in (interpretable) structural representations (see Chapter 4). To see an example of this boot-strapped interpretability, consider a Survive-minimalist syntactic representation for (7), which can be seen in (10).[2] (As before, the material in bold typeface is a copy.)

(7)   What does Chris seem to have stolen?

(10)   [what [does [Chris [**does** [seem [**Chris** to have stolen **what**]]]]]]

Although the syntactic representation in (10) is interpreted by both performance systems, each system "reads" only those concatenations bearing its features. So the SM system will read (10) as (11), where all the concatenations involve SM spell-out features; and the C-I system will read (10) as (12), where all the concatenations involve C-I features.

(11)   [what [does [Chris [seem [to have stolen]]]]]

(12)   [what [does [**does** [seem [**Chris** to have stolen **what**]]]]]

Note that in the SM representation (11) all LIs appear only once and they appear at the point in the derivation in which the final morphophonetic features in their Feature Matrices (FMs) are concatenated. It is generally the case that the most deeply embedded feature in an FM is a phonetic realization feature (as is true of all the LIs in (10)/(11)), so LIs tend to be realized in their final concatenation.[3] There are, however, LIs that have concatenative features more deeply embedded in their FMs than their final morphophonetic features. Such a situation occurs for wh-in-situ elements in English. As with wh-operators, wh-in-situ items have as their final two features a Case-feature and a <WH> feature; unlike wh-operators, though, the <WH> feature for wh-in-situ elements is not a morphophonetic feature (see Stroik 2009a for an expansive discussion of the <WH> feature in wh-in-situ elements). As a result, wh-in-situ elements are not phonetically realized in their final concatenation, which involves their <WH> feature. Rather, they are realized where their Case feature is concatenated, as is expressed in the syntactic representation (13b) for sentence (13a).[4]

(13)   a.   Who did Pat ask to do what?
         b.   [who [what [did [Pat [ask [who [ask [to do what]]]]]]]]

In (13b), it is the most deeply embedded copy (not the highest copy) of the wh-in-situ element that is phonetically realized – which is just the opposite realization pattern that we see for the wh-operator. The point here is that only one of the copies of an LI is phonetically realized, but which copy is realized will depend on the morphophonetic properties of a given language.

While SM representations such as (11) permit copies of LIs (and other syntactic objects) to appear only once for morphophonetic interpretation, C-I representations such as (12), repeated below, allow copies of LIs to appear in more than one concatenation.

(12)   [what [does [**does** [seem [**Chris** to have stolen **what**]]]]]

LIs will be copied into multiple concatenations in a C-I representation if they have more than one C-I feature. In (12) for example, two LIs have multiple C-I features and, therefore, will appear in multiple concatenations: *does/**does*** (which has a <WH> feature and a temporal feature) and *what/**what*** (which has a <WH> feature and a <CAT> feature). Each of the multiple copies of any LI, say what/**what** in (12), must be interpreted separately as parts of concatenations, but they must also be interpreted together (as parts of the same thing). The individual interpretations of *what/**what*** are straightforward: **what** is interpreted as the object argument of the verb *stolen*, and *what* is interpreted as a wh-operator over the entire representation. Furthermore, the fact that these two copies are connected to one another and have an interconnected interpretation (as operator and variable) is also relatively straightforward: the connection is established lexically and the interconnection is established structurally. The LI *what* by itself is both an operator and a variable because it possesses both an operator feature <WH> and a variable feature (its <CAT> feature). Hence, the wh-operator and its wh-variable are lexically fused: they are but variants of the same LI. Being interpreted as an operator and as a variable, however, requires that the LI *what* have its features properly concatenated and licensed for operator/variable interpretation. The CS will ensure that both of the <WH> features are properly concatenated, but it will also ensure, through its iterated local computations, that the copies of the LI *what* are (licitly) structurally linked. In other words, the CS guarantees that the C-I performance system will be able to interpretatively interconnect the wh-operator copy of *what* with its variable copy by following the well-formed structural connections between the two copies.

In sum, SDs build interpretable representations by concatenating interpretable features. Once these representations are presented to the performance systems, all the performance systems need to do is interpret them (see section 6.5 for a discussion of this interpretation).

6.3   Binding-theoretic considerations

Interpreting the structural relations in an SD involves more than providing semantic and morphophonetic values for concatenations. Although concatenations give the local structural information that will establish predication relations and word-order effects, they do not bear any information about how to interpret long-distance relations between constituents. In particular, concatenations do not help determine whether two constituents can (as in (14)) or cannot (as in (15)) be coreferential. (The italics in the examples below indicate a coreferential reading.)

(14) a. *That woman* likes *her* job.
      b. *Her* mother expects *Chris* to run for the Presidency.
      c. *Sam* believes that *she* could solve the problem.
      d. *Pat* admires *himself*.
      e. *Pat's* mother likes *him*.

(15) a. **She* likes *that woman's* job.
      b. **Chris* expects *Chris's* mother will run for the Presidency.
      c. **Each other's* parents believe that *they* could solve the problem.
      d. **That woman* admires *himself*.
      e. **Pat* likes *him*.

Since Chomsky (1973) first investigated the conditions of NP interpretation under the rubric of 'binding' (originally covered under the *Rule of Interpretation, Disjoint Reference, Binding Theory*), there has been widespread recognition that this interpretation involves, among other things, structural conditions – see Chomsky (1980, 1981, 1993), Chomsky and Lasnik (1993), Epstein et al. (1998), Hornstein (2001, 2006), Kayne (2002), Zwart (2002), Hicks (2009) and Lebeaux (2009), and a myriad of others. Most generative theories of binding and coreferential relations proposed in the above works assume a version of Binding Theory, which Chomsky (1993: 43) formulates as follows (with D an undefined local domain):[5]

(16) The Binding Conditions
      A. If α is an anaphor, interpret it as coreferential with a c-commanding phrase in D.
      B. If α is a pronominal, interpret it as disjoint from every c-commanding phrase in D.
      C. If α is an R-expression, interpret it as disjoint from every c-commanding phrase.

The Binding Conditions in (16) specify that the coreferential interpretation(s) for a constituent α depend on the constituent's type, on its structural (c-command) relations with other constituents in an SD, and on a locality domain; current generative approaches to binding relations tend to embrace all three of these specifications. What is not stated in (16), and what is rather controversial about (16), is when, in the course of an SD, these Binding Conditions are applied. Chomsky (1995) argues that all Binding Conditions apply at the LF (logical form) interface; Hicks (2009), who contends that the concept of "local domain" can be built around the concept of "phases," proposes that Condition A of Binding Theory applies in PF (phonetic form) phases and that Binding Condition B applies in LF (logical form) phases; and Lebeaux (2009) maintains that Binding Condition A applies at the LF interface and the other two binding conditions apply throughout the derivation.

Since there are no interfaces in Survive-minimalism, we must reject the proposals advanced by Chomsky, by Hicks, and by Lebeaux for applying the Binding Conditions. For us coreferential relations are relations of discourse interpretation that are determined by the performance systems.[6] As discourse interpretations, coreferential relations are not simply a matter of LF, as Fiengo and Higginbotham (1981) demonstrate in their observations regarding the phonological effects on coreferentiality (see (17).

(17) a. %*John* read [$_{DP}$ books about *him*]
      b. *John* read [$_{DP}$ books about *HIM*]
      c. **John* read [$_{DP}$ books about *'im*]

The fact that coreferential relations are not merely a matter of LF is further supported by Lebeaux (2009), who points out that if binding were determined at LF, then (18a) and (19a) should be ungrammatical because their logical representations (see (18b) and (19b) respectively) have Binding Condition C violations in them. The grammaticality of (18a) and (19a) suggests that some coreferential relations cannot be reduced to LF phenomena; that is, something other than logical representation must be involved in coreferentiality.

(18) a. *John* seems to *himself* to like cheese.
      b. [seems to *himself* [*John* to like cheese]]

(19) a. Pictures of *John* seem to *him* to be great.
      b. [seem to *him* [pictures of *John* to be great]]

But if coreferential relations are not determined at LF, where are they determined? In Survive-minimalism the answer to this question is straightforward. Recall that Survive-minimalism produces for every SD only a single syntactic representation available for interpretation: the C-I performance system and the SM performance system get exactly the same representation for interpretation. For (18a), they both get (20).

(20) [John seems to himself [**John** to like cheese]]

As we have discussed in the previous section, the two performance systems "see" different versions of any given syntactic representation, say (20), interpreting different, system-dependent concatenations; it is crucial, though, to emphasize that the performance systems do receive the same (single) representation for interpretation. When the structural contributions to coreferential (discourse) relations are interpreted/determined for (18a), this interpretation, too, is read off the syntactic representation (20). What is seen by the C-I performance system as it reads for coreferentiality, however, are not individual concatenations, which are used by the performance systems to provide predication relations and word-order effects, but the entire syntactic representation (i.e., all the intra-sentential discourse relations) with two related exceptions: (i) DPs in concatenations that do not check SM features are not visible for coreferentiality computations and (ii) DPs in concatenations that do not check SM features are not visible for Binding Condition C coreferentiality computations (and neither are the internal constituents of the DPs). The first exception arises because discourse relations, as opposed to purely logical relations, necessarily involve some degree of expressibility; that is, discourse relations must be palpable and physically materialized, which means they must have SM content.[7] And the second exception occurs because referential DPs (covered by Binding Condition C) must be able to be interpreted in and of themselves; hence the expressibility requirement for these DPs is all the more pronounced and stringent.

Once we factor the expressibility exceptions into (20), then the syntactic representation for (18a) "seen" by the C-I performance system to determine coreferentiality relations will be (20'), with the DP *John* invisible for discourse interpretation since none of its SM features are checked in the embedded sentence (therefore, it lacks SM content).

(20')   [*John* seems to *himself* [to like cheese]]

In (20'), the DP *John* will be referentially disjoint from any c-commanding DPs in accordance with Binding Condition C, and the anaphor *himself* will be interpreted as being coreferential with the DP *John*, thereby satisfying Binding Condition A.

Not only does our Survive-analysis explain the well-formed coreferential relations in (18a), it can also account for the coreferentiality between *John* and *him* in (19a). The syntactic representation for (19a) will be (21), and the representation seen for determining Binding Condition C coreferentiality relations will be (21'), with the DP **pictures of John** not visible for discourse interpretation because it lacks SM content.

(21)   [pictures of John seem to him [**pictures of John** to be great]]

(21')   [pictures of *John* seem to *him* [to be great]]

Although (21) would appear to have a Binding Condition C violation in that the pronoun c-commands the R-expression, notice that in (21') no such violation arises. In (21') the R-expression and the pronoun can be coreferential without inducing either a Binding Condition B or a Binding Condition C violation; hence, this coreferential interpretation is permissible for (19a).

A somewhat more complicated example of coreferential relations can be seen in example (22), which is taken from Lebeaux (2009: 35). The anaphor *each other* in this example would appear to lack an antecedent, in violation of Binding Condition A. However, if we look closely at the syntactic representation used for interpreting coreferential relations (given in (23)), we will see that the anaphor is appropriately bound.

(22)   *Each other*'s parents seem to *the boys* to be wonderful.

(23)   [*each other*'s parents seem to *the boys* [**each other's parents** to be wonderful]]

If we compare (21) and (23), we discover something quite interesting: that is, while the emboldened DP copy in (21) is not seen in the interpreted representation (21'), the equivalent emboldened DP copy remains a (visible) part of the interpreted representation in (23). The reason that there is a difference between these two DP copies is that the latter DP copy contains an anaphor with a checked <CASE> feature (an SM feature), so the anaphor must be visible for coreferentiality relations (the only anaphors, or pronouns, that could be invisible are those that have not had any SM features checked). Since the anaphor has had its <CASE> feature checked in the lower DP, the DP containing the anaphor will be visible for coreferential interpretation. In representation (23) the DP *the boys* will appropriately bind the anaphor *each other* in the emboldened DP, thereby satisfying Binding Condition A.

And finally, Lebeaux (2009: xv–xvi) argues that the binding difference between (18a) and (24) "poses a conundrum, which . . . goes to the heart of the grammar."

(18a)   *John* seems to *himself* to like cheese.

(24)   *Which pictures of *John* does *he* like?

The daunting problem putatively posed by (18a) and (24) lies in the fact that the binding relations in (18a) are not captured in the logical representation for (18a) (see (18b)), whereas the binding relations in (24) do fall out of its logical representation (see (25)). (Note that in (25) the emboldened DP remains visible for discourse interpretation because this DP has SM content – it receives Case.)

(25)   [which pictures of *John* [does *he* like **which picture of John**]]

As we can see, the logical representation in (25) has a Binding Condition C violation. So it would appear that the illicit binding relations in (24) can be explained in terms of the logical representation given for (24). Lebeaux's conundrum, however, is a spurious one. For us, the fact that the coreferential relations in (24) are expressed at the level of LF is merely coincidental with the fact that the discourse representation for (24) is the same as its logical representation – both representations are (25). From our perspective, Lebeaux misses a crucial point about (18a) and (24): that is, the coreferentiality relations in these two examples are a matter of discourse representation, not of logical representation. Looked at from our perspective, there are no noteworthy differences between (18a) and (24) at all; they are business as usual, at least in terms of binding relations. If these examples do go "to the heart of the grammar," what they tell us is that a single syntactic representation must be able to be seen (and interpreted) by the performance systems in more than one way – as is the case in Survive-minimalism.

Support for our discourse analysis of binding relations comes from the surprising differences between (26) and (27), differences that are surprising because the examples seem to have very similar structures. These examples, however, follow naturally from our analysis of discourse representations. Our analysis of (26) and (27) goes as follows: example (26), which has syntactic representation (28a), will have discourse representation (28b) in which the emboldened anaphor will not be visible since it has no SM content checked in its concatenation.

(26)   *Mary expects *each other* to seem to *the women* to be unhappy.

(27)   Mary expects *each other*'s friends to seem to *the women* to be unhappy.

(28)   a. Mary expects [*each other* to seem to *the women* [***each other*** to be unhappy]]
       b. Mary expects [*each other* to seem to *the women* [to be unhappy]]

Of note, in discourse representation (28b), the anaphor is structurally superior to its antecedent *the women*, so it cannot be bound by its antecedent; hence the anaphor cannot be given a discourse interpretation, in violation of Binding Condition A (which accounts for the ungrammaticality of (26)). On the other hand, (27) has syntactic representation (29), which is also the discourse representation for (27) because the anaphor in the emboldened DP has SM content (it has a <CASE> feature that has been checked) and, therefore, must be visible for discourse interpretation.

(29)   Mary expects [*each other*'s friends to seem to *the women* [***each other*'s friends** to be unhappy]]

In (29), the anaphor is properly bound by the antecedent *the women*; as a result, the anaphor does receive a discourse interpretation. Importantly, the differences between (26) and (27), which cannot be explained under Lebeaux's analysis of coreferentiality, can be accounted for under our analysis.

Some other supportive data for our analysis of coreferentiality and discourse representation come from the data in (30) and (31).

(30)   a. *The Smiths'* mothers seem to *them* to be in trouble.
       b. *Each other*'s fathers seem to *them* to be in trouble.

(31)   **The Smiths'* mothers and *each other*'s fathers seem to *them* to be in trouble.

What needs to be explained is why (30a) and (30b) are well-formed constructions, while (31), formed by conjoining parts of (30a) and (30b), is not well formed. Under our analysis, although (30a) and (30b) both are well formed, they receive discourse interpretations in quite different and incompatible ways. The well-formedness of (30a) follows from the fact that the emboldened DP ***the Smiths' mothers*** in (32a) is invisible for discourse interpretation because this DP does not check any SM feature in its concatenation and, as we have noted, a DP that does not check any SM features in a given concatenation is not visible for Binding Condition C computations (and neither are the constituents of the DP); as a result, the DP ***the Smiths'*** is not able to be bound by the pronoun *them* and no violation of Binding Condition C emerges. On the other hand, (30b) is well formed because in the discourse representation for (30b), given in (32b), the emboldened DP is visible since it contains a reciprocal DP ***each other*'s** that has its Case feature checked and, therefore, it will be available to be bound by the pronoun *them*.

(32)   a. [*The Smiths'* mothers seem to *them* [[(***the Smiths' mothers***)] to be in trouble]]
       b. [*Each other*'s fathers seem to *them* [[*each other*'s father] to be in trouble]]

Given that (30a) and (30b) have incompatible conditions on discourse interpretation, there is no way to satisfy both of these conditions when we conjoin (30a) and (30b) as in (31). Hence, (31) cannot have a discourse representation in which all the DPs receive interpretations that comply with Binding Theory.

Repeating Lebeaux (2009: xvi), we agree that binding relations go "to the heart of the grammar." What we find, though, when we get to this heart is an FL that looks like (1) and that has the Survive-minimalist CS described in this book.

6.4   Scope, Survive-style

The design of a purely derivational syntax along the lines of Survive-minimalism sketched out here not only offers a compelling account of the binding relations investigated in the previous section, but it can also explain other semantic phenomena, such as scopal relations, in a parsimonious and uniform manner. As a matter of fact, Lechner (2009, 2010) argues that a Survive-minimalist account of scopal phenomena is conceptually superior to the explanations provided by other Minimalist models (particularly with regard to how Survive-minimalism compares with attract-based models). Building on the fundamental tenets of the Survive Principle, as originally proposed in Stroik (1999) and subsequently revised in Putnam (2007) and Stroik (2009a), Lechner shows that the "movement" of scope-bearing constituents takes place in the form of a push-driven chain, i.e., in repulsion fashion, rather than being attracted by a higher head (or, more appropriately, feature on a head): he uses the "Survive" concept of feature incompatibility, which he defines as *Type Driven Interpretation* (TDI) in (33), to derive scopal relations.

(33)   Type Driven Interpretation (TDI)
       If a node α is type incompatible, move α to the next higher position type compatible with α.

(34)   a.   A node α is type compatible iff the denotation of α and its sister can be combined by the principles of semantic composition (Function Application, Predicate Modification, etc. . .).
       b. α is *type incompatible* otherwise.

Lechner provides evidence for how a Survive-based analysis of quantifier raising (QR) is superior to attract-based models of Minimalism that employ a variant of the Minimal Link Condition (MLC) (cf. Chomsky 1995). His evidence comes from examples involving inverse linking and multiple instances of QR. Consider the following examples (from Lechner 2010: 19):

(35)   [$_{QP1}$ Two policemen spy on [$_{QP2}$ someone from [$_{QP3}$ every city]]]
       a. $2 > \forall > \exists$ (inverse linking; wide scope for subject)
       b. $\forall > \exists > 2$ (inverse linking; narrow scope for subject)
       c. $\forall > 2 > \exists$ (inverse linking; intermediate scope for subject)

As Lechner observes, what is not immediately clear is why the scope reading associated with the string in (35c) is not possible. To explain (35c), Lechner shows (2010: Section 5.2) that QR as TDI in a Survive-model can affect sub-portions of the tree (composed in the WorkBench) before being integrated into the primary derivation. Lechner argues that this sort of sub-derivational approach driven by TDI requirements is motivated by the insertion of the predicate (*spy on*), which is followed by the object thereafter appearing to the left of the base position of the subject. Prior to the displacement of the object, Survive-based TDI takes place within [$_{QP2}$ *someone from every city*].

Lechner asserts that TDI within a Survive-based treatment of QR is superior to an attract-based version of scope interpretations. Such attract-based systems compute precedence of operations on the basis of a notice of "closeness" like the MLC (Chomsky 1995). Lechner (2010: 21) demonstrates this with the tree structures in (36) below; as shown in (36a), "the two quantifiers *every city₃* and *two policemen₁* are equidistant to the root node – both are separated from the root by a single segment. If distance is alternatively measured in terms of complete containment within a category, then *every city₃* is even closer to the root than the subject, because the former is only dominated by one of a multi-segment category, whereas both *v*P segments dominate *two policemen₁*":

(36)   a. Subsequent to movement of inversely linked QP (*every city*)
        [$_{vP}$ someone$_2$ every city$_3$ someone$_2$ from t$_3$ [$_{vP}$ two policemen$_1$]]
        (Two policemen spy on someone from every city)
    b. Move subject to closest landing site ($*\forall > 2 > \exists$)
        [$_{\alpha P}$ every city$_3$ [$_{vP}$ two policemen$_1$ [$_{vP}$ someone$_2$ t$_3$ someone$_2$ from t$_3$
        [$_{vP}$ t$_1$]]]]

In (36b), the subject does not qualify as the closest node to the root, thus creating a substantial problem for an attract-based analysis of this structure that is based on the MLC: (36b) fails to exclude the unattested scope order inverse linked QP > subject > container. As we have argued throughout this book, we no longer make reference to "movement" in Survive-minimalism, reducing displacement to instances of iterative Copy-Operations. In a similar fashion to our discussions of interpreting syntactic representations in Sections 6.2 and 6.3, the multiple instances of QR must appear in multiple structural positions in order for the C-I module to properly calculate the licit scope reading(s). The SM module simply needs to see the final instance of the Copy-Operation responsible for checking the Case feature (which is in this instance the highest feature in the FM in the subject *two policemen₁*). In a Survive-minimalist model, the intermediate "landing sites", i.e., licit domains for Copy-Operations to take place, are omnipresent at the edge of every successful concatenation of LIs. Following Lechner's arguments that an attract-based account of QR, which is commonly upheld in "mainstream" variants of the Minimalist Program, fails to exclude the inverse linked QP > subject > container, whereas the Survive-minimalist account provides a clear-cut explanation for such phenomena. Although the interested reader is referred to Lechner (2009, 2010) for a more detailed treatment of scope phenomena within a Survive-minimalist framework, this brief exegesis of Lechner's work highlights the conceptual advantages that Survive-minimalism has over traditional attract-based syntactic analyses when it comes to explaining scopal relationships.

6.5   Syntax-semantic mapping issues

Ott (2010: 102) has recently argued that crash-proof syntax is plagued by an essential flaw in that such models, including ours and Adger's (2008), commonly place "the mistaken 'Fregean intuition' of predicate saturation" at the very center of their crash-proof design. That is, as Ott notes, models of crash-proof syntax "are designed to block 'overgeneration'" (2010: 97) by encoding the argument structure of predicates into the lexical structure of these predicates. For Ott, there are substantial problems with introducing any such lexical constraints into syntactic computations. One of these problems is that it is seemingly not possible to determine (or circumscribe) the argument structure of predicates, as is illustrated in (37) and (38), where the verbs *kick* and *buy* have a multiplicity of argument structures.

(37) a. The baby kicked.
      b. John kicked Bill.
      c. John kicked the ball to Mary.
      d. John got a kick out of the new *Spawn of Possession* record.

(38) a. John bought the book.
      b. John bought Mary the book.
      c. John bought Mary the book for twelve dollars.

The indeterminacy of the argument structure for any given predicate, as Ott argues, compromises the ability of crash-proof models to employ lexical constraints on argument structure to regulate syntactic computations. Furthermore, any attempt to deal with the multiple argument structures of the verbs in (37) and (38) by allowing each instance of these verbs to have distinct argument structures would, according to Ott, bring "massive redundancy into the lexicon" (2010: 96) by requiring there to be multiple lexical forms of every predicate in any given language.

The second problem with encoding argument structure into LIs, as Ott asserts, is that predicates with more than one internal argument, as in (37c) and (38b), would have to structure their lexical features hierarchically in order to be able to project this hierarchical information into syntactic structure. But having LIs with hierarchical features would, from Ott's perspective, encumber LIs with "unwanted complexity."

Needless to say, we strongly disagree with Ott's assessment of crash-proof grammars, even though we also agree with him that in our version of crash-proof grammar, LEX permits redundancy and complexity. What we have been arguing is that it is exactly this lexical redundancy and complexity that has allowed modern human language, with its structured syntax, to emerge from protolanguage. Under our analysis, hierarchical features are not an "unwanted complexity" imposed on lexical items; on the contrary, as Tallerman (2009) and Müller (2010) show, there are compelling reasons to assume that lexical features are hierarchically organized. So, incorporating hierarchically defined category (and thematic) relations into a hierarchically organized FM does not produce any orthogonal complexity at all. But even more to the point of our analysis, the consequence of having "complex" FMs, as we have defined them, is that syntax becomes a lexical spandrel. That is, syntax comes for free; there are no syntactic operations, no syntactic units (such as phases or prolific domains), and no interfaces (or rules that Transfer material to interfaces). Syntactic relations, for us, are the by-products of interconnecting lexical (feature-based) relations. As we have argued in this book, the complexity that is "unwanted" is not the contained and limited complexity of having hierarchical features, but the uncontained and expansive complexity of syntactic relations. By reducing syntactic relations to lexical relations, we have made grammar not more complex, as Ott charges, but maximally simple.

But what about Ott's other criticism that a crash-proof grammar might have "massive redundancy" in LEX by requiring LIs to have multiple FMs (to accommodate the multiple argument structures)? Let us agree, for argument's sake, that an LI could have multiple FMs. Just how "massive" would such redundancy actually be? Well, given that predicates rarely, if ever, have more than four arguments, this would mean that LEX could be up to three or four times as large as it would be if every LI had only one FM. Now, we do not deny that allowing this sort of redundancy is not ideal; however, a redundancy of magnitude-4 is also not a massive cognitive load. To see a cognitive load that is actually massive, consider Ott's analysis of the variable argument structures that appear in (37) and in (38). Ott handles the data in (37) and (38) by adopting Pietroski's (2005, 2006, 2008, forthcoming) theory that all LIs are monadic predicates and all concatenations of LIs are predicate conjunctions. Under this analysis, merging two LIs, say α and β, is not a matter of satisfying selection needs of a single predicate; rather, it involves concatenating/merging together two monadic predicates Concat (α, β) and translating this concatenation into a conjunctive semantic form $\|\alpha\| \, \& \, \|\beta\|$ that will then instruct the C-I performance system how to construct neo-Davidsonian event structures.[8] Although Ott's (2010: 102) Pietroskian assumption that "LIs have no Fregean adicity" does neatly circumvent the problem of explaining the variable argument structures seen in (37) and (38), it does so at a huge cost. If all LIs are monadic predicates and, therefore, have no selectional restrictions that limit their concatenability, then any given LI can concatenate (or merge) freely with any other LI, or with any concatenation of LIs. It then becomes possible to concatenate the verb *kick* with any random set of LIs, as in (39).

(39)   a.   *With kick why.
       b.   *The man the woman John kick the door the car.

Having this sort of blind concatenation is deeply problematic for the same reason that having blind NUMs is – it leads to massive overgeneration of syntactic structure. In fact, it leads to unbounded and unprincipled combinations of randomly selected LIs that will have to be filtered by the C-I and SM performance systems, or perhaps be processed and then left as uninterpretable by the performance systems. As we have argued in Chapter 2 and Chapter 3, the effort it would take to process unboundedly many unusable concatenation would be substantial (it is important to recognize that very few randomly concatenated LIs will produce strings that will be usable by the performance systems). Despite Ott's claim to the contrary, the cognitive effort it would take to learn multiple FMs for LIs is not massive, especially when compared with the cognitive load of processing freely concatenated monadic predicates, few con-catenations of which will be interpretable by the performance systems.

While we reject Pietroski's (and Ott's) monadic analysis of LIs, we do find several of Pietroski's claims about LIs to be interesting and deserving of com-ment. For one, as Pietroski (2008: 13) observes,

I have suggested that a better point of departure, for purposes of explanation, is that open class lexical items are semantically monadic. From this perspective, lexical items efface conceptual distinctions, thereby making it possible to treat recursive combination of expressions as a sign of monadic predicate conjunction. This conception of semantic composition helps explain the otherwise very puzzling fact that lexical items are mas-sively monadic. I have also speculated that this conception of lexicalization may help explain why humans have concepts that combine so rapidly and easily.

It does seem that an extensive number of LIs are monadic – so why should this be the case? The answer to this question, we believe, is not, as Pietroski suggests, because all LIs necessarily are monadic, but because modern human language has evolved from protolanguage, in which all LIs (according to Searle 2010) stood as monadic events. That modern human languages continue to have LIs that are monadic reflects the origins of language. The rapid development of modern human language (some 100,000 years ago) has depended, as we have argued, on the emergence of lexical CATegory features, which would allow LIs to be non-monadic. If, on the other hand, LIs have always been and will always be monadic predicates, then it is not clear what minor change in the protolan-guage could have triggered the rapid development of human language. In fact, under Pietroski's analysis, protolanguage and modern human language would be much the same syntactically – each possessing monadic LIs that could concatenate freely. The difference between these two language systems must, therefore, reside in how the syntactic concatenations could be processed by the performance systems. But is it likely that the protolanguage would have had a modern syntax that produced output it just could not use, and our ancestors had to find a way to use this already-available output? And what would the minor adjustment to the performance systems be that allowed syntactic output to become interpretable and that allowed modern human language to evolve rapidly? Until plausible answers are given to these questions, we find the biolinguistic scenario necessary to support Pietroski's monadic analysis of LIs to be extremely improbable.

Another observation that Pietroski makes about LIs we think is interesting is that concatenating LIs conjoins them. In Pietroski's semantic system, the interpretation of any given concatenation involving α and β (Concat (α, β)) is $\|\alpha\|$ & $\|\beta\|$; that is, it is the conjunction of the semantic values of α and β. The reason for this, according to Pietroski (2006: 2), is that "concatenation signifies conjunction." That concatenating two constituents should be interpreted as conjoining them is seemingly plausible, since concatenation and conjunction both appear to do the same thing: bring constituents together. We, however, reject the seemingly plausible "concatenation signifies conjunction" hypothesis. As we have argued in Chapter 5, conjunction is a terminating operation, not a combining one (for us, the combinative effects of conjunction emerge from the structural requirements of the terminated/stranded constituent). While we agree in the main with Pietroski that the semantic interpretation of Concat (α, β) is $\|\alpha\|$ & $\|\beta\|$, we propose that the conjunction operation functions to isolate interpretable predicates. Once the C-I performance system reads β and identifies it as a predicate (which is the sort of predicate that this performance system can interpret), it closes off its reading of β with the conjunction operation, and continues its reading of the concatenation by reading α; that is, after it completes its reading of one concatenation, it closes the concatenation off (with the conjunction operation) and moves on to the next concatenation.

So, our Survive-minimalist framework can accommodate Pietroski's conjunctivist semantics – but it can also build neo-Davidsonian event structures. To see this, let us consider the neo-Davidsonian interpretation for (40), where (41) is an informal interpretation of (40) and (42) is a formal interpretation of (40) – note that we take (40)–(42) from Pietroski (2006: 1–2).

(40) Pat hugged Chris quickly.

(41) there was something such that it was done by Pat, *and* it was a hugging, *and* it happened to Chris, *and* it was quick.

(42) $\exists x$ [Agent (x, Pat) & Hugging (x) & Theme (x, Chris) & Quick (x)][9]

There are three core facts about conjunctivist, neo-Davidsonian representation (42) that are especially noteworthy. First, each of the conjuncts is a predicate able to be given a semantic value in and of itself. Hence, the conjunct **Agent (x, Pat)** will be true if and only if **(for some x) Pat is the Agent of x**. Second, the constituents in (40) are represented semantically within individual conjuncts in (42). And third, the semantic representation given for (40) in (42) does not invoke predicational adicity (or saturation). Importantly, Survive-minimalism is actually compatible with the crucial assumptions and the core facts of this semantics. One very significant way in which Survive-minimalism aligns closely with conjunctivist semantics is in its focus on concatenations. Throughout this book, we have argued that the computational mechanisms used in Survive-minimalism produce interpretable concatenations and that they produce these concatenations without any appeal to predicational relations (recall that we subscribe to Hinzen's 2009a, 2009b and Reuland's 2009 arguments that the syntax creates semantic relations, which requires that these latter relations, including what look like traditional predicational relations, not already be pre-encoded into syntactic computations; that is, predicational adicity cannot be involved in forming concatenations). Hence, given the design of Survive-minimalism, the semantic interpretation of syntactic representations must provide values for concatenations without regard for traditional predicationality – just as Pietroski claims in his conjunctivist semantics. For Survive-minimalism, semantic interpretations are built compositely over the interpretations of each separate and self-contained concatenation, i.e., conjunctively. To see this, consider how we build a semantic interpretation for (4) from its SD (given in (5)). Once we put the parts of the interpretation together (as in (6)), we build a composite semantic interpretation of (4) that would align with a conjunctivist, neo-Davidsonian semantics, as in (43).

(4)   Chris will hire Pat.

(5)   a. [Pat]
      b. [hire [Pat]]
      c. [Chris [hire [Pat]]]
      d. [will [Chris [hire [Pat]]]]
      e. [Chris [will [Chris [hire [Pat]]]]]

(6)   a. $\|Pat\| = p$ (an individual)
      b. $\|hire\ Pat\| = PATIENT\ (hire, p)$
      c. $\|Chris\ hire\ Pat\| = AGENT\ (hire, c)$, where $\|Chris\| = c$
      d. $\|will\ Chris\ hire\ Pat\| = FUTURE\ (hire)$

(43) $\exists x\ [Hire\ (x)\ \&\ PATIENT\ (x, Chris)\ \&\ AGENT\ (x, Pat)\ \&\ FUTURE\ (x)]$

By building semantic representations piecemeal from the SD (concatenation by concatenation), Survive-minimalism produces a conjunctivist semantics, as we can observe in (43), that yields neo-Davidsonian interpretations, which have conjoined predicates that are defined by performance system features (PSFs). In other words, under our analysis, the CS builds SDs that are driven by interpretation-ready PSFs and, subsequently, the performance systems read the derivational output (i.e., syntactic representations). For the C-I performance system, this reading includes interpreting the concatenations that comprise syntactic representations as conjoined PSF-defined predicates.

6.6   Conclusion

This chapter has investigated the question of what happens to syntactic representations when they are used by the performance systems. Since this question is actually peripheral to our core arguments (which are about the structural design of FL and not about the computational and interpretative processes that transpire within the design), we do not pursue the question of how the performance systems handle syntactic representations in much detail. We have attempted, though, to give broad insights into a few of the interpretative processes (in particular, binding relations, scopal relations, and the formation of semantic representations) that await syntactic representations when they are used by the performance systems; and we have emphasized the role that Survive-minimalism plays in these interpretative processes.

7 Conclusions and challenges

7.1   General conclusions

Our version of Survive-minimalism departs from standard Minimalism in two essential ways: in the overall design of the Faculty of Language (FL) and in the computational mechanisms that generate the structures of language. The design differences are particularly dramatic ones. Unlike standard Minimalism (see Chomsky 1995, 2005, 2009), which assumes that the Narrow Syntax (which includes the Lexicon/Numeration and the computational system (CS)) is extrinsic to the Conceptual-Intentional (C-I) and the Sensorimotor (SM) performance systems and must have its derivational output somehow brought into "interface" with the performance systems, Survive-minimalism situates the Narrow Syntax within the performance systems. Given that the protolanguage, as Hornstein (2009) and Reuland (2009) argue, resides within the performance systems, it seems much more plausible that the language faculty that has developed out of protolanguage would remain in these systems, as Survive-minimalism proposes, than that the language faculty would build a completely new biolinguistic system (the Narrow Syntax) that is, on the one hand, extraneous to the performance systems but, on the other hand, must still meet the interface conditions imposed on the output of this new system by the old performance systems, as standard Minimalism proposes. The fact that standard Minimalism requires substantial evolutionary engineering to build both a performance-system-extraneous Narrow Syntax and the conduits to connect the Narrow Syntax with the performance system would argue strongly against the design of standard Minimalism, especially in the face of Hornstein's (2009) observation that the rapid development of human language from protolanguage severely limits the bioengineering required for human language to emerge. Survive-minimalism, then, has the conceptual advantage of reducing the engineering requirement for human language to develop. Not only do the aforementioned design differences tell divergent biolinguistic tales, they also yield radically dissimilar derivational outputs. In the Minimalist framework developed by Chomsky (2005, 2009), Boeckx (2008a, 2008b, 2009), and Epstein and Seely (2006), among others, the Narrow Syntax can generate derivational output that cannot be interpreted by the performance systems – this unusable output is said to "crash." Frampton and Gutmann (2002), Hinzen (2006), Stroik (1999, 2009a), López (2007, 2009), and Putnam (2010) have argued, however, that the Narrow Syntax must be "crash-proof" to reduce the processing demands on the linguistic systems (Stroik has contended, in particular, that crash-ready analyses of syntax would yield few, if any, usable derivations). Although there have been several arguments for the desirability of a crash-proof syntax (see the references noted above), none of these arguments have been able to make a case for the conceptual necessity of having a crash-proof syntax. We believe that our version of Survive-minimalism does make this case, in a simple and direct fashion. By positioning the Narrow Syntax squarely within the performance systems, Survive-minimalism uses only performance system simplex objects (lexical material) and performance system operations (the Copy operation) to produce performance system complex objects (structured lexical material). Under Survive-minimalist assumptions, all the syntactic objects derived by the CS of human language will necessarily be contained in, and usable by, the performance systems. That is, the Narrow Syntax of human language not only *should* be crash-proof (as Stroik 1999, 2009a, Frampton and Gutmann 2002, Hinzen 2006, and Putnam 2010 maintain), it *must* be crash-proof.

The second way that Survive-minimalism differs from standard Minimalism has to do with the mechanisms each uses to compute syntactic structure. Standard Minimalism employs several types of operations to build syntactic structure: a Copy operation that reproduces lexical material from the Lexicon (LEX) and places it in short-term memory (in the Numeration (NUM)); an External Merge operation that moves the material from NUM and places this material in a syntactic derivation (SD); an Internal Merge operation that takes constituents out of an SD, makes a copy of these constituents, places the copied material back into the derivation (replacing the removed constituents), and then places/moves the extracted constituents to a new structural position; Agreement operations that allow the features from a constituent in the SD to read back through the structure to look for matching features that are still active (see López 2007 and Hornstein 2009 for constraints on the agreement operation); a Transfer operation that removes sections of an SD and ships these sections off to the performance system interfaces for interpretation; and some sort of Recompilation operation that reconnects the transferred structural material into a single structural unit at the interfaces, for another round of interpretation. Of particular note here is the fact that much of the computation machinery just described is required because the Narrow Syntax in standard Minimalism resides outside the performance systems, and the output of the Narrow Syntax must be imported into the performance systems. Compared with standard Minimalism, Survive-minimalism has negligible computational machinery. In fact, it has only one operation: the Copy operation. In Survive-minimalism, the Copy operation reproduces lexical material from LEX and introduces this material into NUM, and it also brings recopied material from the NUM to the SD. No other operations are required in Survive-minimalism to build syntactic structure, or to prepare it for interpretation.

7.2   Specific challenges

Although there have been numerous investigations of biolinguistics within the Minimalist Program over the last ten years (see, for example, Jenkins 2000; Boeckx 2006, 2008b; Hornstein 2009; Hinzen 2006, 2009a, 2009b; Bickerton 2009, 2010; Reuland 2009; and Chomsky 2000, 2005, 2009, among others), and although all of these investigations give a passing nod to the importance of Turing's Thesis (that the structural design of systems must obey physical and mathematical laws), these studies have, by and large, ignored the structural design of human language. These studies have paid significant attention to identifying the components of language – settling on a Lexicon, a computational system, a Sensorimotor performance system, and a Conceptual-Intentional performance system; however, they have not examined in much serious detail how these components must be inter-structured to meet thresholds of simplicity, generality, naturalness, and beauty, as well as of biological and conceptual necessity. In this book, we have taken on Turing's Challenge. We have argued that the Narrow Syntax – LEX and the CS – must reside, for reasons of conceptual necessity, within the performance systems. As simple as this novel design is, it provides, as we have demonstrated throughout this book, radical new insights into what the language faculty is and how language emerged in the species. We have called our design of language *Survive-minimalism*.

This book is a sequel to Stroik's (1999, 2009a) work on the Survive Principle and its extensions in Putnam (2007), Putnam and Stroik (2009, 2010), and Stroik and Putnam (2005, 2009), which use a reconceptualization of NUM to simplify the CS of human language. Here we go well beyond the early work on the Survive-minimalist framework. Instead of trying to answer one question (how can the CS be maximally simplified?), we have attempted to resolve a rash of problems and challenges – those given in (1)–(8) and in (A)–(C).

(1) What is the knowledge or Faculty of Language? (Humboldt's Problem)
(2) How is this knowledge or FL acquired? (Plato's Problem)
(3) How is this knowledge put to use? (Descartes's Problem)
(4) How is this knowledge implemented in the brain? (Broca's Problem)
(5) How did this knowledge emerge in the species? (Darwin's Problem)
(6) How could the evolution of language occur in an abbreviated time span? (Hornstein's Challenge)

(7) What is the optimal structural design of FL? (Turing's Challenge)

(8) What is the optimal CS for FL? (Galileo's Challenge)

(A) How does the CS initialize? (Reuland's Challenge)

(B) How does the CS sustain? (Boeckx's Challenge)

(C) How does the CS succeed? (Hinzen's Challenge)

Needless to say, each one of the problems and challenges in (1)–(8) is theoretically substantial and is individually deserving of serious investigation. We, however, have bundled all the questions raised in (1)–(8) and in (A)–(C) and we have pursued a unified analysis of human language able to answer all of them. Importantly, the above questions, we have argued in this book, are interconnected to the question posed by Turing's Challenge: what is the optimal structural design of FL? Answering this latter question is crucial to understanding the FL because it will identify the components of FL and their interrelations, which will subsequently provide insight into the essential nature of what language is, how it has biolinguistically developed, and how it works. Our investigations into the FL, consequently, focus predominantly on Turing's Challenge.

We have approached Turing's Challenge by minimizing both the ontological components of FL and, more significantly, their relations. Following Chomsky (1995), we have assumed that the minimal components in FL include: a LEX containing simplex lexical material in long-term memory; a NUM containing lexical material, copied from the long-term memory to the short-term memory, which will be used to construct complex lexical material; a CS that concatenates lexical material in NUM to construct complex lexical material, and two performance systems (a C-I system and an SM system) that interpret the "meaning" and the "form" of both the simplex and the complex lexical material. It should be readily apparent that from an ontological perspective Survive-minimalism is a version of standard Minimalism. Where Survive-minimalism differs radically from standard Minimalism, though, is in the way it structures the ontological components. For standard Minimalism (see Chomsky 1995, 2005, 2009), all the components are standalone components that are separate from the others, each with its own internal operating system. This means that all the lexical information shared by these separate components must be carried from component to component. Hence, having separate components actually multiplies the ontologies required for FL because not only must there be the components in FL, but there must also be component-to-component couriers in FL. However, expanding ontologies is only one of the substantial problems that arise for the standard Minimalist design of FL. A second problem is the biolinguistic justification problem. If, say, the CS is a system that is completely separated from the performance systems, how and why would it ever evolve? And how would such a complex, separate system ever evolve within the very narrow temporal parameters that Hornstein places on language development? (As Hornstein observes, FL develops rather quickly in the species; therefore this evolutionary development cannot include any major system-building, such as the building of a CS.) Third, if the system components can be as separate as assumed in standard Minimalism, it becomes conceptually possible for these systems to have redundancies and inconsistencies. Brody (2002) makes the case that the performance systems and the CS in standard Minimalism have redundancies in that both have to form chains; and Frampton and Gutmann (2002) make the case that standard Minimalism has an incompatibility between the CS and the performance systems and that this incompatibility produces crashes. Needless to say, the sorts of redundancies and inconsistencies we see in the standard Minimalism model suggest that the design of this model is hardly optimal.

We have argued in this book that we can avoid the design problems noted above if we assume that LEX, NUM, and the CS are contained within, rather than separate from, the performance systems. Under this assumption, all the system components will necessarily be compatible and they will be able to share lexical information with the use of a single Copy operation. Such a design for FL will be redundancy-free, crash-proof, and biolinguistically constructible. If, to meet Turing's Challenge and Galileo's Challenge, language-theoretic optimality requires maximized simplicity and generality, as well as minimized computational effort, then Survive-minimalism is the optimal design for FL.

Under Survive-minimalist assumptions, FL is a biological system, located at the intersection of the C-I and the SM performance systems, that computes complex structures from simplex lexical material. Using this system involves mastering lexical features and their hierarchical organization (as expressed in feature matrices (FMs)). Once FMs for simplex LIs are acquired, these FMs (and not the LIs themselves) are used to compute complex structures in the following way: the CS operates on FMs, structurally projecting the highest unchecked/unmatched hierarchical feature, so the initial LI brought into the CS will project its highest unchecked feature. In the next derivational step, the initial projected feature must be checked for concatenative integrity by a matching feature from another syntactic object, which will be Copied to the SD from the NUM/WorkBench and which will, in the Copying process, build another syntactic structure that will project the highest unchecked hierarchical feature available in the derivation. Subsequent derivational steps will proceed as described above until all the concatenative features of all LIs in NUM have been appropriately checked. At this point, the derivation ends and its crash-proof output (a representation) is ready to be interpreted by the performance systems (see Chapter 4 for an extended discussion of these computational processes). This CS, we have contended, has no need for any of the mechanisms exogamous to the performance systems that we see in standard Minimalism (such as the Phase Impenetrability Condition or the Transfer operation); it is a maximally simple CS that meets Reuland's Challenge, Boeckx's Challenge, and Hinzen's Challenge.

In this book we have further argued that not only does Survive-minimalism provide the optimal design for FL, but it also offers an explanation for how modern human language could have evolved (in a relatively short time span) from a protolanguage. In Survive-minimalism, all the components of FL are "old" components available for use by the protolanguage. This is certainly true of LEX in long-term memory, NUM in short-term memory, and the performance systems; however, it is also true of the CS, which in Survive-minimalism consists of a single operation (Copy-to-Domain) that is not an operation unique to FL. Hence, the protolanguage would have exactly the same system components that FL has and it would putatively have structured these components in the same arrangement that exists in FL. That is, given Survive-minimalist assumptions, the protolanguage should be virtually the same as FL. So what is the difference between the two language systems? As we have argued, the evolutionary development that produced FL is a seemingly small adjustment to the features expressed in a feature matrix. It is the development of CATegory and SUBcategory features, absent in the protolanguage, which dramatically shifted the way language could be computed – from symbolic, non-recursive derivations (in the protolanguage) to non-symbolic, recursive derivations (in FL). Hence, although both the protolanguage and FL could produce complex structures from simplex lexical material, only FL could unboundedly produce such structures. If this is correct, then we have a rather straightforward answer to Hornstein's Challenge: FL could have developed from the protolanguage in a compressed time span because the evolutionary development definitive of FL was systemically a minor one (but one that had profound computational effects).

The final challenge we want to revisit here is Kinsella's Challenge. As we have mentioned in the first chapter of this book, Kinsella (2009: 36) raises the question, "Is the minimalist language faculty evolvable?" By focusing on a single Minimalist assumption – that FL is a "perfect" solution to interface conditions – Kinsella argues against minimalist designs of FL: as she contends, language is an adaptive system and adaptive systems are not perfect. There is little doubt that the imperfections that Kinsella (2009: 63) attributes to biological systems (redundancies, vestiges, and inefficiencies) all show up in human language. We can see large-scale redundancy in agreement systems of language that mark agreement relations on multiple constituents, as in the example *Er war gestern gegangen*, which has subject-verb agreement marked on the subject and on the verb; we find vestiges of a very old expressive system, according to Pinker (2007), in our responses to strong emotional or physical experiences (*ouch, damn*); and we have inefficiencies in language, readily apparent in the limitations of our short-term memory, which allow us to forget the exact details of what we have just said almost immediately. So, Kinsella appears to be correct in asserting that the human language system falls short of perfection. Her arguments make it clear that FL cannot be operationally perfect, that FL is a biological system that cannot achieve anything like systemic perfection. Designs of FL grounded in operational perfection, then, are doomed to failure – among these failures, Kinsella concludes, is Chomsky's version of Minimalism. But what about Survive-minimalism; is it evolvable or it is too yet another Minimalist failure? Since Survive-minimalism is not committed to operational perfection, this version of Minimalism would seem to avoid Kinsella's noose. The reason we come to this conclusion is that the hallmark of Survive-minimalism is not the assumption that FL is the perfect solution to interface conditions; rather, it is the assumption that all animal communications systems perfectly depend on having an overlap of C-I and SM performance systems. Without this necessary overlap, aligning the form and meaning of a message would be at best accidental and communication would be virtually impossible. Whether the communicants are ants, bees, birds, dolphins, or human beings, they all have overlapping performance systems that ensure communication. The types of information these overlapping performance systems contain will, of course, vary from species to species, although the essential design of communication systems will not vary. In this way, Survive-minimalism is not a theory of how human language became "perfect" – instead, it is a theory of how changes in the performance systems of humans have allowed the modern human language system to emerge from its predecessor (proto-) language system.

The challenges this book pursues are substantial ones, but the challenges left behind are equally daunting. Although this book looks at the design of the faculty of language through the lens of conceptual necessity (thereby taking on Turing's Challenge), it does not attempt to investigate in any significant detail the empirical consequences of the conceptual design we propose, nor does it probe in any depth the content or structure of the two performance systems that stand at the heart of the faculty of language. Needless to say, both of these omissions need to be addressed in the future. Questions of empirical coverage, though in many ways irrelevant to the conceptual foundations of the faculty of language, should be pressed forward to demonstrate (as well as to examine) the legitimacy of these conceptual foundations. We will in future work consider such questions and we encourage others to do so, too. And of course, a great deal of work remains to be done on our understanding of the Conceptual-Intentional and Sensorimotor performance systems. Even though some of the research in Relevance Theory, starting with Sperber and Wilson (1986), has investigated the role that syntax plays in computing cognitive effects and even though the recent research in the Theory of Mind (see Baron-Cohen 1995) has opened up new ways of looking at the biological underpinnings of perceived intentionality, we still have a limited understanding of the performance systems. The more we unravel the inner workings of the performance systems, the more we will expose the dynamic processes contained within these systems that give rise to the Faculty of Language.

Notes

CHAPTER 1 THE BIOLINGUISTIC TURN

1 Although Kinsella argues against "perfection" in evolutionary biology, she does recognize that there can be perfection in the physical world, as in the petal-patterns of flowers. She does not, however, connect evolution-formed organisms (flowers) to physical output (petal-patterns), as we are doing. She is willing to bracket off physics from biology. Adopting Turing's Thesis, we are not willing to separate physics and biology the way Kinsella, who embraces adaptationist theories of evolution, does. In fact, our constraint-based views of biological development follow the evolutionary developmental (evo devo) theories advanced by Dawkins (2009) and by Fodor and Piattelli-Palmarini (2010), among others.

2 We are factoring out performance errors, such as slips-of-the-tongue or the manufactured oddities that are (at times, playfully) generated by, among others, poets, linguists, and second-language speakers. As Chomsky has argued, these sorts of errors involve processes outside the Faculty of Language.

3 There is some dispute about the Theory of Mind possessed by nonhuman great apes. Fitch (2010) asserts that nonhuman great apes have only a basic Theory of Mind; and Ramachandran (2011:128) takes a similar position, noting that "This ability to entertain a theory of mind may exist in great apes in rudimentary form, but we humans are exceptionally good at it." Recently, however, Yamamoto, Humle, and Tanaka (2012) have argued that chimpanzees have a rather developed Theory of Mind in which they "can understand conspecifics' goals and demonstrate advanced targeted helping."

4 Ott (2009: 256) formalizes the Strong Minimalist Thesis as the assumption that the linguistic system "comprises only the minimal mechanisms necessary to compute representations that can be accessed by the interfacing external systems."

5 Hornstein (2009: 58) claims that in addition to the Concatenate operation (ia), there is another operation involved in structure-building. This operation, called Label, projects/names the output of the Concatenation operation, as in (ib).

(i) a. Concatenate A, B → AB
     b. Label A, B → $_A$ [ÂB]

For Hornstein, the Label operation – the only unique operation of the language system – plays a central role in explaining the recursive property of human language (HL) identified by Hauser, Chomsky, and Fitch (2002) as the definitive property of HL.

6 Internal Merge (once called the Move operation) is used to explain how an element can enter into more than one grammatical relation in a given syntactic derivation. The

Internal Merge operation can copy an element in one structural position in a derivation and remerge the copy in another position, with the consequence of allowing the element to occupy multiple positions. We can see this in (ia) and (ib), where the objects (Pat) and (who) also show up in fronted positions.

(i) a. Pat was hired (Pat)
     b. Who did Chris hire (who) yesterday morning?

7 Others have argued that Internal Merge is not a "minimal" operation. Among these are Levine and Hukari (2006), who argue that having Internal Merge vastly complicates a grammar: "Such a grammar, in effect, (i) specifies a dedicated set of PS rules corresponding to extraction constructions, e.g., rule for S that specifies a filler category paired with a specially notated clausal category S'; and (ii) adds to every rule R of the grammar . . . a disjunction of rules . . . that jointly exhaust the possibilities of removing exactly one occurrence of an extracted category . . . together with a disjunction of rules . . . [that] replaces [the extracted category] . . ." (3).

8 According to Putnam (2010), the notion of "crash" is not a coherent notion in current Minimalist analyses. Putnam observes that notions of "crash" tend to fall into two crash-types: strict crash and soft crash, defined below.

(i) a. **Strict crash:** If a syntactic object α has any uninterpretable features, α is not usable by the performance systems.
     b. **Soft crash:** If a syntactic object α has any uninterpretable features, α is not usable by the performance systems unless α can be combined with another local derivational unit that repairs the interpretability of α.

Each of these notions, as Putnam points out, comes with a few substantial ontological commitments. Adopting the first notion requires having a Merge operation that is "meaningful" (most likely feature-driven) and that follows a strict version of locality (i.e., Spec-Head) with regard to measuring syntactic relations; and adopting the second notion allows "free" Merge (able to tolerate non-fatal crashes) and it takes a view of locality that includes the notion of c-command (both from a representational and derivational perspective) and the presence of phases, the Phase Impenetrability Condition and Probe–Goal relations.

9 This is not true, of course, for every "mainstream" variant of Minimalism. Boeckx (2007:419) correctly identifies Spell-Out (and in a related sense, Transfer) as a "stripping operation" and rightly points out that if a framework such as Distributed Morphology is ultimately correct, structural stripping cannot be correct because all relevant material is inserted post Spell-Out. Ultimately, we agree with the main tenet of Boeckx's argument that Spell-Out creates significant problems for Minimalist analyses.

10 Jackendoff (2002, 2010) criticizes syntacticocentric designs of human language, such as the Minimalist design, for requiring syntax to mediate all form–meaning correspondences. According to Jackendoff (2010: 70–72), syntacticocentricism leads to the dubious conclusion that there can be no "combinatorial thought" without syntax, which suggests that protolanguage did not permit such thought.

11 Despite similarities between Saussure's proposal and ours, there are substantial differences between these proposals. For Saussure, "the linguistic unit is a double entity . . . [one that] unites . . . a concept and a sound-image" (1951/1966: 65–66).

The two entities – signifier and signified – are parts of separate systems that are brought together, like two sides of a piece of paper, to make a single sign. For us, linguistic units possess both SM features and C-I features. Importantly, these features do not remain separated, as their signifier and signified equivalents do for Saussure; rather they commingle. If we use the piece of paper analogy, these C-I and SM features are aligned as if on a Mobius strip, simultaneously separate from one another (because they are located in different performance systems) and together, in that the SM and C-I performance systems overlap.

12 Saleemi's (2009: 205–207) linear revision of the architecture for FL (in which conceptual structure and illocutionary force features are encoded into lexical items that are brought into the Narrow Syntax through the CI system, building larger units shipped to the SM system for phonetic interpretation: LEX → C-I → CS → SM) suffers from the same logical conundrum that besets architecture (6). Although Saleemi's architecture does not have the output from the computational system sent to the C-I system, his architectural revision requires that conceptual structure does have combinatory (i.e., syntactic) properties, which precede the combinatory operations used by the syntax.

13 In his linear architecture for FL (see note 12), Saleemi (2009) expands the performance systems by placing the Lexicon in the CI system; he notes that the Lexicon "is the linguistic starting point of any derivation and therefore a significant part of the CI interface" (206–207). He does not, however, extend his observation to the SM interface, even though the Lexicon is also the starting point of the SM output and, therefore, a significant part of the SM system. Had he located the Lexicon in both of the performance systems, his architecture for FL would be much more like (9) than like his linear design.

14 These sorts of "uninterpretable" features, as we will argue in Chapter 2, are unlearnable and, worse from a conceptual point of view, they contribute nothing to the performance systems.

15 We are not alone in claiming that lexical features are always interpretable; this position is advanced in most unification grammars (particularly in HPSG).

16 Hinzen (2009a) offers another argument against free External Merge. He contends that this sort of operation cannot be the distinctive/core operation of FL, as advocated by Chomsky (1995, 2005), because it merely linearizes syntactic elements, as in adjunction, and it does not hierarchicalize elements to project "new categories upon merging two given syntactic objects . . . that give us a different kind of object to think about" (2009a: 47).

17 There is another problem with the Transfer operation – that is, the problem of reconstructing the pieces of structure Transferred into a composite derivation. Given the rather detailed structural status of reconstructed, post-Transferred material, it seems ill-conceived to construct, deconstruct and then completely reconstruct the entire derivation again.

18 An anonymous reviewer raises questions about our abandonment of the Merge operation, noting that, according to Chomsky, Merge is a property of any hierarchically organized system. While we agree that structure-building in general requires an operation that connects two (or more) discrete elements/constituents, we do not think that Chomsky's version of Merge – a binary operation which brings two elements A and B together to form a single constituent K that is defined as a projection of either A or B – is that general structure-building operation. We believe

that the structure-building operation, instead, is the sort of adhesion operation that Dawkins identifies in biological processes. As Dawkins (2009) observes, "Cells in general bristle with 'labels', chemical badges that enable them to find their 'partners'" (234). Opposed to Chomsky's binary Merge operation, Dawkins' adhesion operation is a unary operation, in which a constituent A is added to a partnered constituent, say B, creating K, but not projecting either A or B.

19 Stroik (2009a), however, argues that Internal Merge is not a conceptually necessary operation, pointing out that while it is necessary to have some version of First Merge to link lexical material together (to establish a compositional semantics for the performance systems to interpret), it is not conceptually necessary that material within a derivation be moved, remerged, or readjusted, because derivation-internal processes themselves are not visible to the performance systems, only the derivation output is. That is, having more than one type of merging-type operation would be conceptually necessary only if the performance systems interpreted how things are merged, rather than just the fact that they are merged. Since the performance systems respond to computational output, they do not interpret the source of the output (whether Internal Merge is involved, or not). Hence, Internal Merge is not conceptually necessary. Chomsky is confusing the possible operational necessity of the Internal Merge operation with its conceptual necessity (though there are many arguments that Internal Merge is not even operationally necessary – see Kinsella 2009 and Putnam and Stroik 2009).

20 We would encourage the reader to revisit our Preface, in which we offer a critique of Chomsky's (Newtonian) approach to displacement. Our critique of Chomsky makes structural arguments against his action-at-a-distance analysis of displacement.

21 Stroik (1999, 2009a) assumes, following Chomsky (1995), that all the lexical material in the Numeration must be used in the course of a derivation. This means that all the lexical (concatenative) features must be appropriately concatenated. Should there be any lexical item with surviving features at the end of a derivation, the derivation, according to Stroik, will stall; it will not come to derivational completion and, therefore, it will not be usable by the performance systems. We want to point out, however, that although Survive-minimalism allows derivations to stall, it does not permit derivations to crash. That is, Survive-minimalism, unlike Boeckx's (2008b) or Epstein and Seely's (2006) versions of Minimalism, does not submit unusable derivations to the performance systems for interpretation. As Stroik (2009a) argues, if the performance systems had to process unusable derivations, these systems could, in principle, become so clogged with these sorts of derivations that they would only on very rare occasions find it possible to produce meaningful interpretations.

22 Bickerton (2009), Searle (2010), and Fitch (2010) argue that the evolutionary development of a syntax for modern human language involves dissecting linguistic wholes into parts. We can see this in action in pronouns. The existence of pronouns in human languages, including ancient languages, gives good evidence that partitioning lexical material into subparts (features) is an essential property of FL. Pronouns, after all, are interpreted by the performance systems as a compendium of features. For example, the pronoun *git* in Old English exhaustively means <2nd person, dual, nominative Case>. It is impossible to change any of the features of the pronoun without changing the pronoun. What this suggests is that the pronoun is a sum of its partitioned subparts (features).

23 The free Copy operation and the part Copy operations, in accordance with Dawkins' (2009: 234) view of structure-building rules, are both strictly local operations and adhesive operations that map an element A to a domain B.

24 Ridding itself of almost all the operational machinery required in standard versions of Minimalism, especially all the machinery associated with Internal Merge, allows Survive-minimalism to avoid the criticism Brody (1995, 2002) levels at mixed derivational/representational models of grammar, those models that permit operations to reach backwards into derivations to reoperate over objects already in the derivation. Brody contends that such grammars (which include all standard versions of Minimalism) have excessive generative power (beyond the power needed for human language) and that their backward-reaching derivational output will be redundant with the representational chains interpreted by the performance systems. As a purely derivational model of grammar, Survive-minimalism does not suffer from the generative excesses and interpretative redundancies that beset mixed derivational/representational grammars. See Stroik (2009a: 11–15) for an extended discussion of how Survive-minimalism handles Brody's criticisms.

25 Recall that the Copy operation copies material into homogeneous domains. The Copy-to-Numeration (CoN) operation copies material from one lexical domain (the Lexicon) and places it in another lexical domain (the Numeration, a domain in which all the items are homogeneous in that they all have holistically similar FMs <feature selecting <feature selected>>). The Copy-to-SD (CoSD) operation also copies material from one domain (the Numeration) to another (a syntactic derivation). As with the CoN operation, the CoSD operation must copy material to a homogeneous domain. That is, the material CoSD copies to an SD must match the projected feature-domain of the SD, which is determined by the edge feature of SD.

26 Our objective here should not be mistaken – in this book we do not propose that Survive-minimalism offers "fix all" solutions to the problems that other versions of Minimalist theory are vexed by. Rather, our objective is strictly limited to investigating issues surrounding the structural design of the Faculty of Language.

CHAPTER 2 THE STRUCTURE OF THE LEXICON

1 Here we will only briefly touch on the notion of *Select* and its (un)necessity in Survive-minimalism. For a more detailed discussion of this topic, we refer the reader to Putnam and Parafita (2009).

2 Note that Chomsky refers to the C-I and SM "interfaces." For Chomsky, lexical material taken from the Lexicon and compiled by the computational system is eventually sent to the "external" performance systems for interpretation; that is, this material is sent to interface with the performance systems. We do not use the term "interfaces" in our analysis of the Faculty of Language because, for us, all lexical material is always contained in the performance systems. So it never "interfaces" with these systems.

3 As Chomsky (2001) and Hornstein, Nunes, and Grohmann (2005) observe, the NUM could consist of phase-selected sub-arrays of LIs, rather than a single array of LIs. Whether NUM consists of a single array or a set of sub-arrays is not particularly relevant to our analysis of NUM because the problems with the blind selection of LIs, which we discuss at length in this chapter and in the next chapter, are the same in either case.

4 See Adger (2008) for an extended discussion of the matching condition on the Merge operation. However, see Boeckx (2008b), Epstein (2007), and Chomsky (2008) for arguments that Merge should be free-Merge, an operation not constrained by matching conditions.

5 Epstein and Seely (2006) and Putnam (2010) discuss a variety of different types of "crashes" – fatal versus non-fatal crashes – and of the relationship between crash-type and interpretability. Recall, too, in Chapter 1 our brief discussion of the computational burden placed on the performance systems if "crashes" of any stripe are tolerated. We give a detailed discussion of this issue in Chapter 3.

6 See Sigurðsson (2006) and Sigurðsson and Maling (2010) for a similar approach arguing against uninterpretable features within Minimalist theory.

7 In the previous chapter, we observed that one of the unexplained consequences of assuming that the C-I and SM performance systems have "external interfaces" separated from the computational system is that, as discussed by Putnam (2010), a previously assembled derivational chunk must be Transferred and later reassembled at some later stage in the derivation. However, Sigurðsson and Maling (2010) and Putnam and Sigurðsson (2010) note that the PF (phonetic Form)/SM "interface" is shown to have much more syntactic/hierarchical structure than commonly assumed in most Minimalist theories, which suggests that the Transfer operation (and Spell-Out as discussed by Boeckx 2007 and Putnam and Stroik 2009, 2010) prematurely terminate the structural derivation required to satisfy SM interpretation.

8 There are – as we will briefly discuss in section 3 of this chapter – however, certain aspects of exoskeletal analyses of argument structure and event-related syntax-semantics issues (commonly associated with the Distributed Morphology (DM) literature) that can be grafted into our theory of lexical features.

9 Our structural constraint-based theory of grammar differs in substantial ways from lexical constraint-based theories of grammar such as HPSG and LFG (Lexical-Functional Grammar). One key difference is that we follow Boeckx (2008b: Chapter 4) in assuming a derivational analysis of constituent "displacement." Our approach allows for the multiple occurrences of lexical items (something that Boeckx argues to be computationally necessary), which is difficult, if not impossible, to achieve in a lexical constraint-based theory.

10 Tallerman (2009) states that the protolexicon contains "conceptual knowledge and representations" (183) and that one of the key steps towards building the protolexicon is that it "evolved by building on pre-existing conceptual categories, likely shared by other anthropoids" (185). One could interpret her notion of "conceptual knowledge" as being a form of encyclopedic knowledge assumed in Distributed Morphology (DM). In our view, the protolexicon grows out of pre-linguistic, conceptual categories. Although this may also be true for DM-type models with impoverished √ROOTS, we still depart from these theories due to the fact that they appear to limit the Lexicon to those conceptual categories and they need to build a new domain (namely, the "syntax") for emergent categories. Survive-minimalism, on the other hand, argues that the protolexicon evolved, as our hominid brain evolved, producing new lexical categories out of which the computational system (syntax) developed as a lexical spandrel.

11 Chomsky (2010) and Gärdenfors and Osvath (2010) make similar claims about the separation between form and meaning. According to Chomsky, "The symbols of language ... do not pick out mind-independent objects or events in the external

world . . . rather these are creations of what seventeenth-century investigators call our 'cognoscitive powers,' which provide us with rich means to interpret and refer to the outside world from certain perspectives" (2010: 57). And Gärdenfors and Osvath claim that language gives humans the ability to have "detached representations [that] can even stand for something that does not exist at all" (2010: 105).

12 Jackendoff (2002) argues that the crucial stage of syntactic evolution involved the introduction of syntactic categories (as a linguistic category separate from semantic categories).

13 Pustejovsky (1991, 2004) maintains that lexical meaning can best be captured by assuming the following levels of representation:

i.   *Argument Structure:* The behavior of a word as a function, with its arity specified. This is the predicate argument structure for a word, which indicates how it maps to syntactic expressions.

ii. *Event Structure:* Identification of the particular event type (in the sense of Vendler 1967) for a word or phrase: e.g., as state, process, or transition.

iii. *Qualia Structure:* The essential attributes of an object as defined by the lexical item.

iv. *Inheritance Structure:* How the word is globally related to other concepts in the Lexicon.

14 Tallerman (2009: 189–190) raises a critical question here regarding the first cause of the emergence of hierarchical structure in human language: "In the current context, the research question would then be, what drove what? Did the emerging Lexicon (rather, the emerging ability to learn a Lexicon) drive enhanced hierarchical abilities, or did early hominins already possess superior skills in hierarchical processing, which were then exapted for use in the protolexicon? More probably, we can postulate a scaffolding effect, with those individuals better able to handle hierarchical learning in general being in a good position to form a hierarchically structured Lexicon, and the latter providing a basis for improved cognitive skills involving hierarchical processing." We will not address this issue here, but Bickerton (2009), Fitch (2010), and Ramachandran (2011) all have given interesting analyses of how our ancestors might have developed a symbolic communicative system.

15 Conway and Christiansen (2001: 544–545) claim in particular that "apes and monkeys rarely use hierarchical routines in their spontaneous and learned actions."

16 The ramifications of this analysis are far-reaching and cast serious doubt on the universality of Chomsky's (2000 et seq.) notion of "derivation by phase" (see especially Gouskova's 2001 treatment of barrierhood in connection with split-scrambling).

17 See Thiersch (1985), den Besten and Webelhuth (1990), Grewendorf and Sabel (1994), Müller (1998), and Putnam (2007) for similar arguments.

18 In his discussion of FMs, Müller (2010, 2011) distinguishes between two types of features: namely, (i) structure-building features and (ii) features that are checked by derivational-internal mechanisms such as Agree. We find this distinction between these two types of features to be superfluous.

19 As suggested by Ramchand (2008) and Ritter and Rosen (1996, 1998), such a view of event predication being directly encoded in the syntactic structure reduces the central role of *aktionsart* (cf. Vendler 1967) as playing a large role in the decomposition of predicates.

CHAPTER 3 CONSTRUCTING THE NUMERATION

1 Epstein's analysis brings to mind our discussion in Chapter 1 in which we argue that building a biological system that randomly generates biological output that is subsequently filtered by another separate (and external) biological system is not feasible, as Fodor and Piattelli-Palmarini (2010) demonstrate.

2 As far as we have been able to find, no one, except for Collins (1997), has looked closely at the problem of selecting LIs for the NUM in derivational blindness. The statistical problem of forming a workable NUM this way has gone largely unnoticed.

3 Without a feature-match condition on Merge, all the possible 3.6 million structure strings will have to be computed and submitted to the interfaces for interpretation. But, as we mention above, it is unlikely that any of these structured strings will be interpretable.

4 Chomsky (2008) proposes a computational system that does not, apparently, include a NUM. Since he does not offer any arguments for why the External Merge (EM) operation should select LIs from the Lexicon and not from the NUM, beyond the broad claim that EM is unbounded, it is difficult to respond to his proposal. The viability of Chomsky's proposal will depend, in part, on whether or not it can respond to the arguments for NUM that we give in (i)-(v). Argument (v) is a particularly important one since it raises questions about the conceptual necessity of Internal Merge (IM) and since it pointedly argues that NUM must be a component of the computational system if this system lacks IM operations (see Putnam and Stroik 2009 for arguments against the conceptual necessity of IM). Given that the arguments in (i)-(v) have not been addressed, we will continue to assume, as does Hornstein (2009), that NUM exists.

5 One more line of argument against the conceptual necessity of IM operations goes as follows. Chomsky (2004) claims that EM and IM are versions of the same operation, which suggests that these operations should have the same conceptual justifications. However, the fact that EM and IM have similar effects on building syntactic structure is not sufficient reason to construe these operations as versions of the same thing. These operations have two inherent properties that make them incommensurable: (i) they function over very different domains – EM functions over derivation-external lexical domains and IM functions over derivation-internal structural domains – and (ii) they build structure in very different ways: EM adds new material to syntactic structures, while IM does not. From the second property it follows that it is not in principle possible to build syntactic structure without some sort of operation akin to EM; the same is not true of IM. Hence, an EM-type operation is unquestionably a conceptually necessary component of the Faculty of Language; on the other hand, the conceptual necessity of IM is quite in doubt. Furthermore, should it be the case that EM and IM are actually versions of the same operation (as Chomsky asserts), then one must wonder why we must have both of them – which would seem to argue for finding the generalization that allows the operations to collapse into a single Merge (M) operation (given the conceptual necessity of EM, this M operation would have to be much more like EM than like IM).

6 Another problem with having' "portal" features such as edge features is that they have no interface function; hence, they are not conceptually necessary for the interfaces to operate. Under the Minimalist assumption that all design elements of human language must be conceptually necessary at the interfaces (actually, at the performance systems), these sorts of features should be disallowed.

7 In Chapter 5 we offer an analysis of conjunction that differs from that of te Velde; our latter analysis, however, does not reflect on the viability of te Velde's proposals regarding the WorkBench.

CHAPTER 4 COPY AND THE COMPUTATIONAL SYSTEM

1 Bickerton (2009, 2010) contends that words could be combined in the protolanguage through a Sequence operation, which connects words like beads on a string. For Bickerton, the Sequence operation could put together *gray* and *cat* to produce the unstructured string *gray cat*. We reject this operation because it is unable to discriminate linguistic units that are truly strung together, as in countings and grocery lists (see our discussion in the next paragraph), from pidgins, which Bickerton claims uses the Sequence operation to put words together. The linguistic unit *gray cat* and the forms produced in pidgins are meaningful in ways that strung-together lists are not.

2 Fitch (2010: 506) maintains that protolanguage emerged from "meaningless song that was once the main communication system of prelinguistic hominids."

3 Needless to say, the six "big facts" listed above do not exhaust the defining properties of human language. As Ramachandran (2011: 162–163) notes, "we can list a set of five characteristics that make human language unique ..." These unique characteristics of human language, according to Ramachandran, include its enormous vocabulary, its function words, its use "off-line" to "refer to things or events that are not currently visible," its potential for metaphor and analogy, and its recursive syntax. In this book, we are only investigating one of these characteristics in depth – the recursive syntax of human language.

4 We wish to clarify that our version of "crash-proof" differs significantly from that proposed by Frampton and Gutmann a decade ago. Their model sought to constrain every iterative application of Merge and Move/Internal Merge to ensure that each stage in a derivation was well formed. As pointed out by Epstein and Seely (2006: Chapter 5), such an understanding of well-formedness reverts back to a GB-era understanding of the concept. Our version of "crash-proof" differs from Frampton and Gutmann's in that it requires no filters or constraints.

5 For a detailed discussion of how Survive-minimalism circumvents many of the pitfalls that burden "weakly" representational theories such as mainstream versions of Minimalism, see Stroik (2009a: 112–115).

6 See Lechner (2009, 2010) and Chapter 6 of this book for discussions of how the Survive Principle provides a more motivated explanation of scopal phenomena than do versions of Minimalism that use Attract-type operations to account for displacement phenomena.

7 Feature matrices will not be the same for all LIs. Although some LIs may have a full matrix, with SUBCAT, CAT, and PSFs, not every LI will. The only feature that generally must show up in the FM of any given LI is the CAT feature.

8 Hornstein (2009) proposes that what must project is a lexical category label. Hinzen (2009a: 33), however, points out "If labels are LIs again, hierarchy within syntax does not get off the ground." Under lexical projection, as Hinzen (2009b: 133) observes, "Merge will never carry us outside the one-dimensional space that it constructs. Our basic computational operation, therefore, won't be, as I shall say, *ontologically productive*; it will never generate new kinds of objects, ever."

9 For Fortuny (2008), a syntactic operation takes as input two categories or sets included in an alphabet and yields as output the union of these sets. Accordingly, Fortuny argues that the hierarchical properties of syntactic objects derive from the derivational record, a set K (a nest) where the outputs of successive Merge operations are linearly ordered by the strict inclusion relation. Following this logic a step further, hierarchy in syntax is a natural by-product of the successful creation of structure by keeping the derivational information in a record (thus making notions such as Kayne's (1994) *Linear Correspondence Axiom* and phrase structure rules such as X'-theory nothing more than a description rather than an explanation of empirical facts).

10 Notice that the syntactic domain SD-2 formed through the CoSD operation does not project a lexical category label, and therefore does not get trapped in the single (lexical) dimension that Hinzen identifies as being detrimental to building structural hierarchies and new kinds of objects (for new kinds of thoughts).

11 The LI *who* also has a <CASE> feature, which we will not discuss in this derivation because we are not including a *v*-projection in our analysis (and it is in the *v*-projection that the CASE feature of *who* is checked).

12 Here we show how a derivation would be built if all the verbal arguments were subcategorized by the verb, which means that there is no little *v* head. In our next example, we will show how a derivation would be built with a little *v* head.

13 Having verbs brought into derivations by their complements would align verbs with the other spinal heads (*v*, T, C), all of which are placed in derivations after their complements are.

14 The number of left-right orderings possible for any Numerations with n members in it would be 2^{n-1}.

CHAPTER 5 SOME STRUCTURAL CONSEQUENCES FOR DERIVATIONS

1 Chomsky (1981) claims that there is only a small set of thematic relations, expressed as theta roles, that can be assigned to arguments by predicates and he claims that these roles appear to be universal across languages. Some of these theta roles are Agent, Patient, Experiencer, Theme, Locative, Recipient, Beneficiary, Source, Goal, and Instrument.

2 Arguments similar to those just made for thematic coefficients can also be made for Case coefficients, at least for languages such as English. In English, no nominal elements, except for certain pronominals, are overtly marked for Case – not common nouns, not proper nouns, not determiners, and not noun-modifying adjectives. What this suggests is that English nominals lack a Case specification in the Lexicon and, therefore, in the Numeration. If we assume, in line with Chomsky (1981, 1995), that nominals require Case for Sensorimotor (SM) interpretation (the lack of Case explains the ungrammaticality of the constructions in (i)), then it must be the situation that nominals have their Case specification determined derivationally.

(i)   a. I saw a picture * (of) John.
       b. *Chris tried Pat to hire Sam.
       c. *It was hired Sam (where Sam is the object of the verb)
       d. *Pat to hire Sam

Following Chomsky (1981, 1995), we propose that every nominal in English has a Case feature; specifically, it has a selected performance system feature (PSF) for Case. Although in the Lexicon the nominal Case feature is not identified as having a specific Case, this feature must be structurally licensed by a Case-checker (a head with a selecting PSF for Case) that imposes a Case coefficient on the nominal Case feature it checks. That is, the Case-checking heads (Tense, Modal, light verb v, prepositions) will include selecting PSFs that specify the Case that the heads will license for SM interpretation. For example, the modal *will* has a selecting PSF for Case that requires the nominal that it checks to have Nominative Case: <CASE: NOMINATIVE>. In (ii), when the DP *Chris* is copied into the SD, its selected PSF for Case (<CASE>) will be checked by the modal and this selected feature will be given a NOMINATIVE coefficient by its counterpart selecting feature. The coefficient will be part of the material interpretation the DP is given by the SM performance system.

(ii)   Chris will leave soon.

It is important to bear in mind here that since Case coefficients in English are not features, they cannot project in an SD and therefore cannot affect the well-formedness of any derivation. (Note that in some languages, such as German, Case is a PSF, and Case features can affect the well-formedness of derivations.) This means that the coefficient clashes that might arise when a pronoun has a Case feature that misaligns with (and overrides) the Case coefficient of its Case-checkers will not prevent an SD from being interpreted by the performance systems. We can see this in (iii).

(iii)   a. Me and him are leaving.
        b. This is between she and I.

The fact that sentences such as those in (iii) are produced regularly by native speakers of English (even "educated" speakers) shows that although having Case is required, having a particular Case is not structurally mandated. Our analysis of Case, which breaks the Case feature into two parts (CASE and a coefficient, such as <CASE: NOMINATIVE>), is able to account for the structural necessity of nominal Case, while allowing for the variations in Case exhibited in (iii). (For other analyses of unbalanced Case in coordinate structures, see Zoerner 1995, Johannessen 1998, and Progovac 1998.) Needless to say, the analysis we are sketching here is speculative, and must be pursued in much greater depth than we have here if it is to be given any credibility.

3 The kind of lexical information we propose here for LIs has been found to play a role in the language processing mechanism. MacDonald et al. (1994), among others, have shown that grammatical category information, subcategory information, and thematic role information are the kinds of information associated with LIs.

4 In arguing that adjuncts are not predicates of events, we are generalizing Piñon's (2007) argument that manner adjuncts are not predicates of events. For Piñon, manner adjuncts involve a predicate of manners (not of events). We are arguing that all adjuncts involve predicates of adjunct-relations (such as MANNER, REASON, or TEMPORAL) that are ontologically dependent on the verbs and the events they denote. In this way, adjuncts are reified as objects in their own right, while being arguments of adjunct-predicates, as in (15a") and (15d").

5 A reviewer raises questions about our claim that adjuncts, like arguments, do not
   iterate, noting that while "a walking can be quick, dynamic, pleasurable, etc.," no
   such recursion shows up in argument structure. It seems to us that the recursion in the
   given example is a listing of Manner adjuncts that is no different than the listing of
   arguments in "dancing with Chris, Pat, Sam, etc." We can see the similarities between
   adjuncts and arguments in (i) and (ii).

   (i)   a. Pat was walking quickly and pleasurably.
          b. ?*Pat was walking quickly pleasurably.

   (ii)   a. Mary was dancing with Pat and Sam.
          b. *Mary was dancing with Pat Sam.

6 There are two ways to explain (20d). Either the FM of the verb lacks a temporal PSF
   (suppressing it the way some verbs such as *eat* and *read* can suppress internal
   arguments) – hence no adjunct would be required, or there could be a null temporal
   adjunct that is matching the temporal PSF of the verb. We will not try to decide this
   matter here.

7 We discuss this issue in detail in Stroik and Putnam (2009).

8 There seems to be some support for this analysis from the data in (ia), in which a
   quantifier embedded in the left conjunct can bind a pronoun embedded in the right
   conjunct, though this type of binding is not possible if the quantifier is in the right
   conjunct and the pronoun is in the left conjunct (see (ib)). (The data in (i) are taken
   from Zhang (2010: 12).)

   (i)   a. John bought just *one bottle of wine* and served *it* with dessert.
          b. *John bought just *it* and served *one bottle of wine* with dessert.

9 Informants for these data are Peredur Davies, Dorian Roehrs, Jon Herring, Ryu
   Hirata, Noriko Hoshino, Frederik Karlsson, Jan-Rouke Kuipers, Sian Llyod, Ineke
   Mennen, Alberto Rosignoli, and Eirini Sanoudaki.

10 Progovac (1998) also argues that there are no c-command relations between the two
   conjuncts in a coordinate structure, noting that if the left-conjunct c-commanded the
   right-conjunct, then example (ia) should violate Principle C in the same way that
   example (ib) does. The fact that (ia) is grammatical, while (ib) is not, suggests, for
   Progovac, that although the subject in (ib) c-commands the object, the left-conjunct
   in (ia) does not c-command the right-conjunct. We will discuss examples such as
   those in (i) later in this section.

   (i)   a. *John* and *John's* wife are certainly invited
          b. *?*John* certainly likes *John's* wife

11 Lebeaux formalizes the first part of his proposal as the *Homogeneity conjecture*,
   which states that "all negative conditions, in particular Condition C, apply continu-
   ously throughout the derivation" (2009: xi).

12 One could argue, following Chomsky and Lasnik (1993), that anaphors must attach
   to some agreement element associated with Tense. If this is the case, then the
   anaphors in (32a–d) will all relocate to structural positions not c-commanded by
   anything in the conjunction constructions and, consequently, no special mechanisms
   would be required to relocate the right branch conjuncts in these constructions.

(32)   a.   *Mary likes *those men* and *each other*'s wives.
       b.   *Mary likes *each other*'s wives and *those men*.
       c.   *Those men* like Mary and *each other*'s wives.
       d.   *Those men* like *each other*'s wives and Mary.

The problem with this proposal is that the need to re-locate right-branch conjuncts is not limited to conjuncts with anaphors; a similar need arises in conjuncts with pronouns, as in (i).

(i)   a.   *Bob* read a short story to *him*.
       b.   Mary read a poem to *Bob* and a short story to *him*.

If, as we have argued previously, everything in the left conjunct c-commands everything in the right conjunct of a conjunction construction, then example (ib) should be as ill-formed as (ia). The grammaticality of (ib) suggests that the right conjunct must relocate to some position in which the constituents of the left conjunct can no longer c-command constituents in the right adjunct.

13 Sag et al. (1985), Munn (1993), Zoerner (1995), and Progovac (1998) observe that coordinate conjunctions can link two elements that are of differing types, an X and a Y, as in (i). We will not address the coordination of differing types here, but see Zhang (2010) for an extensive discussion of these sorts of examples.

    (i) Pat has become [a banker] and [very conservative] (from Sag et al. 1985).

14 Our analysis not only explains the Principle C violations in (29) and (30), but it also accounts for the pronominal binding in (ia) and (ib). The binding in (ib) is particularly noteworthy because the quantifier is deep enough in the left conjunct that it will not c-command the pronoun in any analysis of coordinate structures, save ours.

    (i)   a.   *Every man* and *his* dog went to mow a meadow. (From Progovac 1998)
           b.   Which politician does Pat think that *every woman* likes and that *she* should vote for?

15 Similar arguments apply to constructions with conjoined subjects, such as (i). In (i), the right conjunct *Chris* cannot be recopied anywhere in the SD to have its CAT feature checked because the only constituent capable of checking this feature (the verb *left*) will already have had its SUBCAT feature checked when the conjoined subject is copied into the derivation.

    (i) Pat and Chris left.

16 A "weak" Principle C violation, according to Lasnik (1990) and Lebeaux (2009), is one that involves two co-indexable referential expressions. "Strong" Principle C violations involve pronouns and referential expressions.

17 As pointed out by Putnam (2010), it is unclear how many non-fatal crashes can be stacked up in pursuit of an eventually successful SD. Although it would seem to be desirable to repair non-fatal crashes at the very next derivational step (i.e., at step $n +$ 1), we cannot tell how these crashes, in general, might be repaired because Epstein and Seely (2006) and Epstein (2007) discuss only crashes (violations) that involve the Theta Criterion.

CHAPTER 6 OBSERVATIONS ON PERFORMANCE SYSTEM INTERPRETATIONS

1 An anonymous reviewer asks why only two of the properties of chains – (9l) and (9n) – are interpreted by the performance systems. As the reader may recall, both theta roles and Case features are PSFs (or PSF coefficients) in our system and thus must be interpreted by the performance systems; hence, the theta role and Case properties contained in (9l) and (9n) will be visible to the performance systems. On the other hand, since none of the other properties of chains involve PSFs, these properties will not be visible to the performance systems.

2 In Stroik (2009a), the syntactic representation for (7) would be (i), not (10). Under Stroik's analysis, all syntactic objects active in the WorkBench remerge into the syntactic derivation to check whether the objects will continue to "survive" or not. This requires active syntactic objects to undergo Remerger until they are no longer active (see Stroik for an extended discussion of this process). A multiple-Remerger syntactic representation for (7) would look like (i).

(i) [what [does [Chris **[what [does [Chris [what** [seem [Chris **[what** [to **[what** [have [stolen **what**]]]]]]]]]]]]]

Here we reject Stroik's automatic Remerge hypothesis because it creates concatenations in (i) in which no features have been checked, which is tantamount to having uninterpretable concatenations (furthermore, the CoSD operation could not create such concatenations since this operation connects constituents with matching features). What we advocate instead is that syntactic objects will be re-Copied into a syntactic derivation (SD) if and only if they feature-match the projection of the SD. Although all available syntactic objects in the WorkBench will be inspected for re-Copy, only feature-eligible objects will be automatically re-Copied into the SD. Of note, it is the re-Copy operation that forces both wh-elements in (iia) into the SPEC position of the embedded CP, as in (iib).

(ii) a. *What does Pat know where to put?
    b. . . .[what [where [PRO [to put **[what where**]]]]]

Since only one of the wh-elements in the embedded CP SPEC position can be checked by the C-head, one of them must be concatenated but unchecked and, therefore, uninterpretable. At this point, the derivation for (iia) will abort because it has an unusable concatenation. This explanation extends to all the sentences in (3).

3 Chomsky (2010: 55) asserts that the SM performance system interprets only the most "hierarchically prominent" position occupied by any given lexical item (or syntactic object). Here we argue against Chomsky's assertion.

4 Stroik (2009a) argues that wh-in-situ elements must be re-Copied in a syntactic derivation to have their <WH> features checked. Some support for this analysis comes from the data in (ia–b).

(i) a. *That man wants Mary to buy a picture of himself.
    b. Which man wants Mary to buy which picture of himself?

The fact that (ia) and (ib) are not equally (un)grammatical indicates that the reflexive *himself* is closer to its antecedent *X man* in (ib) than it is in (ia). In other words, the wh-in-situ constituent containing the reflexive in (ib) must be re-Copied in the syntactic derivation somewhere above the embedded clause.

5 Chomsky's (1993) formulation of Binding Theory is virtually the same as his 1981 version, except for the fact that in the earlier version he defined the local domain D as a "governing category" (1981:188).

6 We are not attempting to give a general analysis of pronoun interpretation; this would require a robust theory of discourse – one able to explain how texts and contexts beyond the sentence level contribute to pronoun interpretations (such a theory would formalize, among other things, how to interpret pronouns in sentences that lack potential antecedents for the pronouns, as in (i)).

(i) Suddenly she left the party.

We will not venture deeply enough into pronoun interpretation to link this interpretation to theories of discourse. Our speculations will be limited to some of the intersections between discourse and syntactic representation, and will focus on intra-sentential coreferential relations.

7 The fact that discourse interpretations involve expressibility (SM content) can be seen not only in (13), where SM content affects coreferentiality, but also in the examples given in (ia–b), where SM content (word-order relations and/or phonetic cues) is crucially involved in establishing discourse relations (for topicality and focus).

(i) a. Beans, I like.
     b. You did WHAT?

8 Pietroski (2006: 1) offers a wonderfully succinct description of his analysis: "Here is the idea, shorn of all the qualifications and supplementations: each complex expression of natural language is the concatenation of two simpler expressions; these two constituents, together with the meaning of concatenation, determine the meaning of the complex expression; constituents are understood as monadic predicates, and concatenation signifies *conjunction*. So, from a semantic perspective, every complex expression is a conjunction of predicates."

9 In Chapter 5 we argue that the semantic analysis of the adverbials formalized in (42) is incorrect. Since the representation of adverbials is not germane to our general analysis of Pietroski's semantic representations, we will leave Pietroski's analysis of adverbials, as seen in (41) and (42), undisturbed.

References

Abney, S. 1987. *The English noun phrase in its sentential aspect*. Ph.D. dissertation, MIT.

Acquaviva, P. 2008. "Roots and lexicality in Distributed Morphology." Ms., University College Dublin.

Adger, D. 2003. *Core syntax: A minimalist approach*. Oxford University Press.

2008. "A minimalist theory of feature structure." URL http://ling.auf.net/lingBuzz/000583, Ms., Queen Mary University London.

Arbib, M. 2005. "From monkey-like action recognition to human language: An evolutionary framework for neurolinguistics," *Behavioural and Brain Sciences* 28, 105–167.

Bach, E. 1964. *An introduction to transformational grammars*. New York: Holt, Rinehart & Winston.

Baron-Cohen, S. 1995. *Mindblindness: An essay on autism and Theory of Mind*. Cambridge, MA: MIT Press.

Beghelli, F. 1997. "The syntax of distributivity and pair-list readings," in A. Szabolcsi (ed.), *Ways of scope taking*. Dordrecht: Kluwer, 349–408.

Belletti, A. and L. Rizzi. 1988. "Psych-verbs and TH-Theory," *Natural Language and Linguistic Theory* 6, 291–352.

Besten, H. den and G. Webelhuth. 1990. "Stranding," in G. Grewendorf and W. Sternefeld (eds.), *Scrambling and barriers*. Amsterdam: John Benjamins, 77–92.

Bickerton, D. 2005. "Language evolution: A brief guide for linguistics," *Lingua* 117, 510–526.

2009. *Adam's tongue: How humans made language, how language made humans*. New York: Hill and Wang.

2010. "On two incompatible theories of language evolution," in R. Larson, V. Déprez, and H. Yamakido (eds.), *The evolution of human language*. Cambridge University Press, 199–210.

Bingham, P. 2010. "On the evolution of language: Implication of a new and general theory of human origins, properties, and history," in R. Larson, V. Déprez, and H. Yamakido (eds.), *The evolution of human language*. Cambridge University Press, 211–224.

Blakemore, D. 2002. *Relevance and linguistic meaning*. Cambridge University Press.

Boeckx, C. 2006. *Linguistic Minimalism: Origins, concepts, methods, and aims*. Oxford University Press.

2007. "Eliminating spell-out," *Linguistic Analysis* 33, 414–425.

2008a. *Bare syntax*. Oxford University Press.

2008b. *Understanding minimalist syntax: Lessons from locality in long-distance dependencies*. Oxford: Blackwell Publishing.

2009. "The nature of merge: Consequences for language, mind, and biology," in M. Piattelli-Palmarini, J. Uriagereka and P. Salabru (eds.), *Of minds and language: The Basque country encounter with Noam Chomsky*. Oxford University Press, 44–57.

Boeckx, C. and K. Grohmann. 2007. "Putting phases into perspective," *Syntax* 10, 204–222.

Borer, H. 1994. "The projection of arguments," in E. Benedicto and J. Runner (eds.), *Functional projections*. University of Massachusetts Occasional Papers 17, 19–47.

1998. "Deriving passives without theta-grids," in S. Lapointe, D. Brentari, and P. Farrell (eds.), *Morphology and its relation to phonology and syntax*. Stanford: CSLI, 60–99.

2003. *Structuring sense*, Vol. 1: *In name only*. Oxford University Press.

2004. "The grammar machine," in A. Alexiadou, E. Anagnostopoulou, and M. Everaert (eds.), *The unaccusativity puzzle: Explorations of the syntax–lexicon interface*. Oxford University Press, 288–331.

2005. *Structuring sense*, Vol. 2: *The normal course of events*. Oxford University Press.

Brody, M. 1995. *Lexico-logical form: A radically minimalist theory*. Cambridge, MA: MIT Press.

2002. "On the status of representations and derivations," in S. Epstein and T. Seely (eds.), *Derivation and explanation in the Minimalist Program*. Oxford: Blackwell, 19–41.

Chomsky, N. 1957. *Syntactic structures*. The Hague: Mouton.

1959. "Review of B. F. Skinner's *Verbal Behavior*," *Language* 35, 26–58.

1965. *Aspects of the theory of syntax*. Cambridge, MA: MIT Press.

1973. "Conditions on transformations," in S. Anderson and P. Kiparsky (eds.), *A Festschrift for Morris Halle*. New York: Holt, Rinehart, and Winston, 232–285.

1980. "On binding," *Linguistic Inquiry* 11, 1–46.

1981. *Lectures on government and binding*. Dordrecht: Foris.

1986. *Barriers*. Cambridge, MA: MIT Press.

1993. "A minimalist program for linguistic theory," in K. Hale and S. Keyser (eds.), *The view from Building 20: Essays in honor of Sylvan Bromberger*. Cambridge, MA: MIT Press, 1–52.

1995. *The Minimalist Program*. Cambridge, MA: MIT Press.

2000. "Minimalist inquiries: The framework," in R. Martin, D. Michaels, and J. Uriagereka (eds.), *Step by step*. Cambridge, MA: MIT Press, 89–155.

2001. "Derivation by phase," in M. Kenstowicz (ed.), *Ken Hale: A life in language*. Cambridge, MA: MIT Press, 1–52.

2004. "Beyond explanatory adequacy," in A. Belletti (ed.), *Structures and beyond*. Oxford University Press, 104–131.

2005. "Three factors in language design," *Linguistic Inquiry* 36, 1–22.

2007. "Approaching UG from below," in U. Sauerland and H. M. Gartuer (eds.), *Interfaces + Recursion = Language?* New York: Mouton de Gruyter, 1–29.

2008. "On phases," in R. Freidin, C. Otero, and M. L. Zubizarreta (eds.), *Foundational issues in linguistic theory: Essays in honor of Jean-Roger Vergnaud*. Cambridge, MA: MIT Press.

2009. "Opening remarks," in M. Piattelli-Palmarini, J. Uriagereka, and P. Salabru (eds.), *Of minds and language: The Basque country encounter with Noam Chomsky*. Oxford University Press, 13–43.

2010. "Some simple evo devo theses: How true might they be for language?" in R. Larson, V. Déprez, and H. Yamakido (eds.), *The evolution of human language*. Cambridge University Press, 45–62.

Chomsky, N. and H. Lasnik. 1977. "Filters and control," *Linguistic Inquiry* 8, 425–504.

1993. "The theory of principles and parameters," in J. Jacobs, A. Von Stechow, W. Sternefeld, and T. Vennemann (eds.), *Syntax: An international handbook of contemporary research*. Berlin: Walter de Gruyter, 506–569.

Citko, B. 2005. "On the nature of Merge: External Merge, Internal Merge, and Parallel Merge," *Linguistic Inquiry* 36, 475–496.

Clark, E. and H. Clark. 1979. "When nouns surface as verbs," *Language* 55, 767–811.

Collins, C. 1997. *Local economy*. Cambridge, MA: MIT Press.

2002. "Eliminating labels," in S. D. Epstein and T. D. Seely (eds.), *Derivation and explanation in the minimalist program*. Marden, MA: Blackwell-Wiley, 42–64.

Conway, C. M. and M. H. Christiansen. 2001. "Sequential learning in non-human primates," *Trends in Cognitive Sciences* 5, 539–546.

Corballis, M. 2002. *From hand to mouth: The origins of language*. Princeton University Press.

2010. "Did language evolve before speech?" in R. Larson, V. Déprez, and H. Yamakido (eds.), *The evolution of human language*. Cambridge University Press, 115–123.

Cox, B. and J. Forshaw. 2009. *Why does E = mc²?* Cambridge, MA: Da Capo Press.

Culicover, P. and R. Jackendoff. 2005. *Simpler syntax*. Oxford University Press.

Darwin, C. 1871. *The descent of man, and selection in relation to sex*. London: John Murray.

Davidson, D. 1967. "Truth and meaning," *Synthese* 17, 304–323.

Dawkins, R. 2009. *The greatest show on earth: The evidence for evolution*. New York: Free Press.

Deacon, T. 1997. *The symbolic species: The co-evolution of language and the brain*. New York: W. W. Norton.

2012. *Incomplete nature: How mind emerged from matter*. New York: Norton.

Epstein, S. 2007. "On I(nternalist)-functional explanation in minimalism," *Linguistic Analysis* 33.1–2, 20–53.

Epstein, S. D., E. M. Groat, R. Kawashima, and H. Kitahara (eds.). 1998. *A derivational approach to syntactic relations*. Oxford University Press.

Epstein, S. D. and T. D. Seely. 2002. "Rule applications as cycles in a level-free syntax," in S. Epstein and T. Seely (eds.), *Derivation and explanation in the Minimalist Program*. Oxford: Blackwell, 65–89.

2006. *Derivations in minimalism*. Cambridge University Press.

Epstein, S., H. Thráinsson, and J.-W. Zwart. 1996. "Introduction," in W. Abraham, S. Epstein, H. Thráinsson, and J.-W. Zwart (eds.), *Minimal ideas*. Amsterdam: John Benjamins Publishing, 1–66.

Fiengo, R. and J. Higginbotham. 1981. "Opacity in NP," *Linguistic Inquiry* 7, 395–422.

Fillmore, C. 1968. "The case for case," in E. Bach and R. Harms (eds.), *Universals in linguistic theory*. New York: Holt, Rinehart, and Winston, 1–88.

Fitch, W. T. 2010. *The evolution of language*. Cambridge University Press.

Fodor, J. A. and E. Lepore. 2002. *The compositionality papers*. Oxford: Clarendon Press.

Fodor, J. A. and M. Piattelli-Palmarini. 2010. *What Darwin got wrong*. New York: Picador.

Fortuny, J. 2008. *The emergence of order in syntax*. Amsterdam: John Benjamins.

Fox, D. 2003. "On logical form," in R. Hendrick (ed.), *Minimalist syntax*. Oxford: Blackwell, 82–123.

Frampton, J. and S. Gutmann. 2002. "Crash-proof syntax," in S. Epstein and T. Seely (eds.), *Derivation and explanation in the Minimalist Program*. Oxford: Blackwell, 90–105.

Gärdenfors, P. and M. Osvath. 2010. "Prospection as a cognitive precursor to symbolic communication," in R. Larson, V. Déprez, and H. Yamakido (eds.), *The evolution of human language*. Cambridge University Press, 103–114.

Gardner, R. and B. Gardner. 1969. "Teaching sign language to a chimpanzee," *Science* 165, 664–672.

Gazdar, G., E. Klein, G. Pullum, and I. Sag. 1985. *Generalized Phrase-Structure Grammar*. Cambridge, MA: Harvard University Press.

Gould, S. and R. Lewontin. 1979. "The spandrels of San Marco and the Panglossian paradigm: A critique of the adaptationist programme," *Proceedings of the Royal Society*, B 205, 581–598.

Gouskova, M. 2001. "Split scrambling: barriers as violable constraints," in K. Megerdoomian and L. Bar-el (eds.), *Proceedings of WCCFL 20*. Somerville, MA: Cascadilla Press, 220–223.

Grewendorf, G. and I. Sabel. 1994. "Long scrambling and incorporation," *Linguistic Inquiry* 25, 263–308.

1999. "Scrambling in German and Japanese: adjunction vs. multiple specifiers," *Natural Language and Linguistic Theory* 17, 1–65.

Grohmann, K. 2000. *Prolific peripheries: A radical view from the left*. Ph.D. dissertation, University of Maryland.

2003. *Prolific domains: On the anti-locality movement dependencies*. Amsterdam: John Benjamins.

Gruber, J. 1965. *Studies in lexical relations*. Ph.D. dissertation, MIT.

Haegeman, L. 1994. *Introduction to government and binding theory*. Oxford: Blackwell-Wiley.

Hale, K. and S. Keyser. 1993. "On argument structure and the lexical expression of syntactic relations," in K. Hale and S. Keyser (eds.), *The view from Building 20: Essays in honor of Sylvan Bromberger*. Cambridge, MA: MIT Press, 53–109.

2002. *Prolegomenon to a theory of argument structure*. Cambridge, MA: MIT Press.

Hauser, M., N. Chomsky, and W. Fitch. 2002. "The Faculty of Language: What is it, who has it, and how did it evolve?" *Science* 298, 1569–1579.

Hicks, G. 2009. *The derivation of anaphoric relations*. Amsterdam: John Benjamins.

Higginbotham, J. 1985. "On semantics," *Linguistic Inquiry* 16, 547–593.

Hinzen, W. 2006. *Mind design and minimalist syntax*. Oxford University Press.

2009a. "The successor function + LEX = Human Language," in K. Grohmann (ed.), *InterPhases: Phase-theoretic investigations of linguistic interfaces*. Oxford University Press, 25–47.

2009b. "Hierarchy, Merge, and Truth," in M. Piattelli-Palmarini, J. Uriagereka and P. Salabru (eds.), *Of minds and language: The Basque country encounter with Noam Chomsky.* Oxford University Press, 123–141.

Hornstein, N. 2001. *Move! A minimalist theory of construal.* Oxford: Blackwell.

2006. "Pronouns in a minimalist setting," *University of Maryland Working Papers in Linguistics* 14, 47–80.

2009. *A theory of syntax: Minimal operation and universal grammar.* Cambridge University Press.

Hornstein, N., J. Nunes, and K. Grohmann. 2005. *Understanding minimalism.* Cambridge University Press.

Hout, A. van. 1992. "Linking and projection based on event structure," Ms., Tilburg University.

1996. *Event semantics of verb frame alternations: A case study of Dutch and its acquisition.* Ph.D. dissertation, Tilburg University.

2004. "Unaccusativity as telicity checking," in A. Alexiadou, E. Anagnostopoulou, and M. Everaert (eds.), *The unaccusativity puzzle: Explorations of the syntax–lexicon interface.* Oxford University Press, 60–83.

Jackendoff, R. 2002. *Foundations of language: Brain, meaning, grammar, evolution.* Oxford University Press.

2010. "Your theory of language evolution depends on your theory of language," in R. Larson, V. Déprez, and H. Yamakido (eds.), *The evolution of human language.* Cambridge University Press, 63–72.

Jenkins, L. 2000. *Biolinguistics: Exploring the biology of language.* Cambridge University Press.

Jespersen, O. 1922. *Language: Its nature, development, and origin.* New York: W. W. Norton & Company.

Johannessen, J. B. 1998. *Coordination.* Oxford University Press.

Johnson, K. 2008. "The view of QR from ellipsis," in K. Johnson (ed.), *Topics in ellipsis.* Cambridge University Press, 69–94.

Kayne, R. 1983. "Connectedness," *Linguistic Inquiry* 14, 223–249.

1994. *The antisymmetry of syntax.* Cambridge, MA: MIT Press.

2002. "Pronouns and their antecedents," in S. Epstein and T. D. Seely (eds.), *Derivation and explanation in the Minimalist Program.* Oxford: Blackwell, 133–166.

Kinsella, A. 2009. *Language evolution and syntactic theory.* Cambridge University Press.

Kitahara, H. 1994. *Target! A unified theory of movement and structure building.* Ph.D. dissertation, Harvard University.

1995. "Target! Deducing strict cyclicity from derivational economy," *Linguistic Inquiry* 26, 47–77.

1997. *Elementary operations and optimal derivations.* Cambridge, MA: MIT Press.

Kratzer, A. 1996. "Severing the external argument from the verb," in J. Rooryck and L. Zaring (eds.), *Phrase structure and the lexicon.* Dordrecht: Kluwer, 109–137.

Krifka, M. 1989. "Nominal reference and temporal constitution and quantification in event semantics," in P. van Emde, B. R. Bartsch, and J. van Bentham (eds.), *Semantics and contextual expression.* Dordrecht: Foris, 75–115.

Kuhn, T. S. 1962. *The structure of scientific revolutions.* University of Chicago Press.

Larson, R. 2004. "Sentence final adverbs and scope," in M. Wolf and K. Moulton (eds.), *Proceedings of NELS,* volume 34, 23–43.

Lasnik, H. 1990. "On the necessity of the Binding Conditions," in R. Friedin (ed.), *Principles and parameters in comparative grammar.* Cambridge, MA: MIT Press, 7–28.

1999. *Minimalist analysis.* Oxford: Blackwell.

Lebeaux, D. 1991. "Relative clauses, licensing, and the nature of derivation," in S. Rothstein (ed.), *Perspectives on phrase structure: Heads and licensing.* San Diego, CA: Academic Press, 209–239.

1995. "Where does the Binding Theory apply?" *University of Maryland Working Papers in Linguistics* 3, 63–88.

2009. *Where does Binding Theory apply?* Cambridge, MA: MIT Press.

Lechner, W. 2009. "Evidence for Survive from covert movement," in M. Putnam (ed.), *Towards a derivational syntax: Survive minimalism.* Amsterdam: John Benjamins, 231–257.

2010. "Structure building from below: More on Survive and covert movement," Ms., University of Athens.

Levin, B. and M. Rappaport-Hovav. 1986. "The formation of adjectival passives," *Linguistic Inquiry* 17, 623–661.

1995. *Unaccusativity.* Cambridge, MA: MIT Press.

Levine, R. and T. Hukari. 2006. *The unity of unbounded dependency constructions.* Stanford: CSLI.

Lieberman, P. 1998. *Eve spoke: Human language and human evolution.* New York: W. W. Norton.

2000. *Human language and our reptilian brain: The subcortical bases of speech, syntax, and thought.* Cambridge, MA: Harvard University Press.

2006. *Toward an evolutionary biology of language.* Cambridge, MA: Harvard University Press.

2010. "The creative capacity of language, in what manner is it unique, and who had it?" in R. Larson, V. Déprez, and H. Yamakido (eds.), *The evolution of human language.* Cambridge University Press, 163–175.

Lohndal, T. and P. Pietroski. 2011. "Interrogatives, instructions, and I-Languages: an I-semantics for questions," *Linguistic Analysis* 37.3–4, 460–512.

López, L. 2007. *Locality and the architecture of syntactic dependencies.* London: Palgrave-Macmillan.

2009. *A derivational syntax of information structure.* Oxford University Press.

MacDonald, M., N. Perlmutter, and M. Seidenberg. 1994. "Lexical nature of syntactic ambiguity resolution," *Psychological Review* 101, 676–703.

Maienborne, C. 2005. "On the limits of the Davidsonian approach," *Theoretical Linguistics* 31, 275–317.

Marantz, A. 1993. "Implications of asymmetries in double object constructions," in S. A. Mchombo (ed.), *Theoretical aspects in Bantu grammar.* University of Chicago Press, 113–149.

1997. "No escape from syntax: Don't try a morphological analysis in the privacy of your own lexicon," *University of Pennsylvania Working Papers in Linguistics* 4.2, 201–225.

2005. "Generative linguistics within the cognitive neuroscience of language." *The Linguistic Review* 22, 429–445.

May, R. 1985. *Logical form*. Cambridge, MA: MIT Press.

Merchant, J. 2004. "Fragments and ellipsis," *Linguistics and Philosophy* 27.6, 661–738.

Müller, G. 1998. *Incomplete category fronting*. Dordrecht: Kluwer.

2010. "On deriving CER effects from the PIC," *Linguistic Inquiry* 41, 35–82.

2011. *Constraints on displacement: A phase-based approach*. Amsterdam: John Benjamins.

Munn, A. 1987. "Coordinate structure and X-bar theory," *McGill Working Papers in Linguistics* 4: 121–140.

1993. *Topics in the syntax and semantics of coordinate structures*. Doctoral dissertation, University of Maryland.

Nunes, J. 2004. *Linearization of chains and sideward movement*. Cambridge, MA: MIT Press.

2005. *The copy theory of movement and linearization of chains in the Minimalist Program*. Doctoral dissertation, University of Maryland.

Ott, D. 2009. "The conceptual necessity of phases: Some remarks on the minimalist enterprise," in K. Grohmann (ed.), *Explorations of phase theory: Interpretation at the interfaces*. Berlin: Mouton de Gruyter, 253–275.

2010. "Grammaticality, interfaces, and UG," in M. Putnam (ed.), *Exploring crash-proof grammars*. Amsterdam: John Benjamins, 89–104.

Parsons, T. 1990. *Events in the semantics of English: A study in subatomic semantics*. Cambridge, MA: MIT Press.

Pesetsky, D. 1995. *Zero syntax*. Cambridge, MA: MIT Press.

1998. "Some optimality principles of sentence pronunciation," in P. Barbosa, D. Fox, P. Hagstrom, M. McGinnis, and D. Pesetsky (eds.), *Is the best good enough?* Cambridge, MA: MIT Press, 337–383.

Pietroski, P. 2002. "Function and concatenation," in G. Reyer and G. Peters (eds.), *Logical form*, Vol. 9. Oxford University Press, 91–117.

2005. *Events and semantic architecture*. Oxford University Press.

2006. "Interpreting concatenation and concatenates," *Philosophical Issues* 16, 221–245.

2008. "Semantic monadicity with conceptual polyadicity," Ms., Harvard University and University of Maryland, College Park.

Forthcoming. *Semantics without truth-values*. Oxford University Press.

Pinker, S. 2007. *The stuff of thought*. London: Penguin.

Piñon, C. 2007. "Manner adverbs and manners," MS, Université de Lille 3.

Pollard, C. and I. Sag. 1994. *Head-driven phrase structure grammar*. University of Chicago Press.

Postal, P. 1972. "Some rules that are not successive cyclic," *Linguistic Inquiry* 3, 211–222.

Potts, C. 2008. "Review article: Hagit Borer's *Structuring Sense* Volumes I and II," *Language* 82.2, 348–369.

Premack, D. 1976. *Intelligence in ape and man*. Hillsdale, NJ: Lawrence Erlbaum Associates, Publishers.

Preminger, O. 2009. "Long-distance agreement without probe–goal relations," in M. Putnam (ed.), *Towards a purely derivational syntax: Survive-minimalism*. Amsterdam: John Benjamins, 41–56.

Progovac, L. 1998. "Structure of coordination, part I," *GLOT International* 3, 3–6.

Pustejovsky, J. 1991. "The syntax of event structure," *Cognition* 41, 47–81.

2004. "The generative lexicon," in S. Davis and B. Gillon (eds.), *Semantics: A reader.* Oxford: Oxford University Press, 369–393.

Putnam, M. 2007. *Scrambling and the Survive Principle.* Amsterdam: John Benjamins.

Putnam, M. (ed.) 2010. *Exploring crash-proof grammars.* Amsterdam: John Benjamins.

Putnam, M. and M. C. Parafita Cuoto. 2009. "When grammars collide: Code-switching in Survive-minimalism," in M. Putnam (ed.), *Towards a derivational syntax: Survive-minimalism.* Amsterdam: John Benjamins, 133–168.

Putnam, M. and T. Stroik. 2009. "Traveling without moving: The conceptual necessity of Survive-minimalism," in M. Putnam (ed.), *Towards a derivational syntax: Survive-minimalism.* Amsterdam: John Benjamins Publishing, 3–19.

2010. "Syntactic relations in Survive-minimalism," in M. Putnam (ed.), *Exploring crash-proof grammars.* Amsterdam: John Benjamins, 143–166.

2011. "Syntax at ground zero," *Linguistic Analysis* 37.3–4, 389–405.

Pylkkänen, L. 2002. *Introducing arguments.* Doctoral dissertation, MIT.

2008. *Introducing arguments.* Cambridge, MA: MIT Press.

Ramachandran, V. 2011. *The tell-tale brain.* New York: W. W. Norton & Company.

Ramchand, G. 2007. "Events in syntax: Modification and predication," *Language and Linguistics Compass* 1.5, 476–497.

2008. *Verb meaning and the lexicon: A first-phase syntax.* Cambridge University Press.

Reuland, E. 2009. "Language, symbolization and beyond," in R. Botha and C. Knight (eds.), *The prehistory of language.* Oxford University Press, 201–224.

Richards, N. 1997. *What moves where when in which language?* Doctoral dissertation, MIT.

2001. *Movement in language: Interactions and architectures.* Oxford University Press.

Ritter, E. and S. Rosen. 1996. "Strong and weak predicates: Reducing the lexical burden," *Linguistic Analysis* 26, 1–34.

1998. "Delimiting events in syntax," in W. Greuder and M. Butt (eds.), *The projection of arguments.* Stanford: CSLI, 97–134.

Rizzi, L. 2006. "On the form of chains: criterial positions and ECP effects," in L. Cheng and N. Corver (eds.), *Wh-movement: moving on.* Cambridge, MA: MIT Press, 97–133.

Rizzolatti, G. and M. Arbib. 1998. "Language within our grasp," *Trends in Cognitive Sciences* 21, 188–194.

Ross, J. 1967. *Constraints on variables in syntax.* Ph.D. dissertation, MIT.

Sag, I. et al. 1985. "Coordination and how to distinguish categories," *Natural Language and Linguistic Theory* 3, 117–171.

Saleemi, A. 2009. "On the interface(s) between syntax and meaning," in K. Grohmann (ed.), *Explorations of phase theory: Interpretation at the interfaces.* Berlin: Mouton de Gruyter, 181–210.

Sauerland, U. 1999. "Erasability and interpretation," *Syntax* 3, 161–188.

Saussure, F. de. 1915/1966. *Course in general linguistics.* New York: McGraw-Hill.

Searle, J. 1972. "Chomsky's revolution in linguistics," *The New York Review of Books* 18.12, 16–24.

2010. *Making the social world: The structure of human civilization.* Oxford University Press.

Sheehan, M. and W. Hinzen. 2011. "Moving toward the edge," *Linguistic Analysis* 37, 3–4.

Sigurðsson, H. 2006. "Agree in syntax, agreement in signs," in C. Boeckx (ed.), *Agreement systems.* Amsterdam: John Benjamins, 201–237.

Sigurðsson, H. and J. Maling. 2010. "The Empty Left Edge Condition," in M. Putnam (ed.), *Exploring crash-proof grammars.* Amsterdam: John Benjamins, 59–86.

Sperber, D. and G. Origgi. 2010. "A pragmatic perspective on the evolution of language," in R. Larson, V. Déprez, and H. Yamakido (eds.), *The evolution of human language.* Cambridge University Press, 124–132.

Sperber, D. and D. Wilson. 1986. *Relevance: Communication and cognition.* Oxford: Blackwell.

Starke, M. 2001. *Move dissolves into merge: A theory of locality.* Ph.D. dissertation, University of Geneva.

Stroik, T. 1999. "The Survive Principle," *Linguistic Analysis* 29, 239–258.

2000. *Syntactic controversies.* Munich: Lincom Europa.

2009a. *Locality in minimalist syntax.* Cambridge, MA: MIT Press.

2009b. "The Numeration in Survive-minimalism," in M. Putnam (ed.), *Towards a derivational syntax: Survive-minimalism.* Amsterdam: John Benjamins, 21–37.

Stroik, T. and M. Putnam. 2005. "The lexicon at the interfaces," Handout. LASSO 2005, Lubbock, TX.

2009. "Surviving reconstruction," in K. Grohmann (ed.), *Explorations of phase theory: Interpretation at the interfaces.* Berlin: Mouton de Gruyter, 161–179.

Stroik, T., M. Putnam, and M. C. Parafita Cuoto. 2008 "Flavors of Merge," Paper presented at the Ways of Structure Building Conference, 2008.

Takano, Y. 2004. "Coordination of verbs and two types of verbal inflection," *Linguistic Inquiry* 35, 168–178.

Tallerman, M. 2009. "The origins of the lexicon: How a word-store evolved," in R. Botha and C. Knight (eds.), *The prehistory of language.* Oxford University Press, 181–200.

Taraldsen, T. 2010. "Unintentionality out of control," in M. Duguine, S. Huidobro, and N. Madariaga (eds.), *Argument structure and syntactic relations: A cross-linguistic perspective.* Amsterdam: John Benjamins, 283–302.

Thiersch, C. 1985. "VP Scrambling and the German middle field," unpublished MS, Tilburg University.

Thompson, D. W. 1917. *On growth and form.* Cambridge University Press. Reprinted and edited in 1992 by J. Bonner, New York: Dover.

Turing, A. 1952. "The chemical basis of morphogenesis," *Philosophical Transactions of the Royal Society of London, Series B,* 37–72.

Uriagereka, J. 1999. "Multiple spell-out," in S. Epstein and N. Hornstein (eds.), *Working minimalism.* Cambridge, MA: MIT Press, 251–282.

2002. *Derivations.* London: Routledge.

Velde, J. te. 2009. "Using the *Survive* principle for deriving coordinate (a)symmetries," in M. Putnam (ed.), *Towards a derivational syntax: Survive-minimalism.* Amsterdam: John Benjamins, 169–192.

Vendler, Z. 1967. *Linguistics in philosophy*. Ithaca, NY: Cornell University Press.

Wallman, J. 1992. *Aping language*. Cambridge University Press.

Wedeen, V. et al. 2012. "The geometric structure of the brain fiber pathways," *Science* 335, 1628–1634.

Weinberg, S. 2001. *Facing up*. Cambridge, MA: Harvard University Press.

Wray, A. 2000. "Holistic utterances in protolanguage: The link from primates to humans," in C. Knight, M. Studdert-Kennedy, and J. Hurford (eds.), *The evolutionary emergence of language: Social function and the origins of linguistic form*. Cambridge University Press, 285–302.

Yamamoto, S., T. Humle, and M. Tanaka. 2012. "Chimpanzees' flexible targeted helping based on an understanding of conspecifics' goals," *Proceedings of the National Academy of Sciences*, 108, 3588–3592.

Zhang, N. 2010. *Coordination in syntax*. Cambridge University Press.

Zoerner, E. 1995. *Coordination: The Syntax of &P*. Doctoral dissertation, University of California-San Diego.

Zwart, J. W. 2002. "Issues relating to a derivational theory of binding," in S. Epstein and T. D. Seely (eds.), *Derivation and explanation in the Minimalist Program*. Oxford: Blackwell, 269–304

Index

For EU product safety concerns, contact us at Calle de José Abascal, 56–1°,
28003 Madrid, Spain or eugpsr@cambridge.org.